To Mom
Love P

HOMESTEADING WOMEN

An Oral History of Colorado, 1890–1950

TWAYNE'S
ORAL HISTORY SERIES

Donald A. Ritchie, Series Editor

JULIE JONES-EDDY

HOMESTEADING WOMEN

An Oral History of Colorado, 1890–1950

TWAYNE PUBLISHERS · NEW YORK
Maxwell Macmillan Canada · Toronto
Maxwell Macmillan International · New York   Oxford   Singapore   Sydney

Twayne's Oral History Series No. 7

Copyright © 1992 by Twayne Publishers
All rights reserved. No part of this book may be reproduced or
transmitted in any form or by any means, electronic or mechanical,
including photocopying, recording, or by any information storage and
retrieval system, without permission in writing from the Publisher.

Twayne Publishers   Maxwell Macmillan Canada, Inc.
Macmillan Publishing Company   1200 Eglinton Avenue East
866 Third Avenue   Suite 200
New York, New York 10022   Don Mills, Ontario M3C 3N1

Macmillan Publishing Company is part of the Maxwell Communication
Group of Companies.

Library of Congress Cataloging-in-Publication Data

Jones-Eddy, Julie.
    Homesteading women : an oral history of Colorado, 1890–1950 /
Julie Jones-Eddy.
       p.   cm.—(Twayne's oral history series ; no. 7)
    Includes index.
    ISBN 0-8057-9103-5—ISBN 0-8057-9114-0 (pbk.)
    1. Women pioneers—Colorado—Interviews.   2. Frontier and
pioneer life—Colorado.   3. Colorado—Social life and customs.
4. Colorado—Biography.   5. Oral history.   I. Title.   II. Series.
F781.J84   1992
978.8'0088042—dc20   91-34302
                                                                CIP

The paper used in this publication meets the minimum requirements of
American National Standard for Information Sciences—Permanence of
Paper for Printed Library Materials. ANSI Z3948-1984. ∞™

10 9 8 7 6 5 4 3 2 1 (hc)
10 9 8 7 6 5 4 3 2 1 (pb)

Printed in the United States of America

To the women of northwestern Colorado, and to my husband, John, whose support and expertise were essential to this project.

Contents

Foreword

It is a paradox that those who lived largely isolated lives would share a common memory. But the harsh and demanding environment of the high country of northwestern Colorado forged a community of experience for the women in that region's scattered homesteads and towns. Through her collection and arrangement of their reminiscences, Julie Jones-Eddy offers insights into the frontier personality of the early twentieth century—people whose experiences were not unlike those of homesteaders in the previous century. The women she interviewed recount their similar attitudes toward childhood and child rearing, schooling, marriage, health care, and work. They recall the relationships between white settlers and displaced Indians, and they detail the network of social clubs and other mutual support that frontier women created. Through their general recollections, they reflect back over their lives and their successes and failures. Amusing, moving, and revealing, their individual stories flow together to re-create the sense of unity that emerged from the struggle to survive.

Oral history may well be the twentieth century's substitute for the written memoir. In exchange for the immediacy of diaries or correspondence, the retrospective interview offers a dialogue between the participant and the informed interviewer. Having prepared sufficient preliminary research, interviewers can direct the discussion into areas long since "forgotten" or no longer considered of consequence. "I haven't thought about that in years" is a common response, uttered just before the interviewee commences with a surprisingly detailed description of some past incident. The quality of the interview, its candidness and depth, generally will depend as much on the interviewer as on the interviewee, and the confidence and rapport between the two add a special dimension to the spoken memoir.

Interviewers represent a variety of disciplines, and work either as part of a collective effort or as an individual enterprise. Regardless of their different interests or the variety of their subjects, all interviewers share a common imperative: to collect memories while they are still available. Most oral historians feel an additional responsibility to make their interviews accessible for use beyond their own research needs. Still, important collections of vital, vibrant interviews lie scattered in archives throughout every state, undiscovered or underutilized.

Twayne's Oral History Series seeks to identify those resources and to publish selections of the best materials. The series lets people speak for themselves, from their own unique perspectives on people, places, and events. But to be more than a babble of voices, each volume organizes its interviews around particular situations and events and ties them together with interpretive essays that place individuals into the larger historical context. The style and format of each volume vary with the material from which it is drawn, demonstrating again the diversity of oral history and its methodology.

Whenever oral historians gather in conference they enjoy retelling experiences about unusual individuals they have met, unexpected information they have elicited, and unforgettable reminiscences that would otherwise never have been recorded. The result invariably reminds listeners of others who deserve to be interviewed, provides them with models of interviewing techniques, and inspires them to make their own contribution to the field. I trust that the oral historians in this series, as interviewers, editors, and interpreters, will have a similar effect on their readers.

DONALD A. RITCHIE
Series Editor, Senate Historical Office

Preface

Northwestern Colorado is a special place to me. Raised in Craig, Colorado, I am the great-granddaughter of early settlers in that area. Although I haven't lived there in many years, I frequently drive through the quiet, lonely country to see the people my family has known for generations.

Several histories of northwestern Colorado have been written, and stories have been told about the cowboys, the ranchers, the miners—the men. But little is known about the experiences of homesteading women. When I was a child, my grandmother's friends had impressed me as dignified, strong, resourceful women. Yet a record of their contributions to their families and communities was missing from any of the published historical sources about the area. Therefore in 1983 I began to collect the names of women who would be good sources of information. My list grew to 90 names.

A letter I sent out to these 90 women, explaining the project and including sample questions and biographical and legal release forms, elicited only about 30 responses. I began calling the women who had not responded and found that until they knew who my parents and grandparents were, they were unwilling to talk with me. Establishing my roots in the community, I finally received responses from 50 of the women, 47 of whom I was able to interview. I completed the interviews in the fall of 1984.

Each interview took place in the woman's home and lasted from one to two hours. I used a list of 38 questions about childhood, adolescence, and young adult experiences, as well as about marriage, childbearing, and working at home and outside the home. I asked only those questions which applied to each woman's experience (e.g., women who came to homestead in the 1920s were not asked questions about their childhoods). All the women were asked the final questions about life's satisfactions and disappointments.

The women's ages ranged from 54 to 95. Forty-five were married. Two had never married. Of those who married, seven had no children and four were divorced. Of the divorcées, three had remarried. Twenty-six of the women had been employed after marriage at some time. Fourteen were employed for most of their adult working years. Twenty-three had lived in northwestern Colorado all their lives. When interviewed, all lived in their own homes, apartments, or senior-citizen apartments.

As a group these women were optimistic. They had coped with the hardships of homesteading in a demanding environment. I had no interviews with women who could not tolerate this kind of life, since most such women had left the area. Represented here are women who succeeded at this kind of life and lived long enough to reflect on it.

I have included a few interviews with women who lived not on a homestead but in one of the four small communities of Craig, Maybell, Rangely, and Meeker, because of the important relationship between the people in these communities and those who lived on a homestead. The homesteaders bought, sold, or traded essential materials in these communities and depended on the skills of those who lived in the community (doctors, midwives, bankers, ministers, priests). In most cases, the women who lived in town had parents or grandparents who had homesteaded in the area.

I have grouped the material by subject (childhood experiences, adolescent experiences, working experiences, etc.). Only those questions necessary to understand the responses are included. Editorial clarifications and explanations are in brackets. To ensure privacy, I have in some cases substituted descriptive words for individuals identified by name in the interviews (e.g., *neighbor* or *rancher*). I have used ellipses only to indicate a thoughtful interruption or pause in a woman's answer, not to show where part of a response has been omitted.

I concentrated on Moffat and Rio Blanco counties, an area of almost 10,000 square miles, through which run two major rivers, the White and the Yampa. These counties are in the far-northwestern corner of the state, along the Utah and Wyoming borders. The time period for which I recorded the homesteading experience was roughly 1890 to 1940. I included some material from the 1940s and early 1950s because in some respects life for these people did not change significantly until the 1950s. Even in the 1950s, some remote rural areas were still using one-room schools. Many ranches had no electricity, and roads were sometimes impassable in the winter. Horses on occasion were still the best mode of transportation.

Acknowledgments

In many ways the Colorado Endowment for the Humanities made this book possible. I received a grant from the CEH in the spring of 1984 to interview 70 women and produce a slide-tape program. For this initial project I collected family photographs from 12 of the women interviewed, and Cinda Roth, a friend and professional photographer, took additional photographs of the area. Colorado College provided the equipment for slide conversion and assembly of the sound track, which consists of portions of the interviews, narration recorded by my sister, Marci Jones Macaluso, and music played and sung by Freddie Blevins, one of the women interviewed. David Armstrong and Gus Mundt of the Colorado College Audiovisual Department were generous with their time and technical expertise. The slide-tape program was first presented to 100 members of the American Association of University Women at Colorado College in March 1985. The CEH later funded the conversion of the slide sequence to videotape with a professionally produced sound track, and eventually the transcription of the tapes so that I could compile this book. For the efforts of those mentioned above, I am very grateful.

Colorado College in Colorado Springs kindly served as fiscal agent for the CEH grants.

I also extend my sincere thanks to the following:

John H. Eddy, Jr., my husband, who spent many hours helping me with the historical aspects of this book.

My parents, Hugh and Margaret Jones, who provided money and equipment.

My Craig high school friend Pam Foster, who provided lodging and helped arrange the interviews.

The tape transcriber, Elaine Schantz, for the great care she took in her work.

Interviewee Virginia Shepherd, my mother's seventh-grade teacher, who provided encouragement and contacts in Meeker.

Joyce and Kenneth Kenney, my husband's sister and her husband, who supplied names of interviewees in Rangely.

Jackie Mock for help with contacts in Maybell.

Robert Dey for help with various details in Rangely.

And librarians Barbara Neilon at Colorado College, Robbie Nickol in Meeker, and Dortha Fae Babb in Craig, who made room for the tape and transcript collections at their facilities.

JULIE JONES-EDDY

I wish to thank Leslie Downs for her assistance in collecting the census data for the afterword and for her unfailing good cheer, to acknowledge my debt to Julie Jones-Eddy for undertaking such a fascinating project, and most of all to express my gratitude to the women who so generously shared their lives.

ELIZABETH JAMESON

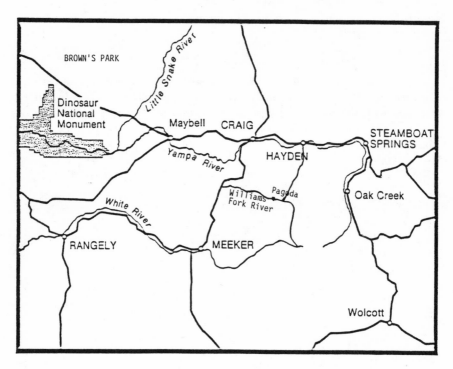

Northwestern Colorado
Courtesy of the Department of Interior

Introduction

The Land in Which They Lived

To understand these women's experiences, we need to know something about the land in which they lived. Unlike the more mountainous areas of Colorado, the northwestern corner has wide expanses of relatively flat land, interrupted by hills and only a few mountains. The land is covered with sagebrush, the hills with pinion and juniper pine, and in years with enough moisture, hardy grasses grow. The climate is harsh at times. Temperatures can drop to 40 or more degrees below zero in the winter, while in the summer, drought is a constant threat. Brown's Park, a valley that borders Utah and Wyoming, is an exception: it often has mild winters, providing winter range for sheep and cattle.

Described as "an isolated empire" by the historian Frederic Athearn,[1] northwestern Colorado has always been remote and sparsely populated. Home to the Ute Indians for hundreds of years, it was explored by the Spanish in the eighteenth century. Not until the early 1800s did anyone but the Indians live there. The fur trappers and traders lived in the area for parts of the year until the 1840s, when the beaver population was depleted and fur was no longer in demand.

Throughout the 1850s and 1860s, a number of explorers passed through the area looking for new overland routes. In 1853 Richens Lacy "Uncle Dick" Wootten trailed 9,000 sheep from New Mexico through northwestern Colorado and on to California. He found it to be a good route and recommended it to other emigrants who traveled through the area.[2] In 1857–58 Captain Randolph Marcy and Colonel William Loring came through the area from Utah, where they had been putting down a Mormon rebellion. They were on their way to Fort Union, New Mexico. Captain Marcy made his trip in December and nearly perished; Colonel Loring had better luck with his wagon train during the summer months.[3]

The 1870s brought geological and geographical surveys of the West to Colorado's western slope. In 1873 F. V. Hayden explored and mapped northwestern Colorado. With the publication of his exploration, the area became known to those who were seeking new, unsettled land in the west.[4] Settlers did not begin to move into the area until the 1880s, however, because it was still the home of the Ute Indians.

The Utes had once roamed much of the land in the western half of Colorado. As whites began settling in the southwestern region, the Indians were relocated to smaller and smaller areas in the northwestern corner of the state. During the 1870s government officials at the White River Indian Agency monitored their movements through the area and sought to avoid conflict with people moving into this part of the state.

In 1878 Nathan Meeker arrived to manage the agency on the White River. Meeker attempted to convert the Indians' nomadic way of life to an agricultural one, creating great resentment among the Indians. As the tensions mounted, he called for troops to protect the residents of the agency. Fighting broke out as the troops moved into the area, and when the soldiers arrived at the agency they found that 11 men, including Meeker, had been killed. Several women and children from the agency had been captured by the Indians but were later returned. As a result of this incident, the government removed the Utes to a reservation in eastern Utah.

In 1880 the land was opened for settlement, but the Indians continued to make return visits to their home in northwestern Colorado until the turn of the century. Their presence made it difficult for homesteaders. Although the Homestead Act was passed in 1862, most of the settlers in northwestern Colorado did not arrive until after 1900, and land continued to be available for homesteading until the early 1930s.[5]

Because of arid land and poor soil, people struggled to survive on the few acres of a homestead. They often filed for additional homesteads or bought land adjoining their homestead in order to increase the acreage. Until homesteaders began to practice dryland farming, irrigated crops were possible only along the river basins. Much of the land went for grazing, and many acres were required to support a few cattle. Indeed, it was so difficult to support a family on the few acres of a homestead that the men often worked in the coal mines or for the large cattle ranchers for part of the year, leaving the women to maintain the homestead.

Those who stayed in northwestern Colorado were determined, independent people who liked living in an unspoiled, sparsely populated land. The region is still relatively remote and unpopulated, if not so unspoiled. Located far from urban areas of any size, most communities in the region lie 250 to 300 miles over the Rocky Mountains from Denver and 200 to 300 miles from Salt Lake City. Roads into the area were few and difficult to travel until the 1930s and 1940s. Earlier, settlers made supply trips once or twice a year south to the railroad stop in Rifle, Colorado, or north to Wyoming. Eventually, in the late 1930s, U.S. Highway 40 was completed, providing a roadway from Denver to northwestern Colorado and on to Salt Lake City.

A railroad through the area was always a dream. The railroad from Denver over the mountains finally reached Craig in 1913 but went no farther. Transporting products from northwestern Colorado to the centers of commerce continued to impede economic growth. Despite these problems, the people in this area built successful cattle, sheep, and wheat operations. They developed their rich coal and oil reserves. And although life has been made harder with the rise and fall in the prices of these products, the people who settled northwestern Colorado remain hardy and persistent. They continue to endure.

Notes

1. Frederic J. Athearn, *An Isolated Empire: A History of Northwestern Colorado* (Washington, D.C.: Government Printing Office, 1982).

2. Duane Vandenbusche and Duane A. Smith, *A Land Alone: Colorado's Western Slope* (Boulder, Colo.: Pruett Publishing, 1981), 26.

3. Ibid., 28.

4. Ibid., 31.

5. Roy M. Robbins, *Our Landed Heritage: The Public Domain, 1776–1970* (Lincoln and London: University of Nebraska Press, 1976), 206–7, 343, 362–63, 375, 387. A person wishing to homestead registered his tract of land with the government, paid a small fee, and promised to live on the land for five years (called "proving up"). Although the first Homestead Act of 1862 authorized 160 acres per homestead, succeeding acts increased the acreage to allow for settlement of the arid western lands. In 1912 the residency requirement was changed from five years to three years.

Near Maybell
Photography by Cinda Roth

ONE

Starting a New Life

During the late nineteenth century and into the early twentieth, many homesteaders made the journey to northwestern Colorado in wagons, often traveling over the Continental Divide of the Rocky Mountains. The trip usually took about a month.

Mary Gates Haughey

In 1907 Mary Gates Haughey and her family moved from Missouri to Alamosa, Colorado. Her father attempted to farm grain and potatoes there, but the venture failed and he decided to move to Oregon. Mary was eight years old. Slowly making their way in a covered wagon over the mountains, they got no farther than the town of Craig: Mary's mother had become ill, and Mary's father decided to settle near Craig.

I went to school in a little schoolhouse they called the Star School at La Jara, Colorado. Then Dad left the farm and we went into Alamosa, and he worked for a while in the railroad shops; then he decided he was going to Oregon. So he assembled Mother and we kids; my brother was a small baby. [Dad] got us all together in a covered wagon, and we were going to Oregon. He had some friends—there were two or three more wagons of them, and one carriage coming. We had quite a lot of fun and adventures and stunts that we'd pull. I remember how it rained a time or two. Mud—oh, brother! [There were] six of us and two dogs and two cats in a covered wagon—it was rather full! But we kids had a ball.

How long did it take?

Well, it was right around the Fourth of July when we left Alamosa, and we arrived in Craig, down here at the old bridge on Bear River, on the seventh of August. There were so many places that there were no roads—[people] just kind of wandered around to find places to go through. I remember a snow slide that—why there was no road around that snowslide, why we went over it, I'll never know. But Dad what he called rough-locked the hind wheels of the wagon so it wouldn't slide [and] made Mother and we children and the dogs and the cats walk down that snow slide to get down there. Dad was scared spitless, of course. Oh, we had a ball, because we could slide on that old icy snow, and things like that.

And also on this trip, another night when we were camped, my brother and I decided we'd go fishing in this little tiny stream. And I caught my first fish there. We saw a little fish—oh, it must have been four or five inches long—and we scared it into a shallow pool and built a dam so it couldn't get away from us, and caught it with our hands. 'Course you can imagine how three kids that age—how wet we must have been. And clothing was a problem.

And then another time we decided we'd climb a hill. So Mahlon, my oldest brother, we got George between us, ahold of his hands, and we went up on this hill, and then we decided it'd be such fun to run down it. Of course, his legs were shorter than ours. The poor kid! We drug him—oh, Mother was so angry with us!

It was hard on your clothes to do those things, too, probably. They got dirty?

Filthy! Well, Mother would puddle them out if she could, and hang them, you know, around so they'd dry a little bit, but the most miserable part of it was when it would rain and we were penned in, in that wagon. Cooking, of course, was done on bonfires outside, and Mother was one of these clean people—she just couldn't stand all this greasy dirt and stuff, and she was eternally scrubbing the kettles and pans and things, to keep them halfway eatable, so we could eat the food. This one night that we were penned in, I remember this rancher coming up to the wagon, and we were trying to eat supper on old cold snacks. He had a great big bundle of fresh vegetables and a gallon bucket of fresh milk that he had brought to us. That's a real fond memory of how nice he was to us.

So your father then decided that Oregon was too far, and he decided to stop in Craig?

Well, Mother took very ill on the trip, and she was very, very sick when we came to Craig. He stopped at Craig, and walked uptown to see if he could find something. The population of Craig at that time was under 700. Well, fortunately he got acquainted—where, I don't know, but acquainted—with a man by the name of Luther Seldomridge. They had brought their son to town because he had chopped his heel with an ax and he had come down for medical care. By the time Dad visited with Mr. Seldomridge, who was a little sawmill owner—or manager, I don't know which—he had gotten himself a job.

The sawmill was up on Black Mountain, at the head of what was Fortification Creek. So Dad moved us all up there—Mother [was] real sick. And on the way up—going up to the place on the old trail, and it was mostly *trail*—we stopped at this McDonald place. Willis came out to see; anybody, you know, moving like that is a stranger and that is an *event*— you got to go see what's going on. So [he] came out and saw that Mother was ill, and Grandma McDonald—his mother—took Mother and us kids under her wing, just like an old mother hen, which she was, a *darling*. And Willis took the team and put them in the barn and fed them, and Grandma fed us. In a few minutes Dad had leased the place, and there we were.

Jenny Brown Spence

Jenny Brown Spence also came with her family to Colorado from Missouri in the early 1900s. She and her family traveled by covered wagon from Colorado Springs, over the mountains, to Meeker.

My parents came from Missouri, although they weren't born in Missouri. My father's sister and her husband had come up to Colorado Springs and were working in the lumber [industry]—they thought it was a new beginning. My mother's parents had died and left the property in Missouri to her and to her brother, so they decided to sell. She was heartbroken; she didn't want to live there anymore and have all those sad memories, with her parents gone. So they decided to sell everything and come to Colorado and work in the timber [business] there in Colorado Springs.

They had a sale, and my father fixed two wagons with mules, and all their household goods that they could bring, you know, in the wagon, and came to Colorado Springs. They had quite an experience in Kansas. They were in a blizzard and couldn't travel for several days. I don't know how they survived, really, and my father—I heard him tell the story, but, being young, I didn't pay any attention. I'm sorry that I didn't ask more questions, and I've often wondered how they *did* survive, because everything was covered with snow and the mules had to have feed. I suppose they had provisions with them for themselves, but he said actually, he didn't know whether they would make it or not.

But they finally did make it to Colorado Springs. And then they wrote a letter back to Missouri, and my brother and my mother and myself came on the train from Carthage, Missouri, to Colorado Springs.

We lived in Colorado Springs, at the foot of Pikes Peak, until June—until the roads got so that we could come on into Meeker. The reason we wanted to come to Meeker was that there were friends from Missouri that had come into Meeker and lived up on Flag Creek, and we were going to visit them on the way. We really were headed for California, but we were just taking in the sights along the way. So my family came on with my aunt and uncle—my father's sister and her husband and their family, they came—so we made quite a covered-wagon procession. We came from Colorado Springs into Meeker and took almost a month to make the trip. We did come over Tennessee Pass, and the roads were terrible, because it was not graveled—they were just country roads, and we had a heavy, heavy load. My father had his tool chest, and I know Mother said she had a cherry bedstead or bed that she cherished, and every once in a while, when they'd come to those steep hills, something would have to be thrown away. They tried to toss their bedstead out up on Tennessee Pass, but finally they would stop. They just would travel through the week, and they would always stop on Friday night and make camp, and stay over Saturday and Sunday. They would rest, and the women would wash the clothes and cook and bake, so that they could go on. We came over the Newcastle Road up White River; Mrs. Howey's two brothers lived up there in a little cabin on this place, and so we stayed there. We were still headed for [the] Howeys' up Flag Creek, so we came down [into Meeker] with the wagon and with all of us.

We got a room at what was called then the Miller House, and the menfolks took in all the sights. Mother was just scared to death. She said she had never seen cowboys, and she'd heard all these stories about the Indians and the bank robbers and all that. She said she was afraid to even put her head out the door.

But we took in the sights, and we parked—everybody came in with buggies and wagons to the celebration. All the events were up and down Main Street. And in the park there, where the courthouse is now, is where they had the picnic, where everybody took their lunches.

We went on in the next day, on up to the Howeys', and they were haying. They wanted my father to work in the hay with his mules, and my mother's brother was about 17 and could help in the hay. Mrs. Howey said that Mother could help her in the kitchen for her board and for Walter's board and my board. Of course, I was just a baby.

Mother said they thought that was pretty nice. They'd get some money for their team and for Dad, and that would help them on the way to California. They stayed there and worked, and Mother said she had never worked so hard in her life.

So when the hay was put up, Mother said she was *so* glad to leave there, because she had never been used to anything like that. They came back up the river and stayed there with Moon and Tom Stith. At that time everything was either horseback or with buggies, to come to Meeker, and that was about 20 miles, maybe more. So Mother didn't come down anymore, but Dad would go back and forth. They always stopped at [the] Wilbers'. That seemed to be where they would stop to feed their horses and feed themselves. They were always welcome, and Dad got acquainted with Mr. Wilber. He was on the school board for Coal Creek up there, and so he asked him—he knew that Dad was a teacher in their conversations and all; Dad had had a teaching certificate in Illinois and Carthage, Missouri—if he wouldn't like to teach [at] the Coal Creek School. He'd get some money, and [we] could have some money and go on to California. So he took the Coal Creek School [job], and we lived up there in a little log cabin.

I don't know how many years he taught up there, but he finally went down and taught in Powell Park. And he taught around until we were— we just never did get to California. He kept teaching, and we kept living out in the country. Well, finally it was time for me to get in school, six years old, so we came into Meeker, and we lived there in those govern- ment buildings [the log buildings where the military troops had been housed in the 1870s].

When the Moffat Rail was completed over Corona Pass in 1909, many families loaded their possessions into a migrant railroad car and rode the train over the high mountain passes to Steamboat Springs. From there the families traveled by wagon to their homestead site.

Janet Mortimer Eberle

Janet Mortimer Eberle was seven years old in 1918 when she and her mother rode the train from Denver to Steamboat Springs. Her family eventually homesteaded on Fortification Creek, which is north of Craig.

We came over on the Moffat train, which we called it, and it was in March. The snow was really deep, and we came over Corona Pass, which was the route of the railroad at that time. They had snowsheds up on top, and it was quite a trip. Some of our neighbors had given us some smelling salts to take in case we would have trouble coming over the high altitude. We didn't take the smelling salts—we got along fine.

How long did it take—do you remember?

Well, I'm not sure. I think about two days, because we were stalled up on top in the snowsheds for a time. We had to wait until they cleared the track in front of us, and then we came on.

Hilda Shelton Rawlinson

When she was 11, in 1916, Hilda Shelton Rawlinson and her family came over the mountains by railroad from Max, Nebraska.

My parents arrived in 1916—February—and we settled in Dry Lake, about 15 miles south of Maybell, Colorado, on a homestead.

You came in February. Wasn't that snowy, cold?

Very cold. The snow was—just the tops of the fence posts were sticking up. There was no wire—you could see no wire—and there was no road, just a trail. We came in on a sled, with a load of furniture—three loads, I think we had. All our possessions, from Max, Nebraska.

10

I think you said you came on an immigrant car?

Your horses, your chickens, all of your possessions was in this car, and they call it an immigrant car, which is nothing but a boxcar. And we unloaded in Craig. The depot in Craig was an old boxcar, and there was no streetlights. It was in the middle of the night when we came in, and we walked from the train with the conductor—he had his lantern, and we walked behind on this trail up to our hotel room. Of course, my dad had come ahead of us, my mother and I and my two sisters and my little brother. We came in the passenger car. We had to come over Corona Pass, way up high, and we were stuck in a snow slide—a snowshed. We sat in this snowshed until they got this snow slide cleaned off so we could come on. I think it took us two days to come from Max, Nebraska, which is just across the Colorado line. It took us that long.

We stayed in Craig the rest of the night, and the next morning we loaded our sleds and we headed for Maybell. We got to the river bridge, Mr. Wilcox's, and we stayed two days there, to let our teams rest, and then we went to his little cabin that he had close to our homestead. We stayed until March in this little cabin—two rooms—and then we moved to our homestead.

Virginia Shepherd

Virginia Shepherd was born in Meeker in 1905. She lived on a ranch near Buford, along the White River, with her parents until 1911, when the family moved to Meeker. Virginia's mother told her what it was like for a native Virginian to move to an isolated homestead in northwestern Colorado.

Well, my mother arrived in Colorado in March [1901], which isn't the best part of the year to enjoy Colorado. She arrived up at the little ranch near Buford, and that was to be her home for a period of years.

Mother was a Virginian. Her name was Virginia Macon Shepherd. She had grown up in rather a protected atmosphere, and I'm sure that life in pioneer Colorado must have been a great experience for her—it must have been a difficult experience.

First of all, she had grown up in Virginia thinking that there were some things that she did very well, like making beautifully light cakes, and another of her favorite dishes was deviled crab. [Here,] cakes fell with her Virginia recipes. Fortunately, my father knew a little about the fact that altitude affected baking, and he promised that they would soon stop at a neighbor's. A neighbor only 12 miles or so away in those days was a close neighbor. So she gradually adapted to that.

I think the loneliness must have been hard too. She had always lived close to people, and here she was, a little more than 20 miles from town, which was more than a half-day's trip behind horses, and that was another adjustment that she needed to make.

And then there were lonely times too when my father necessarily had to be away. I think about what she must have experienced when he was caught in a blizzard up on top of Burro Mountain. He did what people did in those days: if he came to an empty cabin—and there were many through the mountains, that the cowboys used—he went in and took shelter. But you were always supposed to, sometime later, replace whatever you used, and you were to leave the cabin in the condition it was. Well, the blizzard was so bad that night that he sat down and wrote his will, because he didn't think he was ever going to get out. He did, but it was several days later. I think of my mother waiting for him to come home, and his not appearing, and no way to reach her—no telephone up on top of Burro Mountain.

Julia Biskup Kawcak

Many of the families who settled in the Breeze Basin and Elk Head areas near Craig were European immigrants. Julia Biskup Kawcak's parents emigrated from Austria in the 1890s. Her father first came to Rockvale, Colorado, a coal-mining community, in 1894, and her mother followed in 1896. Julia was born in Rockvale in 1899. In 1908 the Biskup family moved to Breeze Basin, near Craig, to homestead near other family members and friends.

We came from Rockvale, Colorado—that's down by Canon City, a coal mine—and we came up to Rifle by train, through the Royal Gorge and up. The next morning after we got off of the train, we slept on the seats in the depot down there all night, and next morning the stagecoach come and picked us up and brought us up to Craig.

How long was that trip?

Two days. And it was—what was his name?—old Mr. Weyand [who] was the stage driver. One of these old ones. And the family, there was Mother and two sisters, and my brother and his wife, and two little brothers of mine, John and Steve. They were all in the coach, and I didn't have anyplace to sit. So I sat up there with the driver! I was in seventh heaven up there, believe me. I'd never seen a horse, just once in a while somewhere at the coal camp. But I sat up there with Steve Hoza. He later became my brother-in-law. He came up and took a homestead in Breeze Basin, way up at the other end.

My father come here; then Mike [Kawchack (Kawcak)] came and took up a homestead. *Everybody* came here because somehow Joe [Biskup, my brother,] found out about all this homesteading land going to be taken up. So Dad come over here with a friend, and they both took up homesteads, and then Dad didn't come back until the next spring. He quit the mine, and when he come back here, he came with tools and everything. Then, one by one, everybody was coming from different coal mines. They found out about us—you know, that [we] found this land—and everybody came.

Mary Birovchak Levkulich

Mary Birovchak Levkulich emigrated to this country from Hudlova, Austria-Hungary, in 1914 when she was 18. In Pennsylvania in 1917 she was married to a young man who was also an immigrant from Austria-Hungary. They lived in various coal-mining towns in Pennsylvania and Ohio until 1926, when they decided to homestead in northwestern Colorado.

Why did you decide to come all the way to the United States?

Because this country is better than Europe—lots better. My dad told me—he says, "Mary," [and] I told him I like to come to United States, and he says, "Yes, I let you go. I get you money." They borrow money from somewhere, people, and they let me go.

13

Picnic near Maybell, about 1917
Courtesy of Hilda Rawlinson

Hilda Rawlinson's family (Hilda is on the horse in the center) at their homestead. Near
Maybell, 1916
Courtesy of Hilda Rawlinson

Were there any other of your parents' children who got to come with you? Or were you the only one?

I'm the only one. I have brother in Czechoslovakia and one brother in Canada; he come to Canada but not United States, so I still have brother there. I was the oldest one.

I had to get somebody [to] sign [his] name in [my] passport. See, when you are underage, you can't come by yourself, so [this] man was coming from Europe, and he signed his name in my passport so he'd take care of me while I'm on the road, you know. But after I come to Ellis Island, they sent him back to Europe because they said he had heart trouble. I was left there, and I was nine days there. They wouldn't let me go, because they say, "You are underage, unless somebody come get you." Well, my cousin came there to get me, but she was underage—she was same age as I was. But she come, and they wouldn't even let me see her. But finally she brought a man with her, and he signed his name, so that'll work; I got out of there. They said they'll send me back to Europe, and I was crying—I didn't want to go back. So that's the way it was.

I lived with some of my friends, European people, and I paid them rent. And I got a job next day, $12 a month doing housework. Then after [that] I got a restaurant job and [a] little more pay. Then I got [a job] in [a] hotel, and I got $25 already a month. That was big money in those days.

How long did you live in New York City?

For three years. Then I come to my cousin, Betty [in Minersville, Pennsylvania]. She wanted me to come for her wedding. At that time I worked for a movie star, and I told her I come back. She say, "Mary, please come back—I want you to come back." But I never did. I met my husband then and married.

How long did you live in Pennsylvania after you were married?

Well, not very long after. We went to soft coal—that's Pittsburgh. We moved a lot of places because wherever mine work, my husband just in mine all the time. After that we went to Akron, Ohio.

When did you finally come to northwestern Colorado?

In 1926. See, his friends were there, with his family, and it was hard to find jobs in Webster, Pennsylvania, and he says, "Let's go [to] Colorado." They [Mr. Levkulich and his friend] heard about Colorado, that they have homesteads. But when they came, the good land was already taken—just not very good, whatever it was, so they had to buy it. My husband got 160 acres, down in Breeze Basin. So he pay $2,200 for that 160 acres [of] land. Twenty acres was wheat in it; the rest was brush, rocks, and everything.

Did you have a house to live in out there?

No. There was no house. We stayed some with friends till fall, and then in the fall he went back to the coal mines to work because he say, "Well, I'm not going to sit around." And we had to make payments on the farm too, so he went to Wyoming to get a job—[in] Rock Springs. And then in the spring again we went to plant some crops, you know.

When the family arrived on the homestead, usually in early spring, they often lived in tents until they could build a dugout or erect a cabin. The land was covered with sagebrush, which had to be removed before planting or building. Because this chore needed to be done as soon as possible, the women and children often helped. Of course, the women were also responsible for the cooking and washing. The cooking was done on an open fire or on the coal or wood stove the family brought with them. Clothes washing was an all-day affair. The family hauled the water from a spring or river in buckets or barrels and heated it over the fire or on the stove.

Hilda Shelton Rawlinson

And you started to work. First thing you did, you got your ax and you chopped the sagebrush—start in, put [up] your fence. And then you went right on, you know.

How long did you live in a tent?

We lived in a tent from March until January, and it was very cold, I'll tell you. My dad had to sit up many nights and keep the fire going so we wouldn't freeze. You know what our wood was? Sagebrush! You cut your sagebrush, and you had to go and haul your wood from the mountains—your fence posts; you cut your fence posts.

You were busy clearing the sagebrush to plant a little garden so you'd have something to eat and you'd have some food for your horses and your cows—we didn't have any cows at that particular time. And of course we made the dugout, which is an earth house, [as] they call them now. That was our home, the dugout, which was a wonderful thing after living in the tent in the cold—we really appreciated the dugout. It was very comfortable.

The dugout was a long building—a hole in the ground, with a dirt roof. And it had windows: two windows and a door in the end—the south end—and a partition with curtains. There was a window in the back part that gave light into the back end, and this window was built up from the roof—extended up, you know. Once in a while it would leak, and you got your buckets—maybe it would be in the middle of your bed or someplace. Sometimes the dirt would fall down on your table and get in the food, but we didn't pay any attention to that. But we were warm, and we always had something to eat. We were never hungry, we were never cold, and it was very comfortable. We had a wood stove for a kitchen stove, you know, and our tables and our chairs, and our beds and the dressers.

We went through the next winter, and the next winter, I think, and then finally we got the house built, which was an adobe house—eight-room house, two stories. And we lived in it two years. Then my dad decided to take up another homestead, an additional homestead, and go and do it all over again. So we did.

Esther Anderson Campbell (Chandler)

Esther Anderson Campbell (Chandler) came to teach school in Skull Creek in 1922. For 30 years she taught in several one-room schools in the Brown's Park area. Her first home after her marriage to Duard Campbell was a dugout near the schoolhouse. Although she has recently remarried and taken the name Chandler, she is well known throughout northwestern Colorado as Esther Campbell.

I realize that a lot of people nowadays, younger generation, don't know what a dugout is. It's just a little hole dug back into a hill—has a dirt roof, dirt floor, dirt walls, and usually sticks up out of the ground far enough that you can have a tiny window up at the top. One window in the front, and in that dugout I think there was one in the back, so it was maybe a couple of feet above the ground—the roof above that. So we were down in—it was nice and warm, comfortable. It faced west so that the window was a full-size window, but it sloped into the hill, you see. The back side was mostly just dirt wall, and the sides were dirt wall.

So you didn't cover the dirt with anything?

No. Not in that house. I lived in another dugout too; that was Duard's mother's dugout—her homestead cabin is what it was. Well, the dirt walls weren't covered there either, but they were hard and they didn't shale off bad. The floors were dirt, but to make them hard we would sprinkle them, and as we walked on it that packed it hard—it became hard as clay or cement almost.

When you sprinkled it, did it make a little bit of mud?

Well, it would if you stepped on it right away. But [the idea was to] not get enough to make mud—just kind of dampen it and pack it in. And then after a while you could use rugs on it.

Our home, after we were married, over on Douglas Mountain was a bigger log house, and we did pack those floors hard and even them up as much as possible. And yet any little rock or stake or anything like that felt sharp, and so we put linoleum down. Of course, people couldn't sit in their chairs like lots of men do and rock back on the hind legs—that would poke through. But just an ordinary chair—and we didn't have many chairs; we sat on stumps and so on—or boxes.

In this first little dugout I remember that if we had company—I don't believe we had any chairs; I don't remember what we sat on, but boxes up on end. I remember whenever we needed an extra chair, we used the washboard. Somebody sat on the top of the washboard.

In this little dugout we had a big cook range—wood-coal range. It belonged to Duard's mother, and it was in one corner. And we had a cupboard made of orange crates, and then our little table was in the next corner, I think, toward the other end, and the bed over across from it, in that corner. I fixed some way to hang clothes—just a rod fixed up some way with a curtain around it for our closet. And behind the door was a big barrel: in the winter we'd gather snow and put in that; we had ice water that way.

Julia Biskup Kawcak

I came here to Craig in 1908, April tenth, with my parents, and they had a ranch out on Breeze Basin. It used to be an old Breeze homestead, or whatever they had then. They had land, and my father got it for $1,500. But there wasn't sagebrush chopped on it, so we had to clean it all.

Our house was an old log house. My father and Tony Backus—[Tony] helped him fix that log cabin up, because it was nothing, just logs, and the windows were broke out and all. Those windows were from up there [gestures] clear to the floor at that time. The windows were so long, you know, and dirt roof. They put in a new floor, and they daubed it—you had to daub it with mud, you know. Then they put oilcloth on the walls and cheesecloth on the ceiling—because dirt would fall! [Laughter.] And if there was a mouse up in that dirt, you could see it running around on that cheesecloth!

[The log cabin] was about 14 by 14 [feet]. That first year, when it rained in the fall, it was leaking everywhere. We had buckets and pans all over. So my father went to town, and he got canvas [and] put them over the beds so we could at least sleep without getting [wet].

Well, next year, after we came here, you see, we had the J. W. Hugus Company down here on the corner [in Craig], across from our old bank. That was a general store. They had everything from toothpicks to binders and plows and everything. Then [Dad] got a chance to haul freight from Steamboat to help pay our grocery bill. They let us have groceries—anything we needed—and he'd haul freight.

There used to be crickets come here by the millions—you couldn't even step anywhere. If you was in the way and they were coming, they'd just come right up your legs. You was always stomping when you was around them. But our neighbors told us about them. They told us that every year they make a noise on buckets and pans and stuff [when] they're coming, so we'd watch. Now the first year we cleaned off five acres of brush. We carried all that brush to the outside and made a fence all the way around it, because we had a couple of cows, and that was our fence around that oats.

We had to watch so [the crickets] wouldn't get into our oats. So when we heard them, it was towards evening, about 5:00, 6:00, or something. We heard them making noise down there. So we get our tubs and buckets and pans—everybody with a stick, you know. We went over to the corner of the fence. We were waiting there for them; we started making noise. Instead of coming straight there, they kind of turned and went around that sagebrush. We just kept a-pounding, and they were getting out of the way. It took a long time for the back end of them to come.

And then when it got dark, they got into that sagebrush, into that pile. So after we knew that they were already hiding, my father and brother Joe, they lit that, burned it. Oh, you ought to have heard the *frying* in there! [Laughter.] Honest! They were horrible!

Did they come every summer?

Every summer there for a while, yes, they did. They come down from the bridge up through there and come all the way through, clear up into where the Lyonses lived, you know, and we got them burnt. The next morning Dad and Joe got up early, and they went out there to see how many were out there—didn't want them in the oats. So they went making noise around there, and they seen them out in the sagebrush, hopping away, and they were very, very thin—wasn't any of them. The next year they come again. Well, we had more lands, and we had to keep them away from the wheat and everything.

They would eat it?

Oh, yes—just eat every bit of it to the ground. You know, grasshoppers do that to some farmers back in the eastern slope. But after a few years later, they didn't show up anymore.

Oma Jensen Graham

The crickets were a devastating experience for Oma Jensen Graham's parents, who homesteaded near the Utah border in the early 1900s. After losing cattle to a hard winter and enduring three years of crickets, they left the homestead in 1927 and moved to Buford, where Oma's father was a foreman for a large ranch.

Dad was a cowpuncher all of his life, and we homesteaded on this outfit. We raised some hay and things like that, and then after the hard winter—I think that was about 1919, 1920—most of the cattlemen went out of business because cattle froze to death and starved to death. And then we had three years of Mormon crickets [black wingless grasshoppers, first encountered by the Mormons in Utah in 1848], and that was about it.*

They ate everything. They'd come to a post and just go right up over it—you couldn't turn them. They stripped all the service berries, the quaking aspen, and the choke-cherry leaves—just left the bare branches. And they went down through the alfalfa field, and all you had was—just looked like a bunch of pencils was sitting down there.

Julia Biskup Kawcak

Julia married Paul Kawcak in 1915 when she was 16. She helped her husband dig the water well on their new homestead in the Elk Head area.

We got 80 acres to start with, because the rest wasn't turned loose. Then later on we were to get 160. Well, they didn't have 160 there, but we had an 80. Then a couple [or] three years later they turned loose that land, so we took that up. We got 360 acres. There was one 40 left there, 40 acres, that was just between everybody, and the government gave it to us. And we proved up on everything. You had to live there three years and have 20 acres plowed and fenced. Well, we had all that, and we proved up on it. From then on we were paying taxes. That's where our county started living—they started building.

We dug our well, him and I. Then [when] we got about 12 feet down, we got into solid gravel. It had to be blown up. I'd go down there on the ladder, help him drill a hole, and he'd put dynamite in and then put a long fuse on it, and I'd come back up the ladder. We had a rope on the ladder so that when he jumped out I could already pull the ladder out of the well. And then we'd run! Boy, rocks would just be blown up everywhere.

Well, then he'd go back down in and load it into that bucket, and I pulled it out. I had to drag it a ways to dump it. But it was just an every-day job, to me. We had to get it done. So then, about 13, 14 feet, I think, there was that gravel, and I had to go down there every time, [to] help

*U.S. Department of Agriculture, *Grass: The Yearbook of Agriculture, 1948* (Washington, D.C.: Government Printing Office, 1948), 274.

him. He left a little wall of that gravel, see, so from there on after we put rocks to rock the well up.

Below that, we come into blue slate, and we got down to 40 feet. I had to go down there and help him drill those holes every time. We had one ladder down to that wall and then the other one from there down into the well. We had a long rope on that lower one, so when I'd come out I got ahold of that lower ladder rope, and he lit it and hurried up that ladder and got on the other one. While he was coming up the other one, I pulled the ladder out of the well. When he got out, he already had the rope in his hand, and he drug the other one and we ran—so we wouldn't get hit by the rocks, you know.

After you got past the slate, did you finally find water?

Yes, but we didn't have too much. We built a reservoir, just with the horses and a scraper, just above where we were going to build our house. We had water in that the next year, and, you know, from that, we got a lot of water in our well. You can get about 1,100 or 1,200 gallons of water at a time out of there.

Then we were up in the mountains hauling logs—he was, and his brother. Hauling logs to the sawmill. [There was] a sawmill up there on Black Mountain, and they sawed the lumber—it was just rough lumber—and while they were doing that, I was grubbing sagebrush. I grubbed out about two acres of brush where we were going to build the house, so there wouldn't be anything to catch fire real close. Well, I had all that dug out and everything when they brought the lumber. Then they were building. First he dug a little cellar under the house. They rocked it, made a rock foundation, just out of rocks, then built the house on top of that. It [had] 14-by-14 [foot] rooms, and we had a pretty high attic. After the kids were big enough to go from downstairs upstairs, they slept some in one end of the attic and some in the other. The girls had a blanket in the middle there, so the boys wouldn't be seeing them. The boys were at one end, and the girls in the other. Just had a spring—a bedspring and a mattress. The mattress was made out of some heavy material, filled with hay.

Chloe Bunker Vaughan

In 1926, when she was 24, Chloe Bunker Vaughan came from Illinois to visit her sister, who lived in Brown's Park. She met Minford Vaughan at her sister's house, and soon they were married. They homesteaded on Zenobia Peak in Brown's Park and later owned other ranchland. Chloe had one daughter.

We came down [from Craig] in a wagon, and we had, oh, 18 or 20 bum lambs [lambs without a mother] in the back of the wagon, and we stopped three times a day to feed them. We camped all the way down. It took us about five or six days. It would be about 150 miles, I imagine. And we took the back roads. We didn't go on the main highway at all. I didn't know anything, because I never rode a horse until I come here, you see. My husband would take me and show me a certain point or knob to head to, and then he would go around the road with the wagon and we would meet over there that evening.

I was all by myself, and I had cows, and sheep, and—well, they'd all go different directions, you know. I got so upset I just didn't know what I was doing, but I kept a-going.

As you were making that trip, how many ranches or people did you see on the way?

I didn't see any, because I was in the back road in the hills.

What time of year was that?

It was in the spring of the year, because I know the feed was coming up and, you know, the stock wanted that grain and feed. And that's what made me so nervous—I couldn't keep them moving.

When you got to this place, what did you do next? Was there a house?

No, no. We just had a little old tipi—a tent—and we slept in that, and I cooked out on the camp fire. And we had a pack—we had a little burro. I had him too, to drive. We had our food and bed thrown over the top; you know how they do. And that's what we used.

We came down to Zenobia Peak, and that summer we had our little tent to sleep in. Then we took the lumber that we were going to use for the roof of the house and made a lean-to, and we put all of our food and things under that. I had my clothes in a trunk.

23

Did your husband start to build the house at that time?

Well, we both did. We had an old crooked saw—had a nail in one end and a handle on the other. We went up there on Zenobia Peak and cut logs for our house. I think it took 48 logs for the house. We made it 20 by 30 [feet]. 'Course, I had always lived in a big home; I guess I thought the cabin, I couldn't live in it, because we made it big—20 by 30.

We had a living room that was about 20 by 20, and then I had a little kitchen, 10 by 10, and then off to the side we had our bed and our little dresser.

When did you get it built well enough so that you could live in it?

Oh, we had it up by fall—with a roof on it and all. Of course, it wasn't really finished, but we had it livable. Then later, up above, there was a spring, and—that was lots of rocks to bring that water over—he brought the water down and put the water in the house.

On the way down, there was a big rock that we could hide behind. And we put up a curtain on one side, and at noon, around noon or 2:00, that water would be so hot that you could take the loveliest showers. And so we—[laughter]. He tried to make it just as nice for me as he could, because he knew that I had always lived in a nice home.

How did you feel about doing that? Were you frightened?

I loved it—I just loved it! The country was beautiful. He never went anyplace without me. He took me everyplace, and we'd just turn our sheep loose and they'd be all right. There was no other sheep up there, and we'd just turn them loose and go ahead and cut our logs and everything. And fix springs—we had lots of springs we had to fix.

What do you mean by that?

Well, for the water. You see, the sheep would all pour in at one time. And so he hollowed out great big trees. He'd cut the middle out; that made the troughs. We'd have a row of those troughs. If they'd be filled up with water, the sheep would come in and drink.

Jayne White Hoth

Jayne White Hoth's grandmother, Sarah Carpenter Farrell, came by herself to homestead in the area around Maybell in 1887. Jayne grew up on the family homestead.

My grandmother came from Cincinnati, Ohio, and she homesteaded about 1887, I think it was. She had 160 acres down by what they call Sunbeam now. It bordered the old King ranch. She met my grandfather, who was a cowboy, because he had been snow-blind and he came over there because she did a little midwifing and some practical nursing. She helped him get his eyesight back again, with medication, which, I think, if I remember correctly, she told me she brewed from cedar leaves for tea, and you used the poultices and it was successful. Anyway, they became engaged, and they were married up at Hahn's Peak in 1890, by Judge Walbridge.

She's the first woman I have heard about who came here on her own to homestead.

Well, she was considered a failure in Cincinnati because she was 32 years old and she was an old maid. She was the only girl, and she had five brothers. She was a little rebellious over the whole situation. My grandmother was a *very*, oh, jolly type of person, lots of ambition. And at her time of life nursing was *not* considered the thing to do. Although she never had a license, she was very, very competent.

She was known as Aunt Sally around Moffat County for years and years. I think she told me at one time that she'd helped 110 babies into the world and never lost one, so I think that's quite a record.

Minnie Eberle James

Minnie Eberle James moved with her family to the Craig area from Michigan in 1910 at age 14. Her parents brought nine children with them. They first lived on a rented ranch and later moved to their homestead.

The house had a dirt roof, which I'd never seen before. On the inside they had papered it with—like we would use paper, they used muslin on the walls. We had four rooms.

How far was it from the river to the house?

About, oh, two miles up the bank. We'd haul the water, I imagine, every other day.

[We heated the water] just in a dishpan on the stove. [We had] a range. I think that everybody had coal more or less, because they could go to Mt. Harris and get it, haul it in. So I think we just used kindling to build a fire; coal kept it going. It was so cold, and we'd get up in the morning and we'd go to the kitchen to get warm. One time I had a burn clear across my leg like that [gestures], where I'd gotten close to the oven door. The oven door was down and it was real hot, and I had an awfully sore leg for a while.

How did you bake a cake in a stove in which you couldn't set the temperature?

You could tell just by feeling in those days—that's the only way you had. You just could tell by how big a fire you had and by feeling the heat if it was hot enough. We did baking, just the same as they did anywhere else, you know. [If it was too hot] then you'd open the door and let the [heat out].

Did you have a garden?

We tried a garden; my dad believed in having fruit trees and things like that, and after we moved over on the homestead he just *had* to have plants. He planted fruit trees and he planted grapes, and Mother planted lilacs. We had flowers and fruit, but it didn't do any good, you know, because of winter kill. We'd have things like turnips and carrots and cabbage and stuff like that would grow. Spinach [too]. There wasn't rain enough. You didn't have irrigation on this place.

Janet Mortimer Eberle

When we were homesteading [1921], there were sizable neighborhoods. In the Sand Springs neighborhood we had 16 or 18 kids in the school. That's a fair-size school. At the Williams School we didn't have that many, but that was a little later, and some of the people were leaving the homestead. But when we were at Sand Springs, that was the peak of the homestead [period].

When people left the homestead, did they finally just give up?

Sometimes. Sometimes they would move to town then and go on with their lives—butcher, baker, candlestick maker—and leave the homestead, and then perhaps they would sell it later. Or sometimes they kept it for a number of years, but sometimes *the* farmer, the farmer in the neighborhood, would buy up that property.

Our homestead was like hundreds of them in Moffat County—probably other counties too. Instead of any kind of a substructure, you hauled in the best rocks you could find and you put the four biggest ones in the corners. And then you put other rocks between the corners. And then it was made out of green lumber—it came from your grandfather's mill up on Black Mountain. We started out with one room, and the house was just board and batting. There was no insulation. There was nothing on the inside, except the inside of the boards. The batting was on the outside. Wide boards were put up vertically and then over the crack the batting. Believe me, they were cold.

Lana Gregory Idol

Although Lana Gregory Idol didn't live in northwestern Colorado until she was a teenager, she later married Loren Idol, whose parents came to the Meeker area to homestead in 1916. Her mother-in-law told Lana about many experiences on the homestead.

My husband's mother was quite a little lady—Nellie Idol. They came out here because they didn't think she could live for a year. She had what they called lung fever. And she lived to be 97!

27

Did she have tuberculosis?

No, she didn't really have tuberculosis. She had a bad heart, but they thought it was tuberculosis. Mr. Idol sold everything they had back in Missouri and came with the train. They brought what they called gondolas, and they loaded all their stock and their furniture and their farm machinery and the whole thing. They homesteaded in 1916 on Strawberry Creek [northwest of Meeker]. And Nellie was very active in everything. She started the first Sunday school. She taught in all the schools around the valley, and she was a good teacher.

They had a bad time. They had a five-room house and had all their furniture and everything; Grandmother had nice things. And it all burned down, the whole thing. They went to a party one night up at Price Creek; some of her relatives lived up there. And when they came home, Loren said he could remember that. He was about nine. He said there was just the four pillars, the four corners of the house were glowing, and that was all that was left. They lost everything they had. So she lived in a tent for one whole winter, and they had a tent as a granary. She did all her cooking in that tent, and they slept in the granary until they could build a house the next spring. They hauled their logs off of Sawmill Mountain, which was about 23 miles. She would ride up on that load of logs and then drive one team while Barnett, her husband, drove the other team. Loren said many times he'd seen her reach over and throw on that brake and it would trip her. She weighed about 95 pounds.

June O'Connell Sweeney

June O'Connell Sweeney came to Moffat County in 1925 as a first-year rural schoolteacher. She married Henry Sweeney the following year and went to live on a ranch near Maybell. She came to know Henry's mother, Mary, who had homesteaded with her husband in the late 1890s.

The only thing I know about Mother Sweeney [my husband's mother] was that she came over from Ireland when she was just a young girl. She was of a good family in Ireland. Her father was a shoemaker, and that was quite a respected trade. They had enough money so she didn't have to come steerage when she came across the ocean. They paid her way.

She came across the country to Meeker with this banker and worked in the kitchen for them. Then she went back [to Ireland]. She saved enough money, and, along with her folks in Ireland, she brought her sister back. And so her sister lived down at Maybell.

When Dad Sweeney went over to buy groceries, where Mary Frawley, as her name was then, was working, the banker had him come over and meet Mary Frawley. That connected the two of them, [and] they were married [about 1890].

If you'd seen the house that they lived in those first years—I couldn't believe it, till I went over. Everything was made out of logs—everything. And [earlier I'd] said to myself, "Well, they couldn't make a table out of logs—they couldn't make a bed out of logs. Boy, it [would] sure be a bumpy bed." When I got over there, of course, [I] saw it. You know how they did it, don't you? They slit the logs in two, so they were flat! [Laughter.] I don't know—it must have been eight by eight [feet] or something like that. She had two children when they moved over on the river.

A bed that was made out of logs must have been hard. What did they put on top?

Hay. That's how they softened it, was with the hay, because there was a natural meadow and they put up the hay from the natural meadow.

That was the old ranch. That was the one that Dad Sweeney filed on as his original homestead [in Axial Basin] in about 1888–89. Then they moved over to the river, and they had to move early [in the spring]. She'd already had two children—two boys—and it was cold. It was March when he bundled her up, and he'd worked all winter on the house on the river. But if they left later than that—and she was pregnant, with my husband—the gulches would be full of water and they couldn't have got there. So in late April—that's when [my husband] was born—why, she and the two boys were in the wagon, and they came through a blizzard to get down to the ranch house that he'd worked on all winter.

When they got to the neighbor's, they had to just pick [Mother Sweeney] up and carry her in and give her some whiskey and thaw her out. But then they had to go on to their own house, which was only about a half-mile away from that place. It was a nice, big house, and it had some hardwood floors. When we were married, she had lovely floors. She said she saved the coffee grounds and took the coloring from the coffee grounds. She got the floor darker and darker, and it just shined and was a beautiful floor. Hardwood. Every year they used to put a softwood floor in, and every year the softwood floor was worn out. So finally Dad

Sweeney got hardwood, and this hardwood, of course, lasted. She always kept it nice and neat; all she ever did was wash and cook.

She'd had an education in Ireland. They'd sent her to school. She could read and she could write, and she started to teach the boys to read and to write too, before they had a teacher for their school. And then she made them learn their catechism. Once a year the priest came through the country, and they had mass at the Sweeney house. The priest told them, "Now this is the catechism you learn to say to me next year."

Then when the cowboys would come, they'd sit around at any kind of paper—it could be a year old—but by the lamp. They'd sit around on the floor, and Mary would read them the news.

She was a woman alone among all men.

Doris Stephenson Warren

Doris Stephenson Warren grew up in Meeker. Her maternal grandparents homesteaded in the Meeker area around the turn of the century. She remembers stories told to her by her grandmother about the trip to northwestern Colorado and life on the homestead.

My mother was Goldie May Wilson Stephenson, and her parents were H. T. Wilson and Minirva Jane Wilson. They had started out to find a new home. They started from Terre Haute, Indiana, and they stayed in Kansas for about seven years. Then they started on to Colorado, and my mother was born in Beatrice, Nebraska, in 1889.

Did she tell you stories about that trip?

Well, my mother didn't tell me as much as my grandmother. I stayed with my grandmother quite a bit as a little girl, and I know I asked my grandmother if they saw Indians on the way. She said no, but she said there were robbers who would rob the people's cattle that were traveling by train, and said they had a horn they would blow at night. Then the cattle would stampede, and they would gather up the cattle. Of course, they had cattle with them, and also mules, because my grandfather was going to raise mules after he arrived in Colorado.

She also told me one time that she had had to make her own homemade soap, which would have been lye soap at that time. She didn't really have a very large supply to bring with her on the wagon, but she said she was washing the clothes and she looked up and her soap was gone. She saw this cow, and the cow had the soap in [its] mouth, and the suds were rolling out of its mouth, and that struck me quite funny. She said she had to chase the cow quite a ways to make it give her back her soap. [Laughter.]

They came to Rio Blanco County and they settled—it's eight miles south of Meeker, up Flag Creek. That was their homestead. My grandfather accumulated, I think, around 10,000 acres before he passed away—which was quite a large ranch in those days.

My grandparents' home was just a log house with a dirt top. I can remember it very well, and they had weeds growing out of the top of the house. They had no lawn, no flowers, and they had well water, which was very hard. My grandmother used to have to what she called break it with lye to get it soft enough to make a suds at all. When she washed her dishes—as a little girl I remember washing dishes there, [and] you couldn't use soap in the water. It was so hard it would just make a scum around. So you didn't use soap; you just washed them in water, and then you scalded them with—you know, poured boiling water over them. It was well water. They had a well, and it all had to be drawn by an iron pump.

[The house] had a kitchen, with sloping wooden floors—because it had settled, they sloped. My grandmother didn't have linoleum on it; she put hot linseed oil on them once in a while, and then you just had to mop them and they looked pretty.

The ceilings were lined with cheesecloth and just painted. I remember as a little girl the mice scurrying across in the ceiling at night. I could see their feet come down through the holes once in a while, and that was irritating! [Laughter.]

But very simple—just a cupboard in one corner, with a cloth on a wire pulled across for the door, and another cupboard with great big doors. It was wooden, but I think it had screen doors. And a great long table, which would be our counters now, with a sink top on it, that they used to roll their bread out on and cook on. And then just a square oak table that they used to eat at. It was quite a large room. [There was] a Majestic stove that had a reservoir for the hot water. And then behind the door they always put up their ice and drank ice water the year round, because the well water didn't taste good. The barrel in the wintertime was in the kitchen behind the kitchen door, and then in the summer it was out underneath a kind of a lean-to shed where it didn't melt so fast, I guess, in the hot weather.

Where did they get the ice?

They put it up off Flag Creek. There were beaver ponds, and they put it up off the beaver ponds; they may have even come to the White River and put up some. Now he had a reservoir farther up that he made with teams and horses and scoops. It was quite a large reservoir. They may have put it up on that reservoir. I'm just not really sure.

They had a dining room, and off the dining room there was a little room that they called the—I don't know what they called it—milk room, maybe. The separator was there, where they milked the cows and separated the milk. Then there was a living room and two bedrooms. It was very oddly arranged. Both bedrooms—instead of having their own doorway, you had to go through one to get to the other one.

What about walls? Were they just the logs?

I think they were logs, with cheesecloth over them. Once in a while she'd take that down and either put up new or wash it, and then they'd put [on] what they called calcimine then. It was kind of a chalky paint, you know. You couldn't wash it; you just had to put it on.

Mary Gates Haughey

These people came in, you see, like a boomtime, to settle [in the Craig area], and they had so much advertising about this part of the country being open for homesteading, and all of this good stuff—why, it's amazing how many came in at the time [about 1915].

Where did they advertise?

Eastern papers.

Do you have any feeling about how many people came and gave up and left? Did most people stay, or did many people leave?

Most left. And the country—I learned this from when I was working in the county clerk's office—there was hundreds and hundreds of acres of land in Moffat County that the county owned. They took it as tax.

You see, the people just couldn't make it. Maybe we'd have a good year, and then there'd be these droughts and they couldn't raise anything. And squirrels were here by the millions, and so were sage chickens, and they kept just a wide area on the edge of the fields mowed to the ground. The people in Great Divide had a terrible time trying to raise beans, because sage chickens sure did love the blossoms on beans.

Most homesteaders had a few head of cattle, and they had their horses, which was a means of transportation at that time, and maybe a sheep or two, and chickens—always chickens. And we did raise immense gardens. I was at a fair at Great Divide, I guess, in 1924. Their fair was equal to the ones they now hold down here, at that one time. Beautiful produce, and the following year was a drought. So that was one reason so many people just gave up.

TWO

Home and Family

Life on the homestead for women in northwestern Colorado at the turn of the century was much like life on homesteads in other parts of the West since the 1850s. These women cooked on coal or wood stoves, hauled water from the river or a well, and depended on food they could grow or raise. Trips to town for supplies and staples were few and far between. For economic reasons, the women made most of the clothing except for the boys' and men's overalls. Basic clothing was sometimes available in town or through a catalog, but it was often too expensive for homesteading families.

Margaret Tagert Jones

Margaret Tagert Jones's grandparents came to northwestern Colorado about 1890. They homesteaded on the Yampa River near Juniper Springs when Margaret's mother was eight. Later they moved to the Powell Park area, west of Meeker on the White River.

The people of that area [Juniper Springs] made trips twice a year to Rawlins, Wyoming, to get supplies for the rest of the year. The men went in wagons, and the mothers and children stayed at home. Sometimes it might take a month to make this trip. [My mother] looked forward to that, though, because it meant all these good things that they would bring home. She told me about Christmas, when they were able to have a fresh orange or two, or maybe half a dozen, which was a *real* treat.

They lived on the banks of the Bear River. They called it the Bear River in those days, but now we call it the Yampa—the Indian name for "bear." They were on the south side of the river and had to ford the river to go north, which was the direction of Rawlins, Wyoming. The men had little boats: canoes, I suppose. Maybe they were flat-bottom wooden boats—I don't know what, but something to transport them across the river.

When they took the wagons, I guess they just forded the river with the wagons and the horses. But they kept this boat so that they could get back and forth, and it was a sort of lifeline, I guess, to other neighbors and to Lay, the only place of any community activity and [one that] served as a stockade.

The men had left on their trip, and my grandmother looked out the window and noticed that the boat or canoe had been washed away from the mooring. They kept it tied to a fence, a wire fence that extended out into the river a little way. The boat had hung up at the end of the fence, and she felt that she might be able to retrieve it but she'd have to climb out on this fence. It was in the spring, and the river was fast and deep. My mother might have been around eight years old. [Grandmother] told my mother that she was going to try to retrieve the boat. If she didn't get back and she fell in the river, then my mother should get the horse, put the children on the horse, and go to the neighbor's, which was about seven miles away—the closest neighbor.

My grandmother was successful at this and she did get back, and my mother would tell me about how disappointed she was, because they very rarely got to play with the neighbor children! That was a real treat; it only happened once or twice a year, and here she'd missed a beautiful chance!

Lois Wells Bair

In 1923, when Lois Wells Bair was 11, she moved with her family from Oklahoma to Skull Creek, near Rangely. Her parents had 10 children.

We bought 320 acres from my uncle. We were in a one-room log cabin with a fireplace. It took lots of wood; you had to keep turning to keep warm. We hauled water in wooden barrels and hauled wood in a wagon. We children rode the horses about three miles to Skull Creek to water them every day.

We lived on a dry farm, and my dad did dig a well down 60 feet and hit good water. It was really good: it was so ice-cold. But around the top there was alkali, and the alkali would fall in the water, and then it made it bitter and also made it give you a kind of diarrhea.

How did you drink the water, under those circumstances?

You could barely drink it when it was just fresh out of the well, because it was ice-cold, and you could get it down, but really it wasn't very good.

Did you have another source of water, then?

We had to haul the water from three miles up the creek every few days.

One summer day Mother and some of us were lying on the bed. She was reading to us, and one of the children was sick. I think there were six or seven of us [children] at that time. When we looked down on the floor, there was a big rattlesnake coiled up and ready to strike. He was looking at our black cat. My oldest sister took the .22 gun and hit the snake in the head.

One day in August, Otis Chamberlain brought us a half a deer and that was the best meat I ever ate. My mother cried and fried some of it in hot grease, and then you could just take it out and warm it up. It was the only meat we had—the only [other] meat we had was rabbits and sage chickens. My dad made chili out of ground jackrabbits. I remember he made taffy candy at Christmastime. It was good.

My mother made us girls dresses out of flour sacks. She dyed them real pretty colors, and we just—you know, didn't have too many clothes, of course, but she kept us clean.

Oma Jensen Graham

Oma was very familiar with wood and coal stoves; she grew up on a homestead in Brown's Park. She was married in 1930 and spent many years working on ranches with her husband.

I would think it would be hard to cook with wood.

Well, it isn't hard to cook if you want a quick fire; why, you get your wood. If you want to bake biscuits in a hurry, you use wood. We always banked our cookstove at night, to keep the house warm. And we had an old heating stove. They're very different than these kind you've got now. They were safer than the ones we've got now, and they had a grate in them. You could bank your coal all night long.

You have some live coals in there. You put your coal, some more coal, on top—you don't want to smother it out, but some pretty good-size chunks. Then you adjust the draft—you always had a draft down there. You had the chimney, and a damper in that, and then you adjust[ed] that damper. You didn't shut it off tight, because your coal would smolder and you'd get this pollution from it. But you always left a crack—you could tell. You always left just a tiny little crack down here [gestures]—your adjuster was just under your firebox—just enough so that you'd get enough draft so it would burn slow. And they banked all night.

Then you had an old shaker, [to] shake the ashes down if you wanted. In the summertime when you didn't bank your fire, why, you shook the ashes into the ash pan and started with kindling on up, is what you did.

But you better have those old stoves, like Majestic or Universal, that would bank, and they had a reservoir.

And the reservoir was for what?

Water—that heats your water. It held a little over five gallons, and it was made out of copper.

Did you use that water just for cooking, or did you use it for washing clothes?

Well, when you wanted to wash clothes, five gallons didn't go very far. You had an old boiler that you filled from the spring or from the ditch, and come in and got it hot, and then you washed on the board. With lye soap.

Stella La Force Rector

Stella La Force Rector came as a young bride to a ranch near Rangely in 1939. She had grown up in Glenwood Springs, Colorado, and had much to learn about the duties of a rancher's wife.

You got up very early in the morning. Jay would get up and build the fire and go feed his livestock, his horses and things that he was going to use that day. I would get up and dress—get the children up if they were awake—and then we would prepare breakfast. And, of course, everybody got up for breakfast; even if you were only nine months old, you sat at the table for breakfast. If it was during roundup time, if you had extra help, you had men to cook for, so immediately you started to bake desserts or whatever you were going to have. If not, why, you had washing and ironing—wash day was a real all-day project. You had to pack the water to heat it and then put it in the washing machine, if you were so lucky as to have a washing machine. And then, of course, you always had your meals to prepare, and in the summertime you had your other things. You had a garden and the chickens and the little chores that you have that go with living on a ranch. And then there was always sewing and mending that had to be done. I made nearly everything that the kids and myself wore.

How many hay hands did you say there were, that you cooked for?

Oh, I think probably the most that I ever cooked for, because we—the high-country ranches, you didn't really have all that much haying, and we probably had maybe three. At roundup time you had a lot more people, because the neighbors helped, and it was usually kind of a potluck affair for branding and roundup. Sometimes there would be 15 or 20 people, and if some of the neighbor ladies came, they always brought something, [which] made it a lot easier.

Were there neighbors close by—did you see other women often?

Well, not all that often. Most of the people you saw were cowboys that were looking for a cow and would stop by. When I was first married, being raised in town most of my life, I would invite them in and visit with them. And then Jay would come in, and he would really get upset with me, because the first thing you're supposed to say to them is, "Have you eaten?" and I didn't [laughter].

So anyway, I learned. Donna and Jerry Hill lived in the wintertime out close to us, and when we lived out in the Dragon area. And then, of course, it was 20 miles in here to the river in the wintertime. On holidays or maybe once a month or something, we would go to the neighbor's ranch to visit or just for the company, and that's the only time you ever saw another woman.

Was it lonely?

Well, not really. When I first moved to Rangely, it was so arid, compared to the Glenwood Springs area, and, of course, I think too, as I look back, that probably the lack of people [was hard for me]— because I was real social and enjoyed being with people, and I still do. I hated Rangely for the first two years I lived here. And did a lot of crying! [Laughter.] But after that, I don't remember being lonely and dissatisfied.

Since you didn't grow up on a ranch and didn't learn to do all those things, was that adjustment difficult?

Well, probably the most adjusting part of it was just being very young—when I first came to the ranch and was so isolated and everything, and having to learn all these things for myself. And I never did really like to cook. Having to cook three meals a day was a *real* hardship. It was something that I didn't really enjoy all that much. But it's something that you do because you love your husband, I guess. And I eventually learned to be a pretty good cook. Jay's mother helped me a lot, because she was a good cook.

As a younger person, I enjoyed the outdoors. I would rather have been outdoors than indoors. Gardening and being with the animals and helping take care of them and things—that was more fun and enjoyment for me than taking care of the household duties.

Jennie Steele Mott

Jennie Steele Mott lived with her parents and 11 brothers and sisters on a homestead they started in 1931 on Little Foundation, 30 miles south of Rangely, Colorado.

They built a two-room cabin on the homestead.

And how many children did they have at that time?

Let's see. My sister just after me . . . about nine.

How did your mother manage on that homestead with that many children?

I made the remark one time about taking care of her and paying her back for taking care of me when I was a child, and she said, "I didn't take care of you—the older girls did." My earliest memories was just of her doing her regular housework and whatever else needed [to be] done on the ranch. If Daddy was gone, she would do the irrigation and milk the cows or feed [the animals] or whatever had to be done. Until us kids got up old enough to do it for her, why, she was out doing whatever had to be done.

Did you live there in the winter?

Yes. We lived there in the winter, and at that time it seemed to me like we had much more snow than we have nowadays. I can remember looking out across the yard, and I would say that the drifts across the yard was at least four feet deep. They was even with the bottom of the windows, and one winter in particular we had to put an extension on the top of the corral bars to keep the horses out of the hay corrals. The snow was so deep that they was walking over the top of the fences.

We didn't have cars, so the snow didn't bother us. We rode to school on horseback. We went about three and a half miles to school. One year I believe we had a sled that we went out in. One year we went out in the hay wagon.

When you were going to school on a horse, that must have been around 1936, 1937?

Yes, I started school in 1936.

Did it get quite cold?

Yes, as I remember, it got extremely cold, particularly when you was riding—your feet would get extremely cold. However, when you're young like that, cold don't bother you like it does now.

How was the house heated?

By a coal stove. They had what they call the old potbelly stoves. I can remember there in the old log house at the ranch, they had it sitting in the corner, and behind it was this bench. We'd come in with our feet cold and everything, and we'd pull everything off and take our shoes or—well, we didn't usually take our shoes off. We'd sit there and rest our feet on the bottom ring around the bottom of the stove to warm up our toes—and usually wind up burning them. But all we ever had was just the coal heat, both for the kitchen, to cook on, and for the heat.

Were the bedrooms very warm?

The bedrooms were in the front room and the kitchen when I was real small. We had a two-room house. We didn't have extra bedrooms like that. And when we were small, we slept three to a bed sometimes, and we just had the beds in the house. We had a cot thing that my uncle built that was made out of quaky [aspen] logs and a dried cowhide, that we kept in the kitchen, as a kind of a couch and an extra bed.

Later, when we built the new house, it was never completed the way they had intended when they started it. We got a front room and the kitchen and one bedroom, which was Daddy and Mama's bedroom. Us kids used the old house for our bedroom. Then we had the old bunk-house that was one of the original buildings on the place, [so] that if my older brother came home or anything or had any friends, why, they usually would sleep out there. It was a little ways out from the house—it wasn't right close to it. But you couldn't say we had bedrooms.

Ila Bowman Powell

Ila Bowman Powell's parents were the second homesteaders in the Douglas Creek area, south of Rangely, in 1908. Ila homesteaded with her husband during the early 1930s on Douglas Creek, and they raised 10 children.

It didn't get near as cold up there up Douglas Creek. It's a lot warmer, it's hemmed in by the mountains, and it's warmer up there. But we had a good, snug, warm cabin, and we had a little coal mine we dug our own selves. We then eventually got a little school up there, you know—Douglas Creek School. My son went to school up there, and we had a snug, warm cabin and were always comfortable. We had milk cows, and horses, and a team or two—things were quite comfortable up there.

When it was in the summer up there and you had a lot of things to do, could you paint me a picture of what a typical day for you might have been?

Well, I don't think you could probably hack it, if you had to live like I did then. My husband worked away in the summertime. He usually worked on the county road, and then sometimes he worked for a rancher that lived 5 miles down and 10 miles up another creek. I can't remember but one summer, the first summer we was on the homestead, did I ever milk less than five cows. I don't remember what I milked all those cows for—I guess because the calves didn't take all the milk, because I made butter out of it. I had a great big old tub I made a fire under and put it up on blocks, and I used all the leftover milk or milk that got sour in this tub. And I raised a lot of chickens always, and I made cottage cheese out of that milk. I seldom bought any food for the little chickens, and I fed [the cottage cheese] to the chickens. And I'll bet you, lady, I have dumped $2 million worth of yogurt in this ditch right out here [gestures]! But then I got so I just skimmed it, and what we couldn't use—and what the animals around here, like the pigs and the things, didn't eat it up, and the dogs—I dumped in that great big ditch.

But my typical day was—I milked all those cows, and I always raised a humongous garden. I had strawberries to pick of a morning—every other morning I picked them. And as long as my husband's mother was alive—they lived down below us—I'd usually get up early and go down there and help her, because she wasn't well at all. I picked her strawberries and brought her vegetables from the garden, and, if it was haying time, I helped her get dinner. Then I'd walk back that one mile. I didn't need any exercises or dieting in those days. I sometimes shoveled a half a mile of ditch; if we didn't shut the headgate down when the storm hit in the top of the thing, it would run our ditches full of sand. But that was my day. I'd run back and forth, probably a quarter of a mile each time to the garden and back to tend to the water and change it on the garden and so on. After the children began to come along, why, it was quite a feat. I had to get up early in the morning to get all those chores done before they woke up. So it wasn't easy, and I never got off that creek very often.

Did you have to watch the weather, because the roads were bad?

Well, sometimes, yes. Sometimes the roads were bad, and in the wintertime it isn't like now—they didn't have maintainers and Cats [bulldozers] and stuff to clean off the roads. When you got snowed in up there at Douglas Creek, you were *there,* until the snow melted in the spring.

We'd always try to have enough provision. But if we ran out of something, why, some of them would take a packhorse or maybe two packhorses and come to town and get bare necessities—what people needed, like coffee, or sugar—and pick up the mail. Sometimes it would be three months at a time we didn't get our mail up there.

What about wild animals—did they ever bother you?

There was quite a few mountain lions, and when I was a little kid there was lots of wolves in the country. My dad trapped one winter—he caught 76 coyotes and 4 wolves in six weeks. Now, you know, they were pretty thick in there. They used to surround the cattle, you know. They could just kill a cow and eat it up in no time, that many wolves.

Jennie Brown Spence

Although Jennie didn't homestead with her husband when they married in 1918, they did live on a ranch on Piceance Creek near Meeker. Her activities as a housewife were typical of those of many women in similar circumstances. Some women were expected to maintain the house as well as work outside with their husbands, while others, like Jennie, confined their responsibilities to the house and garden.

My father felt sorry for my husband, because he said I was just a fudge cook—I could make candy and cakes—and he didn't think I was much of a farmer's wife. But I learned. Joe was great. He had bached [as in *bachelor*] a lot, you know; it seemed like the men did in those days. A lot of times the women had to move to town to send their kids to school, and the men had to bach. He was a good cook—he could get up and get breakfast, and I'd take care of the baby. He helped me a lot, always, and taught me a lot, you know. And then, I was willing to try.

But we had as nice a place as there was to live, but no conveniences of any kind. We had coal oil lights. And we had to carry our water in and carry it out and heat it on a cookstove. And we had to take care of the milk—you couldn't buy milk, you had to have cows, and you had to either separate your milk or strain it up in pans and make your own butter. And I made my own soap—I learned to do all of that.

I had hay men to cook for, because it was summer and you went right into haying. You get up early in the morning and cook breakfast and wash the dishes and take care of the milk—and figure out what you were going to have for dinner.

'Course you had dinner at noon, and you had to have a big breakfast. You hardly ever had pancakes. We usually had biscuits—I'd like to have a nickel for all the biscuits I've made. You had bacon and eggs, and you had your own bacon—you cured your own meat in the spring. Your pigs, you butchered so many, and you had your bacon and your ham. And eggs—you had chickens, so you had your eggs. Or if you could possibly sneak a deer and keep it a secret, you could have fresh meat and gravy.

You had your big meal at noon, and that was always meat and potatoes and a dessert. That was one thing my husband said when we were married: "Now, I run the outside, and you run the inside, and I don't care what you buy in the way of groceries, but I want a dessert twice a day." [Laughter.] So I always said the first thing I think of is what to have for dessert.

They ate, and ate a lot, and then you'd do up those dishes and perhaps work in the garden a little bit, but not much. I wasn't too much to do work outside. And then you'd have your supper, at night, and then you'd do your dishes and go to bed. That's what I told the girls. I said, "Usually you'd go to bed early, because you were tired. You'd had a big day, and you have to get up early the next morning and do it all over again."

Usually you'd wash on Monday, and that was a big deal. At first I had just the board, washboard, and Joe would help me. In the wintertime he'd help with the long underwear and the sheets and things. And then finally we got a washing machine, but it was one that you had to turn by hand. And then you'd have to iron. Everything had to be ironed. In those days, they ironed *everything*—pillowcases and, of course, the sheets.

You didn't go very much, because you had to go a distance. We had to go about 10, 15 miles to get our mail. And we had a telephone, but you had to go through Rio Blanco, and half the time they were out and they wouldn't hear the phone and they wouldn't connect you. When I was there that summer, I got pregnant, and all that winter I didn't see a woman or talk to a woman over the phone until I came into town [on the] Fourth of July.

I had all kinds of cowboys [stop by]. They rode for cattle all winter, to gather them, because there would always be some strays that would stay out in the snow. You always had one person extra to cook for and maybe three or four. You had to be free with your meals; everybody was free to stop and eat. If you weren't, when they were on the range and they saw your cow or your calf that needed attention, they'd just drive by it and not pick it up.

Hilda Shelton Rawlinson

Hilda recalls the soap- and quilt-making processes she used while growing up on her parents' homestead in Dry Lake and on her ranch when she was an adult.

I generally used lard, plain old grease from sheep, you know. We'd butcher our sheep, and we'd use the tallow. We used the lard, you know—we used that to cook with.

From the sheep—the lard?

No, from a hog—pigs—we always had our own hogs, you see, to make our own bacon, sausage, and ham, and all that bacon, and all that good stuff.

And you wanted to know how to make soap? Well, you used lard. A can of lye to so [many] pounds of lard, or grease. And if I used the mutton tallow, I had beautiful soap flakes. I'd stir this lard and that would put the air into this soap, and finally, as it got cooler and cooler, it looked like Ivory soap flakes—beautiful.

Did you make quilts? Did you make them with other women, or individually, at home?

Individually. Just for home. I generally pieced blocks. I never pieced very many quilts. I think three nice [quilts]. I always put wool. We had sheep, so—you butchered a sheep, or one died or something; you skinned it; and I generally clipped the wool off myself and washed it. I didn't know how to card it, but I just kind of pulled it apart and placed it together and made a mat out of it—batt, we called them.

And you just sew that inside the squares?

Yes, and then I quilted it. I still have them. I sleep on it every winter. I put it under my sheets in the wintertime. And a wool quilt on top of me.

Velma Burdick Deaver

Velma Burdick Deaver's parents came to the Meeker area in 1898. Velma grew up on ranches along the White River. She remembers what wash day was like in a family with many children.

I can remember we would get up early in the morning, and as soon as the breakfast was over and dishes cleared away, we'd begin washing. And, of course, it had to be done on a washboard. And from the time I was big enough to reach to do it, I helped with the washing. It would be an all-day affair, by the time we washed—we had *huge* washings. And then we'd, of course, have to hang them on a line outdoors.

Did you have to heat the water, too?

We had a big boiler, and we'd heat it on the stove. We used to put them through three tubs of water. First, wash them in one suds, and then put them in and wash them in another, and then have a big tub full of water to rinse them in. And we were careful about rinsing them. We always kept fresh water in it.

What was it like in the wintertime?

We had just as many clothes—maybe more, because there [were] school clothes. They had to be hung outside. Sometimes they'd have to stay out overnight, and it would take them two days to dry, because they would freeze.

Julia Biskup Kawcak

Julia and her husband raised 16 children on their homestead on Elk Head.

We were never hungry. My son Nick, he'll tell anybody, "There was a lot of us. We might have not had fancy clothes to put on, but we never went hungry, never." He said, "Even if we just had noodles mixed with fried cabbage or something, we ate it, and it was good."

We'd buy bacon, big slabs, and I'd buy eggs from somebody until I got chickens, 10¢ a dozen. Oh, I fried bacon and put eggs over, and [we'd] have bacon and eggs. We always had enough to eat.

Did you have a garden?

Well, from the beginning we didn't have too much. It wouldn't grow too good on the side where the house was. But after later years, I had about a half an acre on the other side from the house; it was on the side hill. I had corn, beans, carrots, beets, lettuce. Before I left there, I used to can up to 600 or 800 quarts of stuff. Some of those would be peaches in the fall [from Grand Junction], and a lot of it was garden stuff. My boys would bring a jar of beans out of the cellar and just take a fork, after they opened it, and stand there and eat. They just *loved* those home-canned beans, you know.

But we always had enough to eat. We had cows. I milked up to five cows. Finally I got Paul [my husband] to think, "Well, maybe I could milk too." So I got him to thinking about it, and finally he started, so then we both milked. I'd milk three while he milked two.

Did you do a lot of baking?

Lot of bread. I'd make as high as 12 loaves of bread a week. We had fresh butter from the cows, and I'll tell you, everybody ate like there was no end. I'll tell you, that fresh butter was something on fresh bread.

What about clothing? How could you get that many clothes together?

Well, my husband would go to town and he'd buy me some material. Two kinds—I had a bunch of the girls. So he'd bring maybe 20, 25 yards of one and 25 of the other, and I'd sew the girls two dresses [each]. With what they had and what I sewed, they had enough to go to school in. We'd wash them, and they wore them to school. But when they come home from school, they took them off, kept them nice, you know. He'd go to town in the spring [and] get me some kind of nice material to make the girls's Easter dresses—maybe be yellow, pink, or white. I'd put ruffles on them, and he'd get pink ribbon or blue ribbon for a belt and that'd be their church dress for the summer. They'd go to school, and the teacher would say, "Oh, what *beautiful* dresses." None of the other kids had any like that, you know.

How did you have time to do that?

I done it. I'd maybe work till midnight sometimes. I'd be ironing till midnight before we could go to church. Otherwise, they'd put on something without ironing to go do things outside. But I'd iron everything so we'd have it nice to come to church. We'd have to come on the wagon, you know. We'd leave up there at the ranch about five in the morning, to get down here for ten o'clock mass.

What did you do in the winter? Did you come?

No, we didn't have church in the winter. Just summertime.

What was the winter like up there?

Lots of snow. You hardly ever seen a fence. Years ago there was lots more snow than now. We just had your horses, and we plowed through then. You could just turn them loose if there was a blizzard; they brought you home. And you'd cover up with blankets.

Alta Fox Martin

Alta Fox Martin came to the Great Divide area, which lies northwest of Craig, with her husband and seven children in 1929 from Brighton, Colorado. Her husband's brother lived in northwestern Colorado and convinced him to homestead in that area. Shortly after they arrived, her husband and one child died of strep throat, and Alta was left with six children to raise by herself.

What did your husband do when he came here?

Well, he didn't live very long after we came out here. We came the second of May 1929, and we'd only been here six weeks when we lost our second boy [to] mountain fever and strep throat. At that time they just—people died and they didn't have any cure for it. And now you hear of people having it, and there's no problem.

We started to have a homestead there, but it was too much. The children were too young, and I couldn't go out there and work all that land for a homestead.

Alta then moved with her children to a house near the Great Divide
School and the Community Center.

We didn't have too much there. We had to raise our garden, and we
had a few cattle, and that provided us with our meat, and we kept chickens and milked cows. We did sell cream for a while, but that played out.

And your husband was gone then, so that you were by yourself?

Yes. So the children and I made it. They worked out—we all worked;
we made a dollar however we could. Now that big house, big community
hall there at Great Divide, you know, where they had everything from
church to dances: the children and I always cleaned that [hall] every
Sunday morning, because usually there always would be Sunday school
during the summer months, and sometimes there would be preaching
too. Oh, I can't say just how soon after Easter we started—you know,
when the snow left, so people could get around.

Then in the fall, when it began to snow, why, we didn't have any school
or anything in the winter. We had school in the summertime. The children went to school at Great Divide.

The older boy, Wayne, he used to cut hay on shares, so we'd get hay
for our stock. The mailmen—they couldn't make the trip in a day.
They'd stay overnight, and we had a barn there, and they had a place to
put up their horses. I think that's the reason why Wayne put up so much
hay—we had to have hay for those horses, to keep them overnight.

How far was your place, approximately, from Craig?

They used to say 29 miles.

And the roads were dirt?

Yes. Now they keep a road open. Of course, the mail carriers never
thought of coming any way only with team and sled in the wintertime,
you know. And of course, sometimes in the fall, when it would rain and
rain and, oh, it would be dreadful muddy, they'd have to have team and
buggy then, or wagon or something. And so the Great Divide was the
store, like here [gestures], and then the road come up here. Our house
was right here.

We usually kept two or three pigs around, because we had milk cows,
you know, and we had milk and could feed the milk to the sow.

49

Did you have electric lights or indoor plumbing?

No, we didn't have any electric lights. We used gas lights, gas lanterns, you know. We had a sink, all right, and a well just out from the house a little ways, and we carried the water. And then we finally got gas, and so then we had our gas refrigerator and stove.

Before you had gas, how did you keep things cold?

Before that we had a cellar. We went down in the basement, and that was very cool. We saved our milk in the morning and put it in that cellar, where there was always a breeze through there, and it was cool. That was the morning's milk we'd have to save. If you saved the night's milk, it was too warm and it didn't cool off and we'd have problems with milk souring.

How did you keep meat over a period of time?

Well, most people, they put it down in brine. And then there was a time when we canned our meat. We canned beef every year. And, of course, we had our chickens.

When you had a deer that you'd killed in hunting season, or a cow, how did you save that?

Seems like when we butchered a beef or any of the meat, we canned—we did can some pork that you had to take care of it, you know, right away. I've canned beef and pork and lamb—canned all of that stuff. Canned meat was for summer. If we butchered anything in the wintertime, it was cold enough [so] you didn't have to have any place to keep it much, only hang it up somewhere so it would stay cold, and it would be frozen. Sometimes if it come a warm spell, it thawed it out; then you had to get busy and can it.

Was washing clothes kind of hard?

Oh, not—I had a washing machine. For years I had a power washer run with a gasoline engine. Before that, I'd wash like this [gesture].

On the washing board?

Not on the washboard, no. Not me. [I] had the washing machine with a—it had a wheel on top of it, and it was a stick or something. I don't know how long it was now, but we could stand there. And it had a foot pedal on it. You could use your foot and hand, both. It was easier that way. But some people I knew, they'd put their washboards on—but that washboard would just kill me off. With seven kids?

Did you make any of your children's clothes?

I made everything. And right now, it hurts me that I can't make my own clothes. I can't do it any more.

Did you make underwear and everything?

Yes, I made underwear. For summer I made it out of flour sacks. [For winter underwear] I had to buy some of that, of course, and then some I could take old underwear that was not worn too bad—you'd be surprised what you could make out of that too.

Did you make girls' dresses and boys' . . .

Shirts. And I made the boys' overalls, up until they got old enough to go to school. Before my husband died, he went to town one day and he said it seemed like denim was getting so high. He said he was going to buy the boys some overalls. They just looked like they was poked in a big old sack, four times too big. I made their overalls until they were old enough to go to school.

Janet Mortimer Eberle

We wore lots of clothes—long winter underwear, and then on top of that we had bloomers, full bloomers that came below the knees. We had long cotton stockings, and those were held up by a harness or something that we wore from our shoulders down, to hold up our stockings. If we wore a dress, we had a petticoat, a heavy one in the wintertime: flannel petticoat and a heavy dress and we stayed reasonably warm.

We had a coal stove. We had two stoves. We had a kitchen range that we cooked on, and we had a heating stove. And so on a cold night you'd fire up as much as you could and then you'd turn around. You'd get one side warm, and then you'd turn and get the other side warm. And you were never *that* far away from the stove. If there was any dampness in the house that would freeze on the glass, on the windows. Naturally, that would make it even colder in the house.

Do you remember the way you cooked and if it was a difficult thing to do— making cakes, bread, pies, and all that?

They turned out remarkably well. You had to be a marvel at knowing your stove. There was no indicator on most ovens as to the temperature in the oven, so if you were baking a cake, you made a little "try cake" to begin with. You had a little pan and you'd put some batter in that, and if it burned you knew it was too hot then. If it didn't get done, then you waited until the oven was right. But you learned your stove.

We were very self-sufficient. There was very little that we bought from the grocery store. And we were not alone—everybody had a garden, and we also had wild fruit. What we bought from the grocery store—if we drank coffee, we bought our coffee, and our tea and our sugar, and never any shortening, because everybody raised their own hogs and slaughtered them. We rendered our own lard. So you didn't buy that many things, and you didn't go to town that often.

How do you render lard?

You cut the fat off the hog up in small pieces and you put it in a pan on the stove, and it renders out—it liquefies. And then you put that in buckets, and then it solidifies. It would be good for a couple of years, if you kept it that long, but you probably didn't. You used it. Everything was made with lard. At that time there wasn't any such thing as vegetable oil.

What about any kind of refrigeration?

We put up our own ice from the pond. There would be a place on the creek where they could make a pond, anticipating that this is what they were going to do. When the ice on that pond got thick enough, everyone in the neighborhood would come, and they would cut the ice into blocks.

You would take your ice home, and you had an icehouse, either with sawdust or coal slack, it would keep most of the summer.

You put the ice in the top of the icebox because cold goes down. We had ice-cream freezers, and we made a lot of ice cream. In the wintertime, of course, you didn't *need* anything; you just kept it in the house. Goodness! It wasn't going to spoil in the house, as cold as the house got.

Ethel La Kamp Chrisler

Ethel La Kamp Chrisler's father arrived on the South Fork of the White River near Meeker by team and wagon in 1883. Her mother came to this area in 1900 from Iowa in order to recover from consumption. Ethel's parents were married in 1903 and lived on a homestead on the South Fork where Ethel was born.

We sure had a nice cool spring. Dad built a box, with screen, with a floor and a roof and screen all around. And boy, things would keep just perfect in that spring—your butter, cream, milk, and your fresh meat. Of course, fresh meat wouldn't stay too long. You put it in an airtight container, and then that case. It was just, oh, about as far from the house as from here to that house over there [gestures]. It was just a step.

Everyone had a cellar, and that was another good place to keep things cool.

Oma Jensen Graham

Usually you had a ditch or a stream, and you made what we called a screen box. It was screen all around with a solid bottom, and [you'd] immerse it in the water until it was about this deep [gestures]. And then you took gunnysacks and spread them and fringed them and let the ends hang in the water. The breeze would come through, and it would keep it cool.

Where did you put the gunnysacks?

Over the top of it, to keep the sun off. But then you'd let your fringe—
so just the strips would hang down in the water, so it would let the air
go through, see, and still shade your food.

> The settlers sometimes had encounters with the Ute Indians. After
> being moved to the reservation in Utah in the 1880s, the Indians often
> tried to return to their familiar home and hunting grounds. They were
> permitted to hunt in the area every autumn into the early 1900s.

Margaret Tagert Jones

> Fanny Tagert told her daughter stories about her family's experi-
> ences with the Ute Indians in the 1890s near Meeker.

The Meeker Massacre was an [Indian] uprising caused because Captain Meeker had been sent in by the government, he and his troops, to
help with the Indians. It was not called Meeker at that time—it was just
an army post. Captain Meeker ordered the Indians' racetrack to be
plowed up, so that caused a great deal of trouble over there, and there
were many people killed, including Meeker. His daughter and wife were
abducted. After that, the Indians were supposedly sent to a reservation
in Utah. However, they did get away and they tried to come back to their
home territory. My grandparents were living in the Powell Park Valley,
where all this had occurred, just west of Meeker.

They did encounter the visits from the Indians, when they came back
[to hunt]. Sometimes these were hostile visits, and if that happened and
they were afraid of some unpleasant incidents, the families packed up
and went to Lay, which was on the Yampa River. They would stay there
until the Indian scare, as they called it, was over.

One of the times that my mother has told me about was after the birth
of her little sister. It was the day after the baby was born, and this Indian
scare was going on, so the families were packing to go to the stockade at
Lay. My grandmother and the new baby were just packed into the back
of a wooden wagon, and made the trip, which was about 30 miles to the
stockade. All of the children, of course, were born at home, usually with
midwives.

Ila Bowman Powell

In the early 1900s, the Indians visited the area on Douglas Creek where Ila's family lived.

I had a little black mare that my dad got for me, and I took a lot of trips they didn't know that I took, because I'd go a little farther each time, you know, and look things over. I used to go by myself so much because my brother was two years younger and they kept him pretty close around the house. There was a lot of Indians in the country at the time, and I can remember seeing the Indians come in the fall of the year to hunt deer, and then they dug the red clay out of the hills up there to make their war paint with. They'd be there for days sometimes, digging that out.

Nellie Warren Parks

Nellie Warren Parks grew up on her parents' homestead, located 17 miles from Meeker. It was filed as a preemption in 1891, and Mr. Warren received two 40-acre tracts.* Nellie recalls the Indians who sometimes visited her home around the turn of the century.

They come to the house. This one outfit, he used to always come, and he wanted coffee and he'd say, "Coffee, coffee, coffee." Well, if Grandad would give him coffee, then he wanted sugar too. Yeah, that's what made it an attraction, was that sugar. He loved that. Then one time he wanted sugar in it, and Grandad says, "No, you have to just drink it like it is." He wasn't going to give him any sugar. He wasn't very happy about that, either.

---

*Paul W. Gates, *History of Public Land Law Development* (New York: Arno Press, 1979), 238. The Preemption Act of 1841 allowed people to settle on 160 acres of public land, improve it, and pay the government $1.25 per acre at a specified time. People continued to preempt land even after the Homestead Act of 1862 because preemption was extended to unsurveyed public lands. The Homestead Act applied only to surveyed public lands.

Jennie Spence's parents, Charles and Rose May Brown. Near Meeker, about 1905
Courtesy of Jennie Spence

Were you frightened of the Indians?

No, because they never acted like they would hurt a soul or anything.

And when they came through this area, were they here for the hunting?

Yeah, that's what they come for, was to get that meat for themselves, you see. Then, of course, to test those laws—they allowed them so much meat.

But they couldn't come just anytime?

No, it was just a certain time that they came, and a certain amount of meat that they'd let them have. But they never seemed to be disappointed about it—they accepted it and got what they was allowed and took [it] with them.

Did they ever bring their women with them?

I can't remember ever seeing a squaw, no. I can't remember *ever* seeing one.

Ruby Rector Kirby

In 1898 Ruby Rector Kirby's father traded his hotel in Rifle for a ranch near Rangely. He married Ruby's mother in Missouri and brought her to northwestern Colorado. They raised their three children there. Ruby married a homesteader, and together they built a large cattle ranch.

Do you remember any stories your mother told you about her life on that ranch?

Yes. I can tell you two Indian stories that to me were most outstanding. The Indians were coming up the river on the mesa across from the big ranch when one of the squaw's horses ran away with her. She had a papoose strapped to her back. The strap broke, and it dumped that baby into the rocks, seriously injuring it. They brought the baby over to Mom,

57

and Mom did first aid on it. Of course, the child died, it was hurt so seriously. In appreciation, they later brought Mother a gift of a very fine mare, for helping that baby.

Another incident: one of the old Indians, a Chief Shavano, came to the ranch. It was springtime, and the river was very high. The Indians had been drinking at a little saloon in Rangely, and he ran out of money. So he came to the old ranch to borrow some money to go buy some more firewater, you know, [as] they called it.

When he came in, he started out, "Missy Rector, my good friend, husband have plenty of money." And Mama told him no, she had no money. Well, he repeatedly wanted money. So finally [when] Mom hadn't given him any, he decided he'd sing to her. And lo and behold, that old Indian sang "Jesus, Lover of My Soul" and "Work, for the Night Is Coming." And Mom said he had such a booming voice you could hear him for a mile away.

Well, finally, to get rid of him she gave him a $10 gold piece—you know, gold was what you kept in those days. So he left and she thought maybe he'd fall off his horse and drown in the river, but he made it. But [as] a parting remark he said, "Maybe so, 10 days, paper send it."

And sure enough, in a couple of weeks she got a check from that old Indian for $10. Dad always said if you treated an Indian fair and square, he'd treat you the same way.

So all the stories about bad Indians were certainly not your experience?

It was not true.

Oma Jensen Graham

The Indians often rode through the area in Brown's Park near Oma's home when she was a child (ca. 1912).

Did your mother ever mention that there were Indians during that period?

Oh, yes. They killed a dog of mine, old Sandy, when I was about two and a half years old. We came through an Indian camp at the lower end of the place. My dad was raised with the Indians; he came from Jensen, Utah; and Jensen is named after my grandad, [who] run a ferry four miles below Jensen bridge. And so Dad was more or less raised with the Indians. We got started on the way, and looked back, and the dog wasn't there. So Mother and I came on, went on to the cabin, and Dad went back. And they'd already killed the dog.

Did they eat it?

Oh, sure they ate it! Yeah, that's what they ate.

Were there deer in that area?

Well, they mentioned mostly antelope. They said there was some deer, but they mentioned mostly antelope. However, while I was growing up there, I never saw an antelope. The deer came.

Did the Indians come through there to hunt?

Yes, they'd get off the reservation. [A] lot of them was leaving the reservation, you know. They'd get belligerent and decide to move, and when we had the homestead there at Connie Springs, one time we looked up and thank heavens we had the reservoir full, because the Indians always had a bunch of horses. If we hadn't had the reservoir full, they'd have run out of water, and I don't mean maybe. I don't know how many there were; of course, Dad knew the most of them. And they went on then about a quarter of a mile from the house and camped overnight. But then [the authorities would] go and round them up and take them back.

Some of these women worked outside on the ranch, as well as inside the home. Often, raising chickens, milking cows, and tending the garden were considered part of a woman's job. When the ranch work was especially demanding, women sometimes helped with the plowing, sowing, and harvesting of the crops. In the early years of a homestead, the husband was often away from the homestead working at another job, and so the wife was left with all the ranch work. A few such women preferred the work outdoors and worked either alongside their husbands or by themselves, taking care of the animals and the crops.

CeCelia Sullivan Knott

CeCelia Sullivan Knott's mother came to northwestern Colorado in 1910 at age 17. She married a homesteader on the William's Fork River, southeast of Craig, and had 13 children. CeCelia spent most of her adult life in Craig.

My mother was a very ambitious person. She did everything, inside and out. She wasn't the cowboy type, really, but she took care of the cattle and she would do the chores such as milk cows, take care of chickens. Well, I guess when they had pigs, they took care of pigs and that type of stuff. Raised a monstrous garden. Canned an abundance of garden produce and fruits that were available. Well, it was an "able" job—you got going as soon as you were able, and you went as long as you were able.

The people of today would not do it. That is hard work, when you hoe garden and so forth. And, of course, the men of that day weren't as many men [are] today. That wasn't a man's job to come in and assist with the meal. You [women] may work in a hay field all day and [like] that, *but* you also came in and you got the meals, not just for you and your family [but] for whatever men there were—say, my father [and] any hired men they may have.

Chloe Bunker Vaughan

We raised the sheep, the lambs at Zenobia, in that country, and then in the fall we moved to the Sand Wash country, which was probably 10, 15 miles from home. And we lived in the sheep wagon over there.

For how long?

Through the whole winter. We had a big canvas that we put all the way around the bottom of the sheep wagon to keep the snow from blowing in—you know, keep it warmer. Then we put our meat and our wood and things like that under the canvas to keep it warm—dry.

Is this before your daughter was born?

Well, I had her in the sheep wagon one winter, when Minford [my husband] was so sick; he had an operation, and he couldn't ride a horse.

And so I was determined to keep on with the sheep, and I told him if he would take care of Elmora in the wagon—she was about two years old—I said, "If you'll take care of her, I'll herd the sheep." And so I herded the sheep that winter. I had an old stallion horse I rode, and I was scared of it, because every time it run into a bunch of wild horses, why, it wanted to go with the mares, you see, and I had quite a time with that old horse.

But anyway, that spring, after Minford got so he could get out and do things, he went for the bucks. We had the bucks in a pasture. He went to get the bucks and he left me there alone, and I thought, "Well, I just believe I'll clean up our wagon, really make it nice for when he gets back."

As I washed everything up and cleaned it up, along about five o'clock I looked out. I kept seeing the sheep out there—I thought they were sheep, and I kept seeing them out there on the hills. They were so far away I couldn't make out just what it was. So I set Elmora in a sandpile. She had a bunch of little tiny cars, and she would always sit there and play until I got back.

So, I scooted off on the horse to get my sheep. I started to yell. I'd always yell real loud, and they'd bunch, you know. And I started to yell, and they run off, so I didn't do that anymore. I rode up to where I could see them—I had been herding a bunch of antelope all day long! You know, the whole backs of them are white and I could see those white backs and I thought it was sheep!

I was scared to death I had lost my sheep, but I went out there and I whooped and yelled, and finally, over a hill, I spied them. And they were coming to me.

How cold did it get in the winter?

There was always a lot of snow. And it got pretty cold, but the way we did, we kept a fire in our little stove all night. We'd wake up and we'd be kind of cold, and we'd stick a couple of pieces of wood in.

Did you cook on that same little stove?

Uh-huh, same little stove. It had a little oven in it. It had four burners—four rounds on top—and it was about this big [gestures], little sheepherder stove.

How big was this wagon?

Oh, dear, I don't know. Behind there [gestures] was a bed that went clear across the wagon. Then there was a board that went up above that.

And on that we kept our suitcases and things up there. We didn't have anything fancy with us, you know, just what we really needed.

On this side [gestures] there was a little table that I used to drop down, and then you could sit on the bench. And there was a little table I could pull out from that bed too. Behind the stove there was shelves built to put everything on. 'Course, it had a covering and you could fasten it, because we moved the wagon. We'd move camp. If the sheep run out of food, then we'd move the camp to a better place.

During those winters, did you visit with other people?

Well, I went out to the Sand Wash with Minford one winter. That was before Elmora was born, and we were alone. From the last of November to the first of April, I seen five men and two women.

And that didn't bother you?

It didn't bother me a bit, because I had lots of books to read and we'd go for our mail. We got our mail at the Two-Bar Ranch. We'd go for our mail maybe once a week or twice a week. But many times we went there and we never seen anybody. And their doors were always open, and they told us that we could come in the commissary, where all the herders got their supplies. They told us that we could take anything we wanted to out of the commissary and write it down and then pay them later.

Did that sheep wagon ever seem to get kind of small?

No. I was outdoors too much. I loved the open spaces. I spent most of my time with Minford. Out. Horseback or something.

Jennie Brown Spence

Well, I happened to go on the roundup with Joe [my husband], because my folks lived in Meeker, and my brother's wife was pregnant and had her little boy, and the town was full of flu. I couldn't go to town, because I'd probably get the flu, and I couldn't stay alone, because I never did learn to milk. Mother never would let me milk, and Joe wouldn't. He said, "If you don't know how, you'll never have to stay alone; you'll never be left with the chores." Well, a lot of women would be left with the chores if the men would go on the roundup or if they would go to Rifle for supplies. But he never would let me milk, so I never had to stay alone. I just went with him on the roundup, to ride, and I was riding all the time anyway.

When did the roundup start?

It started in September.

And so you went out in September, and you got back to the ranch when?

At Thanksgivingtime.

You were out that long?

Oh, yes. In the fall the weather was nice, but a lot of times it was a lot of snow out there at Rio Blanco and really about 30 below zero—cold.

And you lived outside?

Yes, they cooked outside, just out in the open. And one of the fellows that rode—they were an older couple [and] she went along as cook. And we had what they call pup tents: it was just a little tipi, just large enough for a bed, you know, at night, and you'd just put that up and you slept right on the ground. Of course, there was floor in it, a canvas floor, and we had all these big—they called them sugans—quilts, and they were made out of old overalls and old clothes, old woolen coats, you know, patchwork quilts, and then there would be a batt, a cotton batt in between. We had about three of them over us, and I couldn't turn over. They weren't eiderdown, like they are today, or sleeping bags. It was just those heavy sugans.

Julia Biskup Kawcak

When you were at home and working either outside or inside, what did you wear?

Dresses!

Never wore pants?

Never *did* wear pants, and I haven't yet! I leave that to the men. I did— I wouldn't wear them! You know, my legs feel like they're smothered. I'd be out there at our ranch, and in the wintertime [my husband] was always gone up to Mt. Harris to work, because we needed the money. I stayed home, took care of the cattle, horses, and everything. Pumped water for them and all. Well, after we had a few head of cattle, I had to hook up our team of horses and haul the straw out—we didn't have hay; it was straw—and pump the water and slop the pigs and take the kids to school when they started and—

All in a dress?

Oh, I sure did. But when it was 30, 40 below, I'd put a pair of overalls of Paul's—my husband—on.

I'd always help out in the field, you know. I'd maybe disk the ground in the spring, after we plowed in the fall, and [my husband would] get out there and just throw the wheat or oats or whatever we planted, by hand. We didn't have drills then. It was quite a few years before we got a drill. And so they broadcasted it, and we'd work behind them, harrow it and everything. After Steve [my eldest son] got big enough that he could drive some horses, I'd be plowing with a gangplow: that's two furrows at a time, four horses, and Steve would have four horses.

Mary Birovchak Levkulich

I got up five o'clock in the morning and go in the garden and work and took care of my chickens. I used to have 300 chickens and baby chicks, you know. Make fire in the stove—I burn it up one time. I order them [chickens], and I put them in the brooder house to get warm. I make little fire, in the stove—you know what kind of potbelly, a little stove. It was a little spark come from the thing, and I have straw and paper around to keep it warm. I turn around, my chicken house on fire! Ah, well! So I told my husband, "Oh, my gosh—my chickens are gone!" I always wanted chickens. I raised all the time chickens. What's the use to live on a farm if you don't raise nothing? And so I had to order me some more, but they got a little bit bigger, you know, two, three weeks old.

What did you do with the chickens? Did you sell them, after they got big?

Yes, fryers—they were mixed, fryers and pullets. And after they lay eggs, I have some for eggs, and fryers.

So you didn't sell any of those to anyone?

Sometimes people ask, yeah, I did—sometimes I did. And sometimes in the store—Safeway asked me about bringing some chickens, so I did dress them out. It was a lot of work to dress a chicken.

What about the eggs?

Yes, I sell eggs. That time was 7¢ a dozen, so when I have a lot of eggs I says, "My gosh—for 7¢ a dozen!" So I give my kids—I say, "Hey! Eat them!" Because it's—no money in that.

But sometime if I have too many I send to Safeway to Denver—I got 25¢ a dozen when I send a whole case. Here in the store they wouldn't give me enough.

How big a garden did you have?

I have more than three acres. I get up early in the morning and [work in it] before mosquitoes started, and after it got hot I come in the house. I had to do my work in the house, because you got to keep the three meals a day. But when I went to bed, I was tired.

Mary and her husband had some problems with their crops in the first few years on the ranch.

[The] crop burned up. Now first year we have a nice crop and the Fedinic family come and help us—we didn't have no horses, no machinery, nothing to help us, you know, stack it up. And we call Elmer Mack. He was a nice man, and he have a threshing machine, those old-fashioned ones that runs by spark—well, [a] fire engine of some kind on it. A spark started [the] fire. We got bushel and a half threshed—the rest of everything burn up. Well, it was gone, and his machine was gone too.

So [the] next year my husband says, "Well, this time it won't burn, because we already got in the granary the wheat." Well, that next day, granary was on fire. And how that started—from gasoline. He had a barrel there by the granary, and that gasoline—I don't know; we don't know how it start. Somebody throw match or something. We see—our granary was burning.

I say, "My gosh, George—the granary!" He come; he was going to try to save it. I carried water, but by the time I pumped the water into the buckets and I fall down with buckets, I said, "Get off that roof, because you going to burn up!" He was waiting for water. And that's the way it burned everything.

So that's the way we have a loss, you know. I'm telling you. So my husband says, "Looks like I have to quit farming—I just can't do it—nothing." And our friend, neighbor, he says, "George, don't give up." He says, "Try again—you'll make it!" So he try again, and we did have crop then.

But I said when people work, you never run out of work on a farm—that's for sure—because you have everything. Some farmers nowadays don't raise nothing. But I raised chickens, turkeys, ducks, because they have water with the ditches and everything like that, you know—even geese, one time I have.

Did you raise them so that you could have food?

Sometimes I sell it, but the turkeys—it was nice for Thanksgiving. [We] raised all kinds of stock—even pigs, we used to have—[and] set the hens on the eggs, you know. Sometimes I order but sometimes we set the hens. And one time I went to see where my chicken is and she was "Squawk, squawk, squawk," and a snake, he takes after her.

We fight rattlesnakes there—all kinds of foxes come after chickens, you know, and other stuff. Oh—what the heck you call them?—skunks! We got four skunks in a trap. Always something after chickens. One night they killed 35 fryers—they were such a nice [size] already. Laying all over—they just sucked the blood out of them. So I throw chickens away.

Did the rattlesnakes ever bother the people?

Oh, yes—I remember I killed one. I told my girls, I say, "Let's kill this thing, because it'll be dangerous if we go in the barn and he'll be there, you know." So we tried to kill him. I'm scared of those things. He was so big—great big thing—and he curled up, you know, and I say, "Oh, my gosh!" We took the big hoe to kill him, and we hit him and he jumped. I was so afraid that he come after us, but the snake don't come after people.

I say, "Let's kill him till he's gone, because we not going to let him go."

So we hit him till he was killed, and we hanged him on a fence so my husband see it, because he wouldn't believe me I killed a snake, because I was scared of them.

All kinds of things you had to fight over there that time. Gophers, they eat the grain, you know—oh, just everything.

What did you do to get rid of those?

We had to poison. [Put] all over. My son, [when] he was small, he used to drown them. He'd pour water in [the hole]; then he'd drown most of them. But in the field they eat a lot of grain, and so that's the time when I see this rattlesnake again and I run from them. I told my daughter, "Run!" I thought the rattlesnake going to run after them, but my neighbor, Mrs. Sadvar, was there and she send the boys to kill it. Oh gosh! I tell you—does this person ever forget?

I poisoned gophers; then after I got scared of that snake, I throw the poison in the wagon, and our horse came in and ate it. So I killed the horse instead of snake. Mrs. Sadvar tried to save him, you know, pour milk in him, with the eggs, but he die anyway. It was the best horse we had.

So it was just that kind of start we had. We have all kinds of bad luck!

Leona Kaloris Papoulas

Leona Kaloris Papoulas emigrated from Greece to Helper, Utah, in 1913, when she was eight. Her parents and many other Greek families came to Colorado and Utah because the land was suitable for raising sheep. After her marriage in 1928, Leona and her husband established their sheep business in northwestern Colorado.

[We] would trail the [sheep] up this way [toward Craig]. [We] would leave [Vernal, Utah, on the Colorado border] the last part of March. The shearing started in April, and then the lambing began. Some of the time we lambed here [near Craig], and some of the time on up [near Mt. Harris]. [We] would stay here a month and a half, two months, and then on up farther [to] summer range up by Hayden—Sage Creek and Oak Creek.

I flagged sheep for them when they were trailing, so people [on the road] wouldn't run into the animals. We didn't truck sheep then; everything was trailing. The men rode horses, and I pulled the wagon. I learned to drive finally in 1928.

When you got to Craig, where did you live?

We would rent a house for a couple of months, whatever time we spent here. In Hayden we stayed up in the Sage Creek area in the summer. We had a little wagon and some tents there. When we went to Oak Creek we had a house [on our homestead].

[In Hayden] the cooking wasn't hard; we had a cookstove. We had our kitchen in a lean-to shack. We had a sheep wagon and a tent with a floor; we had it fixed up real nice. The water was from here to the corner of the block [gestures], and I would go there. [So] you would heat the water and do the washing.

[Later,] when we moved on up to Oak Creek to the homestead, to wash I'd have to go down to an area where there was a spring. My husband fixed a place there and we had the tub—light the fire underneath, and I would do the washing there.

How many people were you washing clothes for?

Our four children and we two: that's six. And I had my husband's cousin [and] my uncle.

Oma Jensen Graham

June [my husband] was living down working for Paul Dunn and Jake Hauskins at Schuta Gulch. So we went down there and stayed until the first of May and [then] started up with the cattle to the old Dunn place at Marvine. We took care of the cattle the first year. Seventy-five dollars a month, and we had to board ourselves.

And then that fall, P. C. Dunn came down. June was a good hand with a team, and he [Mr. Dunn] said, "I'll give you $5 a day to come up and skid logs and Oma can run the cattle." Oh, man—we thought we were on top of the world! I took care of the cattle, and June skidded logs.

So he married the right woman, I think.

Well, we both liked to dance; we both liked to ride horseback; we liked the same things.

We run the cattle then. And then that fall we brought them back, because you have to feed in that upper country. We had $80 to go into the winter with. We lived in a cabin about the size of that carpeted place [gestures]: 12 by 14 [feet], let's say.

Did you stay warm?

Well, of course we did! We were tougher than they are today. And we didn't have insulated underwear, either.

Then we went to work for the club [One Hundred and One Club, a membership club for hunters and fishers], waiting table, and June had shod horses at the club before that, and then drove to pick up the dudes.

So we worked at the club that summer. I was getting $50 a month. Of course, I was getting my room, my board, and I could do my own laundry, but then I made better than $100 a month, because at the end I had $5 more in tips than I'd made in wages.

Then we moved to the old SC Bar [Ranch] above Buford. [Then] we had the concession at the Buford store for horses for hunting season. After that we moved back up to the SC Bar.

It sounds to me like you didn't ever really have a house where you spent year after year—you just moved from one place to the next, depending on where the work was with the cattle?

Yes, correct. [We moved] about three times a year.

Most of the places, they had what you'd call a bach hut, [where] they always had a stove and beds and things like that. You didn't have all this junk that you've got today. You didn't buy everything that you saw that you wanted. You just got along with the necessities. That's what you did.

We took our horses, and we always had a milk cow with us. We'd trail those along with us.

I can't imagine living during the winter with all that snow.

I know, but it wasn't that bad. You never had a cold. You were out from eight o'clock in the morning till four o'clock in the afternoon feeding cattle.

Did you get to town very often?

No, we didn't get to town very often! June would come to Buford every two weeks to pick up the mail. [But] not to Meeker. He made one trip to Meeker, had to come down. That's the only trip we made in the wintertime. You bought enough groceries to last you for four months, which you better do, or you run out.

Did you see other neighbors very often?

Our closest neighbors was four miles down through the fields. We'd go down there about twice a week and get the elk out of the haystacks— holler at them, and they'd scatter out. And we'd go down there and play cards until, oh, three or four o'clock in the morning, and come back.

How many elk would you see at night?

Well, a thousand head. They just scattered all over the place. By the time we got moved up there, they'd already eaten up six stacks of hay, and I imagine that the stacks of hay [were] probably at least 15, maybe 20 ton to a stack, and they had just eaten them out like toadstools.

You'd fix the fence up, and the next morning the elk would have it tore down. We had one stack down there in the bottom, and the elk kept breaking in. We got down there one morning, and it had upset. And June said, "I hope we've got about 10 head of elk under there." Dug the thing out, and we had 4 head of cattle.

Catharine Craig Coles

In 1916, when she was 15, Catharine Craig Coles came to the Steamboat Springs area with her father, stepmother, and four brothers and sisters. They lived on several ranches that her father leased.

Well, my father had never thought that women had any business being out in the ranch work. Being a rancher, he had very decided ideas about what was women's work, and working out in the field was not one of them. So I never worked out in the field, and I think the only time I ever *tried* to help was when we were at Steamboat Springs on the big old

[Wollery] ranch, and help was so hard to get during those First World War years. I tried to drive a sulk[y] rake,* and I just had *no* talent—no endurance, no ability whatever to drive that sulk[y] rake and pull that lever at the right time. And so I just quit, and Dad understood, and it didn't make a great deal of difference.

Although life was somewhat easier for those people who lived in the small communities of Craig, Rangely, and Meeker, their daily life was similar to that of those who lived in the country before the arrival of plumbing and electricity.

Jennie Brown Spence

Jennie's family moved to Meeker when it was time for her to go to school, in 1903. Her parents opened a novelty store that had living quarters in the back for the family.

They had a little money, I guess; you know, they never did talk about money. But anyway, the folks started a store—I guess maybe from Dad's teaching and from her selling the place in Missouri. I never did know how they got their money here. They must have brought it with them, because I don't think they had a bank account or anything, and the banks weren't operating, like they do now. But anyway, they started this store, and we lived in the back of it, and it was a novelty store. They had jewelry and candy and thread and ribbon and toys, dolls, and hats. Mother started then to send for hats, and she sold hats in Meeker for years. She sold ready-made hats, and she made hats. One time she was uptown and sold the hat that she had made right off her head to a certain lady.

By that time my father's unmarried sister from Missouri came out to visit. She was a teacher, and it was in September and they didn't have a first-grade teacher. Dad knew the school board members, and so he said, "Well, Chat, why don't you stay and teach?"

All winter Mother and Chat were sewing to go back to Carthage [Missouri] to visit. Mother was so homesick—she hated Meeker. Even the

*A sulky rake was a one-seat, two-wheeled carriage/farm implement that was pulled by horses.

71

mountains were so depressing she just couldn't enjoy the mountains. I guess she had a lot of headaches. She kept the blinds down all the time.

We were there in Carthage [when] my brother got sick. Mother didn't know what was wrong with him. Took him to the doctor, and the doctor couldn't find anything wrong with him. He said, "I think he's just homesick." He said, "I think the thing to do—it's hot, and I think the thing to do is just go back to Colorado."

So we did. We just stayed a month, and we came back to Colorado. And then by that time they were letting homesteads out to be filed upon. So [my father] took up a homestead on Flag Creek. We had to live up there in the summer, to prove up, and he taught in the winter and my mother ran this little store. And we just stayed and stayed. We never did [get to California].

It sounds as though your mother was not too enthusiastic about living in Meeker?

She was so homesick for Missouri, [but after] they went back, of course, it was all changed. Her parents were gone, and there were so many changes. That just seemed to cure her of Missouri, and when she came back she just was never homesick again. She just fell into the way of life of the country and loved it. She was a very versatile person. It just seems like there wasn't anything she couldn't do. She made hats, and she ran the store, and sewed—she made all my clothes, because you couldn't order clothes in those days: the first ready-made dress I had was when I was teaching. And then she would sew for other people too. She always had a boarder. My dad was bookkeeper at Hugus and Company [the general store] for years, and the young men would come there to work in the bank. And they were always sort of homesick. So Mr. Moulton would ask my mother to take them and let them eat with us, you know.

I don't remember what the boards [were], how much they paid, but it was home cooking. We had the homestead up about 10 miles south of here, and we'd be out there, and, I don't know, Mother would just take them in as one of the family.

At that time, of course, Meeker didn't have a hospital, [but] I think we had a doctor. Perhaps he brought your mother into the world; I wouldn't be surprised. He would call on Mother to assist him, and she would go. I don't think she gave the anesthetic, but she could help, you know, and she never would faint or anything. She could always be right there to help. She said she'd hold their hands or hold their feet or do whatever, and she was great with babies.

We had a family here that the husband used to drink a lot, and the mother, the wife, would have to go and get him—to Glenwood or to Denver, wherever he was. She had several babies, and she'd bring them down any time of night at the house and leave them. [My mother would] take care of those children, and I always enjoyed that.

And then we had another little man that worked here that had a child. We kept her in our family for about a year. We never did adopt her or anything; he just paid for us to take care of her. Finally her relatives came from the East. And when they took her back, it was just like a death in the family, we loved her so. But Mother was always doing that, and she always had money, spending money. I know her pocketbook was always open to my brother and myself. We could go anytime and get whatever we wanted—you know, like for ice cream. In those days you went uptown and sat at the table and ate your ice cream. We didn't have cones or anything of that sort.

She was great, to help nursing, or helping with sick people. I don't know how many people that she made shrouds for.

What's that?

Well, that's when they die, it's like a robe. Usually they were made out of white material, usually cashmere or some soft wool or material, and a little lace around the neck—just a loose robe, and they were called shrouds. She used to help with what they call "lay out" people. They didn't have a mortuary here for years. The man that ran the secondhand store, in the back, he had caskets. I don't know if they embalmed them then or not. I don't think they had to, because they were kept in the homes and friends sat with them until the funeral, day and night. Mother would help bathe them and dress them and fix them in the casket, you know, and make the shrouds. She'd bring scraps of the material home for me to have for my doll clothes. And nursing—she used to go and nurse when they were sick. And help deliver babies.

Did she get called out during the night when people would be sick?

Oh, yes. She'd just go and stay with them. I don't know how many babies she helped deliver. She would go anytime that they called her. Emergencies.

Do you remember her telling the particular things she had to do?

Well, no, not particularly. You know, they kept things like that away from me a lot. I know my friend—we were always together, [and] we'd observe different young women and decide between us, "Do you think they're going to have a baby?" And we'd watch them, and pretty soon there would be a baby. But they *never* told you.

Freddie White Blevins

Freddie White Blevins's mother lived on a homestead with her parents two and a half miles from Craig. They filed one of the earliest homesteads, in 1903. Her mother later married and lived in Craig, where Freddie's father was the first clerk of the district court of the newly created Moffat County. Freddie remembers what Craig was like when she was a young girl (about 1915 to 1920).

Oh, I remember how cold it was in Craig, when I was a little girl. I can remember Mother having to mail a letter—it was very important that it went out that night. We used to have the mail go on the train in those days, the Moffat Railroad. She had to get this letter out, and it was *dreadfully* cold. So I said to my mother, "I don't like for you to walk alone to the post office—I'll go with you." We really had to cover our mouths and noses up to keep from freezing them. But we walked along very briskly, and the next morning we heard that it was 59 below at the refinery, which was west of Craig at that time. So I know what it's like to be cold. But it is a dry cold.

Do you have something you'd call a first childhood memory?

I have a memory at that place of the milk cow. At that time we had chickens and milk cows, and some people even had horses in Craig, because this was in the teens.

I can remember I was so frightened of that cow, and Mother took me to the barn one day and showed me the cow. But I could not bring myself to come close enough to touch that cow. And she showed me how gentle the cow was. Of course, she milked it, and this seems odd to me now, because, you know, you wouldn't think of a town like Craig ever having their own chickens and their horses and their cows right there.

My father's family had an old horse that they ran the ice wagon with, and one of his brothers, during the summer, delivered ice—chunks of ice that they harvested in the winter from the river. They had what they called an icehouse down on the river: they just stored it in there with a lot of sawdust, and it kept; it was insulated in that way. I can remember they delivered with a team and wagon. He'd come up the alley—we had iceboxes then, didn't have electric refrigerators.

One of my fondest memories is when we moved to a house [from] where we'd been living for some time until I started school. We moved to a house that Daddy had built on Barclay Street—it was a new house. He sold a car that he'd won at a raffle for a down payment—a seven-passenger car. In those days, a car was really something: very few people had cars in Craig. But he asked Mother which she'd rather have, and she said a home. So they sold [the car] for a down payment, and he built this new home. We moved in January, and my grandmother Aiken, my mother's mother, was so elated with it—especially the bathroom; she took me immediately to the bathroom and showed me how the toilet worked, showed me how I could take a bath. I remember this so vividly because she was so happy with it you'd have thought it was her home.

Lena Ely Stoddard

In 1921 Lena Ely Stoddard came to Hayden, a small town 17 miles east of Craig from Illinois, with her husband, who was the new school superintendent.

My husband was a schoolteacher. When he returned from the First World War we lived in Illinois. Ferry Carpenter wrote him and told him that [there was] a new high school in Hayden, Colorado, and wanted to know if he'd be interested in coming and being the superintendent. So in 1921 we came to Hayden, with a three-month-old baby. [My husband] had written ahead to get a house—he said he'd like to have a house with two bedrooms and a bath. And he said, "I wish you'd have a load of cobs in the basement." We always started our fire in Illinois with cobs and— kerosene, I think it was.

There wasn't any house in Hayden at all, so when I came in September I had to live at the Hayden Inn. Upstairs it was, and in a bedroom. And it was in September, and I nearly froze coming from Illinois to a cold Colorado climate. But we lived through it.

We lived at Hayden for six years, as superintendent. We took up a homestead, and because of his overseas duty we only had to live on it seven months and we got the 640 acres. Hayden was a small town, maybe 300 or 400 [people]. There were only two bathtubs we found in town:

one in the barbershop and one in the Hayden Inn. That made a problem, of course; with a three-month-old baby, I had to carry water up and wash the baby's clothes in a bowl, an old-fashioned bowl-and-pitcher kind.

It was after Christmas, I think, that year that the house next to the Hayden Inn was vacated and we moved into it. But there was no running water. It was just a hand pump in the kitchen, with a drain that you drained the water into a pail and carried the water out. The toilet was out in the backyard through the pen that they kept the cow in. So you had to go outside. [And you] met the cow every time you went! [Laughter.]

Of course, the snow was deep. I think it was like our snow that we had last winter, maybe three, four, or five feet. We went to a—I guess it was a party, the lady teachers and I, about a mile out of town, and we skied. They said I could get along, because you just slide along, you know. And we slid along over the fences, it was that deep, the snow. We had a sled with a box on it to put the baby in to go out.

The roads weren't too good. I remember too, once when we were in Hayden, we came to Craig to a basketball game. We had a car then, but people had bobsleds, and, you know, the track they make is just narrow. Well, we got on the road to come, and there was a bobsled ahead of us. The snow was so deep we couldn't turn around off the road to pass. So we had to follow that bobsled all the way to Craig. I thought we'd *never* get there. Even after we came to Craig, there were sleighs and bobsleds.

Lena and her family stayed on the homestead just during the summer while they lived in Hayden. In 1927 they bought the *Empire Courier,* the newspaper in Craig. They sold the homestead to a sheep rancher and moved to Craig.

When we moved up here from Yampa Avenue, there was no sidewalk, no pavement, and we'd have to park the car down on Taylor Street because this would be just a sea of mud. Here in this house we'd wake up in the morning surrounded by sheep going "baa." They had this as a sheep drive down Ranney [Street]. They'd drive them down to the stockyards, you know, early in the morning. We'd just be surrounded. When we moved here there was no bushes or trees or grass or anything. It was alfalfa. This was the end of town, right here. [It] was quite primitive.

We didn't have to lock our doors—never had a key. And we could call down to the grocery and order our groceries; they'd deliver them.

During [the time] when the banks were all closed and you didn't have any money, people used to bring chickens and vegetables and things to the office [the newspaper] to pay. That was the Depression. We look back and we weren't unhappy about it, you know—we all had plenty to eat. I think as long as you've got plenty to eat, things aren't too bad.

One day here our telephone service—you know, you always have to ring Central? I was calling some woman, and the operator said, "Mrs. Stoddard, I think that you can't get her now, because I just saw her go by the office."

Virginia Shepherd

Were there automobiles in those years [1918]?

There were, beginning largely, I'd say, in the twenties, because the road [to Rifle] was very narrow and very muddy. When they began using automobiles, I can remember hearing one time that the mail truck had been stuck in the mud, and when they tried to pull it out, they pulled it apart! So it was isolated, to the degree that the travel was difficult.

In Meeker, in town, I hear that they had to put the cars away in the wintertime because they just wouldn't run in all that snow. What year was it when they were finally able to use cars in the wintertime?

Well, I'm not sure, but I expect it was the late twenties or early thirties. I do remember that there was considerable consternation when it was possible to go 30 miles an hour between Meeker and Rifle—that was a shocking speed to make between the two places! I do remember that the streets were not very well kept. They were not surfaced. I know that people had the experience of having cars stall too, and having to spend the night on the road between Meeker and Rifle. So it took considerable courage—and an understanding of weather and climate and being prepared for any eventuality—to survive some of those years.

When you put the cars away in the wintertime, what kind of conveyance did people use then?

Well, they used to use the so-called hayracks. They put runners on the hayracks in the wintertime, and people came to town on runners. There were also so-called cutters, which were smaller conveyances, usually one-horse, to carry two or four people, probably; that was a lighter rig. Of course, there was always horseback, and there were wagons of various kinds, and buggies, and the so-called trap that the people in the backseat couldn't get out until the people in the front seat got out. It was largely horse conveyance in the wintertime.

THREE

Children's Lives

Everyone but the very young had to work on the homestead. When they were old enough, girls helped their mothers with the housework, cooking, tending of gardens, and taking care of barnyard animals. Some did this and more. They also helped plow and harvest the crops, herd the sheep and care for the cattle, build fences, and dig irrigation ditches. They did whatever agricultural life demands. Some of the girls preferred these chores to those in the house, but if they were the oldest child, their help with the outside chores was often essential.

Ila Bowman Powell

Oh, we all had the things that we had to do. I remember when I must have been in the seventh or eighth grade when the sheep came in here—1925. My brother got out and gathered bum lambs. There were days when we'd go to the sheep camps, and then if it rained and was bad weather especially, we'd always have lambs. We raised 157 bum lambs one spring—milked the cows, you know, and took care of them. Then finally we got some calf meal to help out on the food end of it, and we had to mix that and feed those lambs three times a day, and the little ones more often.

But we had to take responsibility—we learned to milk cows at a very early age and [to] do all the things that had to be done, because my dad had to be gone some and work out to make a living. We weren't that well fixed financially, and we had to help Mother take ahold and do the garden work and take care of the animals and shovel out the ditches and all that sort of thing. It just had to be done, and we all learned to work.

Were there different chores for the girls and for the boys?

Well, we all just had something to do outside. I remember I baked my own birthday cake when I was seven years old, and from then on after that I always helped with the cooking. My dad and I always planted the potatoes, because the boys thought it was funny to throw potatoes or something at Dad while he was driving the team, you know—just old walking plows them days, was how we planted the potatoes. That was one of the special things that I did that was outside chores—was to always help my dad plant potatoes.

And then he'd make the boys go to the house and help Mother, and that *really* got them down, to have to wash dishes and carry water from the well and chop the wood and pick up chips and sweep the floors. Whenever they didn't help with the work we were doing, like planting potatoes, they had to go to the house and help Mom while I came and did the other work.

Did you like to work outside better?

Yeah—I'd still rather work outside.

What kinds of things did you wear when you were growing up?

Little girls in those days didn't wear pants and slacks and all that stuff. We wore dresses all the time.

We always got in and helped Mother with the washing. We washed every two or three days. If we let it stack up, we'd never got it done, because you had to do it on the washboard. We never *did* have [a washing machine] as long as I lived at home.

[We heated the water] on [the] cookstove, and then we had to take the washboard and scrub the clothes when the water got cool enough we could put our hands in it. Then we always had a big old copper boiler—clothes boiler, big oval, round, you know—and we always boiled the white clothes and the tea towels and [the other] towels and the underwear and all that stuff on the stove. Then we took a big old stick and lifted them out of the water into the rinse tubs and—it was quite a procedure, believe me.

How did you get them dry in the wintertime?

Sometimes we'd have them out on the clothesline—usually up there it was pretty easy to dry things. They had a pretty good wind, but sometimes it was just cold and they would hang. We'd bring them in, and they'd just be stiff as boards. And we'd hang them up on the lines in the house. We always had some lines in the house, made out of a cotton rope or something, and we'd hang them up there. The air from the stove, the heater and all, would get them dry.

What about ironing—did you have to do that?

You had this old iron that kind of had a spring in it, and you put it over a little rod that went across this whole iron, and it caught under that rod; then you could lift it off and iron. When it began to get cool, too cool, why, then you had to put it back and get another iron. We usually had five or six of those irons. My mama used to turn a great big cast-iron skillet over our irons so they'd heat faster on the stove.

Sometimes when my dad was gone and all, we'd get out and hunt the chips up and the wood, and have it all ready. So we'd just keep firing up and firing up until we got through with the ironing. It wasn't fun, but we did it anyway.

Did you just iron clothes, or were there other things to iron?

We ironed things that people don't think about ironing today, like our pillowcases and all of our aprons. Of course, all this stuff now—it doesn't wear as well as the old cotton stuff used to. A lot of our things were made out of flour sacks. We had cloth sacks, in those days, that flour came in, and we made our clothes out of flour sacks—our aprons, some of our panties, petticoats, and things like that—because we used a lot of flour. Everybody baked their own bread, of course. I didn't know they had such places as bakeries until I was 14 years old and I went to Fruita [Colorado] to go to high school. Aunt Hattie, the lady I stayed with— she sent me up to the bakery to get a loaf of bread, and I said, "Where?" But that's the first time I was ever in a bakery.

Katherine Warren Rector

Katherine and her sister, Nellie Parks, grew up on the family ranch that her father began with a preemption of 80 acres in 1891.

Do you remember when you were a child growing up that you had responsibilities or chores to do every day?

My dad and mother separated when I was 12 years old, and I said I can't remember being a kid very much—I was a housewife, forever and ever.

Did you have a washing machine?

No, of course not. That scrub board around the corner there [gestures] is the one I used. We didn't have no washing machine, I never had an electric washing machine till—oh, it was gas, I should say, till 1938.

Did you have brothers? Did they help with the chores?

I had two brothers. I didn't know my older brother much, because he was gone, but I had a younger brother. He wasn't very good help. When there was anything to do, he was usually elsewhere.

I used to help feed sometimes, which took a little while.

How did you get out to the sheep and cattle in the winter to feed them?

We had the sled and the horses.

Were there other things you would rather have done around the ranch than worked in the house?

I worked in the field. I worked everywhere. I had the whole thing! I worked in the hay field, milked cows, and anything there was to do.

I have a lot of good memories of my dad. Even if I *was* his "hired man." I really enjoyed it up at the ranch. We used to go to Sleepy Cat [a ranch] and pick raspberries. Dad had a thing he made with a gunnysack, and he had three pockets here and three back here [gestures], and you picked in these jars. You picked them berries in them jars, and that's the way he took them home. He had quite an invention, because most of us wouldn't think about—we'd probably get a bucket, and then we'd drop the bucket and spill all the raspberries.

How often did you get to come to town or see other people?

Oh, we didn't come to town very often. I think in earlier years that they come to town more than we did through that period of time. Of course, later on we had a car. I remember my younger sister and I used to come to town on horseback. It was 12 miles.

Ethel La Kamp Chrisler

I drove a stacker horse. When they had these old stackers, you put the hay on this stacker with a buck rake.* Then the stacker horse would have to pull [the stacker] up and flip [the hay] on the stack. That's what I did, was lead the stacker horse.

In the summertime I'd help hay. And, of course, we had our chores. We had to help carry in the water, get the wood, feed the chickens and gather the eggs, and sometimes milk the cows.

Did you have brothers and sisters?

[I] had one brother, five years younger than I.

Did he do certain kinds of chores, whereas you did other kinds?

Oh, we did them together, as a rule—everything, just kind of together. 'Course, he was younger than I; he didn't have the strength that I did.

I loved to work outdoors. I hated to cook—and still do. I'd help [my mother] pick the peas and fix them. But the main cooking she always did—I didn't. But I'd help my dad.

What else did you do outside, besides stack hay?

Well, when he'd cut posts he'd make me snake them with a horse. He didn't make me—he'd ask me. You take a log chain and hook them around two or three or four posts, usually from a saddle horn. And then

---

*A large rake used for raking hay.

you'd get on the horse and snake them to where you could get to the wagon to load them on the wagon.

Oma Jensen Graham

As you got a little older, were there chores you were responsible for?

If there was a poddy calf on Blue Mountain, they saw to it that I got it, because I was the only girl. A poddy calf is a calf that his mother's died, and we call them poddy. And I usually had three or four, and it was my job to feed them, and I don't mean maybe! Milk, in a bottle, and fed them about four or five [times a day]—that's all I got done for about a month after I got them, was filling the bottle and feeding those calves. Occasionally Mother would say, "Well, now, you can go with your dad and ride." But 90 percent of the responsibility was mine. I was probably about six years old.

When you did ride with your dad, what did you do?

Punch cows! I've been punching cows all my life, because Mother would pack me or Dad would pack me, and we punched cows from the time I was born, I think. They had a goose-feather pillow, and they'd put it in front between Dad and the saddle, and he'd pack me most of the time; they'd take turns, see. If anything came up that Dad had to rope something, he'd give me and the pillow to Mother. I'd wake up and go to sleep and wake up thinking I never was going to get off that cotton-pickin' horse!

When you were little like that, how did your mother feed you?

She must have nursed me until I was two years old, because, I don't know, what kind of a lunch would you serve a kid?

I don't know! Did you help your mother in the house too?

Sure. She taught me to cook, and my grandmother taught me to sew. After I got a little older, Mother would say, "All right, it's time to cook today," and so she'd pull me off and I'd stay home. And as I say, I helped to raise my brother and sister.

CeCelia Sullivan Knott

To say that my job was to do this, and this, and this, no. By the time there were other children and so forth, there was no other way. Every child in my growing up worked. And you worked as soon as you were able.

We helped carry in the coal and the wood, and you started helping with the housework, even to the cooking, at a very, very young age: I know that I could cook before I started school. As I said, my mother worked outside a great deal, and before I was seven she was hurt, because a cow attacked her. It injured her back, and she was down for a long time. My older sister Mary was the nurse and the caretaker of the family, but I was to do the cooking, the dishes, and, I guess you'd say, keep house. I remember sweeping the floor, but I can imagine how well I did. But I did know enough to know how to peel potatoes, or scrub the potatoes, and how to cook a piece of meat. I can't say that I knew how to make bread—yeast bread—but I could make biscuits and muffins and cook them in a coal stove. My job was to do the dishes and do the housework. My sister Mary helped with the laundry during this time, but I was to do so much laundry each day so that we could keep clothing for that many people. A child can only wash one tub of laundry.

Did you do any of the outside chores?

A little later on I did, not quite that young, but it was just chores. I never worked in the hay field, nor anything like that. But my brother older than I [and I] would feed horses and feed the cows that were around the corral, and milk, and that kind of stuff. I would say that was in the 8- to 10-year-old bracket. By that time my father had sheep, and I always raised in around 20 bum lambs a year. That was my project, was to raise these lambs. It was passed on down to the younger members of the family as they got a little older. They took over my job, which I was glad to get rid of.

Where did you get your water?

From the river. It wasn't a tremendous ways. Looking back on it through a kid's eyes, it seemed to me like a hundred miles to the river, but it really isn't all that far. But I would say that it was probably as much as five blocks, six blocks from the river. As children [we] either carried the water by bucket or we had barrels on what they called a stone boat [a flat bottom sled]. [We'd] get a workhorse and go to the river and fill these barrels with water and haul the barrels of water with the horse. It's a slow process of filling up—I'm assuming they were 50-gallon barrels, but they were like a big old liquor barrel would be.

During the spring it was especially bad, because the river was high and riley, and dirty. If there'd be any rain, you caught the rainwater off the roof for your laundry. It was almost impossible to do laundry during that period of time.

What about drinking water?

It's a wonder we didn't die. But I guess things were pure then—I don't know. But you would let [the water from the river] settle overnight or sit in barrels for a period of time: overnight or a couple of days. It was amazing how this [sediment] would settle to the bottom of these barrels. The water wasn't clear, [but] it had cleared immensely and we did drink that.

Audrey Ruckman Oldland

Audrey Ruckman Oldland grew up on a ranch that her father and mother had begun as a homestead shortly after the turn of the century. She was the fourth of 10 children. As in most large ranching families, the children had many chores to do, inside and outside the house.

Every child as they grew up was given a responsibility and they were held to that responsibility. I can remember that I had the chickens to take care of when I was only about—maybe four or five years old. I had to see that the chickens were fed and the eggs were gathered. Then as we grew up and became more capable, we assumed other responsibilities, and each child was responsible for that. On Saturdays I had the lamp chimneys to clean and the lamps to fill with kerosene and dirty clothes to gather up, because Saturday was usually wash day; with that many children, wash day was on a day when everybody could help.

And I had all of that to do, and the beds to change, and things like that. And as you grew up, your responsibilities got greater. I was expected to always help in the hay field as soon as I got big enough to drive a team of horses, which I loved.

I inherited the stacker-boy bit at one time. Dad said to me many a time, "Get behind that old horse. If you can drag that old horse and that load of hay up and dump it on the stack, we won't need the horse—we'll just turn him loose and you can do it. So—get *behind* him!" And the horse was smarter than I was—he was a great big old stallion horse, but he was gentle and he knew what he was doing, better than I did. But we grew into our responsibilities, and each and every one was expected to do what they knew they should do. I helped with the milking and helped with those chores when I was in high school. I'd have to get up early in the morning and go and help milk and then catch my horse and hitch him up to the two-wheel cart. Then Carrie and I drove to high school that way.

Did the boys and girls in your family do all the chores, or did the girls do certain things and the boys do certain things?

Well, there were chores the boys did and chores that the girls did too, but it always seemed to me like I wasn't considered a boy and I wasn't considered a girl!

I worked in the hay field, and I would go out and buck-rake hay or rake hay all day long. Then at night when we came in, why, the boys got to sit down but I had to help with the dishes; I had o help the girls do these too.

I worked for Clair Pearson for 50¢ a day. I walked over to her house in the morning, got there around eight o'clock. She helped in the hay field, and I got the meal, did up the breakfast dishes, and got the noon meal and everything.

How old were you?

Twelve years old at that time. The next year after I worked for her, Boyd Crawford's mother and father died, and he was keeping the ranch down there, and I went over and worked there. It meant cooking for about four or five hired men. I had the vegetables to dig and the meat to cut and everything.

[But] I enjoyed it. I enjoyed it. I'm thankful that I had that rounded-

87

out life that I had. I've always told all of my kids, "You learn to do it—whether you will ever *have* to do it or not, you learn to do it, and then if you have to do it, you know how." I think that's missing in the world today.

Hilda Shelton Rawlinson

Were there chores that the boys normally did and chores that the girls did, or was that intermixed?

Seems like we always had to work together—boys and girls. I was the oldest—of course, I always had to take the boy's part. My oldest brother was next to me. But we always had to be out and take a man's place. Everybody helped build fence. I was always the flunky, the cowboy—breaking horses and all that good stuff.

Did you have hay or plant any crops?

Oh, yes. That was our job, to mow hay—plow first. It was with a walking plow, two horses hooked to it, and you walked behind it and you held those handles. And plow the sagebrush—it was a lot of fun.

How did you mow?

Well, you had an old mower—a horse mower, with two horses on it. You pitched it onto a wagon with a fork. Mother and I and all of us would all get out and pitch the hay, load it onto the wagon, and haul it to the stack, and you stacked it.

What did you wear for clothes during those years?

Well, we mostly wore dresses, but when I worked outside I wore knickers—they called them knickerbockers. My mother used to make them. They come down to your knees, and they had a band on it, with a button on the side. And bonnets—she always made our bonnets and hats and so forth.

Children who grew up in town had some of the same household chores as those who were raised on the homestead. But for the former life was somewhat easier because they didn't have ranch work to do as well.

Freddie White Blevins

From the time I was 9 or 10 years old, I could cook a meal and often did. We were expected to make our beds, and my brother didn't always do this, but we made his bed for him. He was supposed to bring in the coal and take out the ashes, but sometimes we had to catch him on the fly or he didn't get it done. Then we also were expected to clean the whole house on Saturday—my sister and I—which we did, because Mother worked. [Her mother worked in her father's office.]

Jennie Brown Spence

I don't know if I had any chores; I don't know what I did. I don't ever remember cooking. [Mother] liked to do the cooking. I didn't do any of that until I got older, and then it was just baking cakes or fancy things— it wasn't regular cooking. And, of course, like most girls, I didn't care much about dishes.

We didn't have a dairy here in Meeker, and that's why there are so many barns around, or old shacks, because people had horses, and most of them had cows. And Mother had a cow. That's the first thing she did was buy a cow, and she wouldn't let my father milk it—she milked it herself. She used to pin up her skirt—she had a long skirt, and she'd fold it up and pin it back—and put on an apron and go out and milk the cow. We sold milk. That was one chore I had. I don't think I ever went to school that I didn't have a pail of milk hung on me. I had to deliver milk every morning, and I delivered it in five-pound pails, a quart. Mother sold 20 quarts for $1. She made little tickets out of a shoe box, and when you put your bucket out for the next day, if you wanted 2 quarts, you'd put two tickets in. I always had customers that I had to [deliver milk to]—well, my brother did too. We both delivered milk on our way to school.

We lived up here in this end of town a lot, and on the way to school it was deep snow I was in—I could hardly wade through it, and I had this milk and I spilled it. I decided that I'd just fill it up with snow and take it on, you know. But the lady I took it to was a friend of ours, and I took music lessons from her. Of course, she knew right away what I had done. But my mother didn't punish me for it. I guess she gave Mrs. Adams another quart of milk. But I didn't get in trouble about it. She gave me music lessons—and that was one thing I had to do. Seems like everybody in those days gave their children music lessons or had a piano. My brother had to take lessons too. I had to practice, and that was probably my chore—that I had to do.

Most children had time to play and have fun. They explored the country on horseback, played games, utilized common materials for toys, and used their imaginations to create whatever they wished.

Ethelyn Whalin Crawford

Ethelyn Whalin Crawford spent her childhood years on a homestead near Meeker. Her parents arrived in the area in 1912, and they eventually had eight children. Ethelyn was the oldest daughter. Her vivid imagination provided many hours of entertainment.

In the summertime, whenever it was possible we climbed the hills and we laid in the shade and watched the clouds and made mansions out of the clouds. I remember once [my brother] Wilbur said the angels were bucking in the sky. We made pictures out of the clouds. One day we climbed to the top of the hill—the first time that we had ever climbed to the real top of the little hill; it wasn't very high. We'd only gone as far as the ledge of rocks before, but this day we were real adventuresome. And so we climbed over to the top of the hill, and it was different from what I had expected, completely. You could just see . . . we could see Bear's Ears up in Wyoming. It was a real summer day, and I remember the smell of dust and sage and kind of an animal smell too. And all together—the smell of the sun on all of it. It was magnificent. I just stood there when we got to the top. Wilbur ran on ahead of me, down some path the animals had made, and pretty soon he called to me, and he brought me out of a regular trance of . . . worshiping, I guess, what I was seeing. [He said,] "Come on, come on, let's go and see this or that or something." And I went, but I have never forgotten the feeling I had at the top of the hill.

We rode horseback; we walked; we climbed hills; we walked fences;

we climbed trees; we climbed clear to the top of box elder trees and sat on the highest branches we thought would bear our weight and whittled. Each of us had a pocketknife. And we'd sit up there and whittle. We thought we were with the birds, you know. We thought we were something.

What did you do in the wintertime?

Winters weren't so bad, except that we always wanted to get outdoors and play, and so often we weren't able to go outdoors and play in the winter—the snow would get so deep. But we made our own playthings. Mom had lots of postcards. We built houses with them—palaces—and then we wrecked them and built more. Also, we didn't really have paper dolls most of the time, but I cut out paper dolls. Dad taught me how—out of catalog paper. And Wilbur and I together would build regular farms out of these things with pasteboard boxes. Ah, I wish you could have seen those ranches full of cattle and sheep and what-have-you . . . we had fun. We were never bored.

Ila Bowman Powell

I remember when I used to go fishing with my dad. He was a good fisherman, and he'd fish and he'd have a sackful of fish. We always took a flour sack or something, tied a thing in the corners and carried it, and when he got through and said, "Sis, I'm tired of fishing. Why don't you fish awhile?" I always thought, "Boy, that was really neat"—you know, my dad would let me take the pole and fish. And, of course, we didn't have fishing poles in those days. When we got up to where we fished, we tied our horses up and cut a willow. Then I'd take my old battered-up hat and I'd go through the prairie until I'd find a grasshopper, and then we had it made from then on. But that was fun for me—and just being with the family.

We had our first homestead, and then this old man that homesteaded above us up Cathedral Creek, he didn't like it up there. So Dad and him traded homestead land. My dad relinquished his ground and filed on 640 acres up where this old man was. We had to clean all the bushes off of there then, because he hadn't done anything—he was just an old bachelor, and he just come and went as he pleased. And so we thought that was really great. [Dad would] go back and forth—he took the wagon and hitched a 2-by-12 on the back with chains, and he would drag it across the brush in the spring of the year when the brush was wet, and they'd come right out by the roots. Dad would say, "Now, while I'm working today, you kids get a whole bunch of those sagebrush cleaned up."

That was our kids' job: pile them in a great big pile and then we'll see who has the biggest bonfire tonight. So we'd have separate piles. And then he'd let us set them afire at night and burn them, and whoever had the biggest bonfire, why, they was the one that really won the prizes, you know.

And that's the way he got us to work for it, is to pile up that many brush today and then tonight we could have the bonfire. And we did lots of things like that.

We used to make jerky. We'd kill the deer in the summertime. We'd slice up a lot of the meat—like the hindquarters and the loin of the backbone—real thin, and put quite a lot of salt and pepper on them. [Then we'd] string them on a wire, and make jerky, like the Indians. They taught us to make jerky. We'd have great old sacks of dried deer meat [made] into jerky.

I remember Sam Wear [the game warden, as well as the editor's great-grandfather] used to have an old roan horse, and he had dogs with him. We'd see him—he didn't come down in our country very often, but once in a while he would. So oh, Lord, my brother and I was alone there one day, and we had jerky on the clothesline—you wouldn't believe it. [My brother] come tearing in and says, "Oh my God, Sissy." He said, "We got to get this jerky down here somewhere." He said, "He comes old Sam Wear." So we took the wires undone on the clothesline. We's pretty smart little devils—we wasn't very big, but he wired them around my waist, and I went down the trail [to the] creek bottom [while] he followed, holding the wires on this end [gestures]. And we took them way up the creek and wired them up in the deep willows in the creek bottom. But when we got back, it *wasn't* Sam—it was an old fellow that lived over on the other creek, and he was off hunting bear and he had these hound dogs with him. But we could see him way down farther than from here to the road [gestures], and we knew that he was riding this roan horse and we thought that was who it was.

Oma Jensen Graham

Along about that time [ca. 1918], why, there was some cattle rustling going on [at] Blue Mountain. And so I rode along. I had a good horse then; they'd traded horses for me, and I had a good horse. And I'd imagine, "Now, I'm going to catch those rustlers." I'd tie my horse up, and slip down through some brush, and [then] gallop home like they were after me! [Laughter.]

And, of course, the guys were always jawbin' [teasing] me. They were building a fence around the homestead, and they came home at noon and said they were ready for the dead man. Now that's the rock that you bury in the ground to hold the corner post. They call them a dead man. And man, I got really excited. I went out and I caught my horse and I went down with them. Here they put this rock in there—talk about disgusted. I come home a-gallopin'—Mother never said a word. She said, "What's the matter?" And I said, "That wasn't any dead man—that was just a rock they put in the ground!" [Laughter.]

Were there other children for you to play with?

Not too many in the summertime. There were very few then. I had one boy. He was about two years older than I was. And he and I rode the roundups together with his stepdad and my dad. And, of course, we'd always get in a little mischief—not bad, but . . . we could think of more things to do.

We were over at Stoot's reservoir during the cricket time. They always sent Martin and I—I guess to get rid of us. We'd have to make our circle, you know, to bring the cattle back, and [it] seemed like we always got more than the other guys did. But anyway, we'd got ours in and they were there on the reservoir. [One of the cowhands] was laying there, sound asleep with his mouth wide open, and snoring, and Martin looked at me and—we could use mental telepathy; I knew what he was going to do. So I got his horse around, and he just reached over and took a big cricket and put it in [the man's] mouth! He crunched down on that thing, and by that time Martin had hit the saddle! [Laughter.]

Did you ever play with dolls?

Well, yes, I had a nice set of dolls. I changed their clothes on Sunday and put them back to bed. For the week they were setting on the bed. I'd rather be out walking on stilts. Did you ever walk on stilts? Oh, brother—it's sure a lot of fun when the mud gets about three feet [deep] and you fall down and have to crawl out of the road to a fence to get up!

I used to go over to Chew's in Pat's Hole. If I worked real hard, I could go over there for my vacation. She had kids from 3 on up to 25 years old. There were so many there—I think there was three girls, and three boys about the same age. We all had our work cut out for us. They raised a big garden and everything like that. You all done your work and got everything under control, and then you could take lunch and take off. We'd go down to where Echo Park is now, and when we'd ford the river we'd just fall off of the horse—tie the reins around the saddle horn, fall off, and catch him by the tail or the stirrups. We just took our shoes off and went in with all of our clothes on, and they'd dry on us. Then we'd come to the river again and do the same thing.

How long did you stay there, and how far was it to this place?

[I stayed] about 10 days. It was about 20 miles, [but] we were in a little hurry and it was good trotting country. Lulu Karen used to go with me, and then Mrs. Chew had a granddaughter the same age as I was [14]. I never had an aunt of my own, so I adopted Julia Mae's mother and father, and so their kids acted like my cousins by adoption.

CeCelia Sullivan Knott

When as a child you had time to play, what did you do?

Play, Julie? What is play? To say really play—no. That's why I say, "Play? What is play?" With a family of that size—and I mean the size wasn't all that great. You see, I was into high school before two younger brothers were born. But still, just to keep the family unit going, everybody had work to do. I'm sure, though, that we *did* play, because I can remember vividly my brother that's older than I am and I having these imaginary friends and that. So we undoubtedly played. But to say that we got up games of ball of any kind or anything like that—no.

Audrey Ruckman Oldland

I remember I loved to climb. I was a tomboy. I loved to climb around and I loved the horses, and [it] seems like I was always doing something

94

that wasn't very constructive. It seems like I was always doing something that I was going to get paddled for, but I went ahead and did it anyway! [Laughter.] Like I said, I loved to climb in the trees, and if I'd get a whipping for something, I'd go and climb up in the tree and get away out on the limbs where they would rock me. It seemed soothing for me— rocked by the trees.

I never will forget when I caught the horse. I have no idea how old I was—I must not have been more than seven or eight years old. The horse had a bridle on, but he had no saddle on, and I loved to ride. So I got the horse and was riding, and Carrie, who is two years younger than me—I thought she should enjoy it too. So I got up on the chicken house, or the fence, or a wagon, and got Carrie on behind me on the horse and went for a ride. I got out on the road, which was prohibited too: I knew I shouldn't be on the road, but I was riding on the road. We went way up to the Bernstein Hill and turned around and came back. And when we came back, I saw Mama in the lane, and she was waving her apron and hollering at me to come in. I knew what she wanted—she wanted me to get off that horse. But I thought, "Well, just a little bit more. As long as I'm going to get it, I just as well get it good."

So I went on down past the lane and ignored the fact that I even saw her, and when I turned around then and came back, with Carrie protesting that we should go in, she was waiting for me. And so I got a thorough going-over with a willow, and then I got tied to the foot of the bed, which was the part that hurt the worst. The whipping didn't last long, but I was tied to the foot of the bed, and I was denied supper. That was the only time that any of us ever got a discipline like that. I don't know what brought it on. I was naughty! I just—oh, I don't know—I was defiant. I knew I was going to get it, because I rode right by.

Most of our play at home when we were children was taken up [with] playing like we were women. Carrie, my younger sister, and myself—we played we were women. We were always Mrs; it was "Mrs. This" and "Mrs. That." In order to play and take care of the kids, why, I was Mrs. So-and-So, and I had the youngest ones—I had Jennie and Stubby and the baby. And Carrie was Mrs. So-and-So, and she had the older ones to take care of. And we had playhouses—one in the granary and one in the icehouse, or something like that. We'd invite one another over and have raw carrots and things like that. That was our games of play.

Did you have any dolls or other toys of any kind?

Our teacher gave us dolls when we were in about the fourth or fifth grade. Carrie and I were given these two little dolls, in little white coats.

They were only about eight-inch dolls, and they had little white fur coats, with blue-and-white dotted belts around them and everything. These were our first dolls. I used to make clothespin dolls, and clothes for the clothespin dolls. But those were our first real dolls—were the ones that were given to us by our teacher.

And I loved my doll. I took it to bed with me, and I let it fall out of bed. My brother Morris came down the next morning and saw it laying on the floor, and he took it and hid it. I shed enough tears with that doll to drown him and me both! He never brought it back. I found it in three or four days in the cow barn, up behind the pigeon nests. He used to give me clues as to where it was. We'd go near every day. He says, "You gather eggs right there," and he says, "I don't know why you don't find it." And he kept giving me clues until I finally found it, but by that time it was getting pretty snuttzy looking.

We were aspiring actresses, Carrie and I. We made up our plays, and we had the stairway in the house. It is in the hall; it goes up from the hallway, and we used to use that as our stage, because we could get everybody conglomerated on the stairs. Then there was the hall here [gestures] that went into the front room, and there was a door here [gestures] that went into the bedroom. So those were our dressing rooms, and we could act here [gesture] in front of the stairs.

We had a play that we put on. I don't know how old we were. We gave it at home, and we had so much fun doing it. The teacher at that time, she thought it was real cute. So we gave the play at the community Christmas program; we gave it for the Odd Fellow program, and—oh, we were aspiring actresses!

What was this play about?

Couple of women gossiping. I can't remember only one line—that was after we had finished our cup of tea and she had gone home and I said, "Oh, that terrible Mrs. Bailey—I think she's the worst old gossip in this town, don't you?"

We made our own amusements. We hadn't a lot of toys—we never had a lot of toys. We used to have our own band—used to have a drummer, and play combs. All of the kids, we'd get together and we'd play and sing.

Iris Self Lyons

Iris Self Lyons grew up in a family of seven children on her parents' homestead on Spring Gulch, near the Williams Fork River, south of Craig.

We'd play out at night, hide-and-seek, and then in the wintertime my mother used to go out skiing with us. My dad never did, because he didn't care much about skiing.

Where did you get the skis?

They made them. They had one-by-fours, and they'd boil them and then stick it in the log cabin [between the logs] and wait until the end turned up. But they made their own skis. They were slick, and, of course, they'd put paraffin or something, wax, whatever they had, on them. Sometimes lard.

One night we were ski-riding in the moonlight and there was one pole out in the field. [Mother] said she knew she was going to hit that post, and she did, head-on. So that took care of her skiing. She wouldn't go skiing with us anymore.

Did you ever play by yourself or play inside at different things?

Oh, yes. In the wintertime we used to get strings behind the old cook-stove and then make little farms and string it around, you know, like fences. Cut out paper dolls, and make rocking chairs out of paper. Just cut paper, then bend it down, and bend one paper up and one down—and you had a little rocking chair.

Did you have any dolls?

Oh, yes. My dad was a good provider. He bought us dolls. The most enjoyable Christmas is when we lived over on a bluff on the south side of [the] Yampa River, and we didn't have a great deal of money, so they got out the Montgomery Ward catalog and ordered little 10¢ and 15¢ gifts and put them on the tree. That was the most enjoyable—I remember a little lady's shoe that had a little knife in it. My sister still has hers, but I lost mine.

Most rural children attended one-room schools until the 1950s, when the school systems were consolidated and began busing children to town. Many women have fond memories of their rural school days, except for the cold weather, which generally made the ride to school miserable. Other women lived in town and walked to school.

The rural schools offered grades one through eight. When students graduated from the eighth grade, they were sometimes sent to town to board with a family during high school, while other families moved to town during the school year. Some children were unable to attend school after the eighth grade and consequently stayed on the homestead to help with the work.

Hilda Shelton Rawlinson

I want to tell you about the schools. We had children—there was us kids and neighbor kids that had lived there, and their mothers taught them. There was no school closer than Maybell, which was 15 miles. The school board would furnish the lumber if the people could build the schoolhouse. So they built the school house, and we had school. It wasn't that summer—it was the next summer—but we got a school. I think we had about 25 or so kids in this school the next year, as the homesteaders came in with their children. I think there was 25 or 27, and then gradually the people starved out—I guess you put it that way. They couldn't make a living, and they'd leave the country. Well, we left the country too and went to this other homestead, up by Wolf Mountain, and no school again. So—same procedure—go through building another schoolhouse, because there were other children in the community that didn't have a school and their folks were teaching them. They weren't without schooling; they were taught by their parents.

Mary Gates Haughey

We usually started [school] the early part of May, as soon as all the snow left so that we could walk. We walked about three-quarters of a mile from our home to the school. And the schoolhouse was a little log cabin, and I mean *cabin,* unfinished, just like our homestead houses were. It's always been a question in my mind why it was put in the loca-

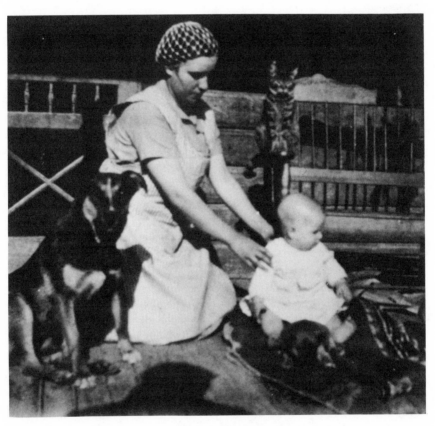

Mary Haughey and son, Clarence. Snake River, 1927
Courtesy of Mary Haughey

tion it was. It was put in an open valley, right down where the sun beat down ferociously in the summertime, and we had to walk quite a distance, carry the water in water buckets. If they had put it on the other side of the creek, in the shade, the spring could have been in the backyard of the schoolhouse. But they didn't think. They figured it was open there.

And there were several of us. There were students from first grade through the eighth.

When you were a child and went to this one-room school, can you think of some of the things you did for entertainment or fun, or did you work hard?

Oh, we played baseball, which we called "workup." There never was enough for a team—you know, to have two complete teams. So we'd play two or three to bat, and when they were put out, why, then they went to be catcher, and so on, till we worked up through. We did that at recesses and noon. I went down and played in the creek and hunted birds' eggs, and we ran up on the hill and picked flowers and got away from the schoolhouse as far as we could. The boys were guilty of going swimming in puddles.

How about some pranks? I think you mentioned some pranks that you—

Well, some of them were that kind of stuff—kept the teacher in a tizzy. The very first teacher we had up there was Ernest Cline, and he only taught maybe a month or six weeks. He sent one of the girls and I down for a bucket of water, and we didn't want to go. But we went, and we played down there too long. We decided that it would be real clever to fill the water bucket partly full and then put several frogs in and take it up to the teacher. We did. And we didn't get tanned for it, which we should have, but we didn't. So he just emptied the water out and sent a couple of boys down.

I'm sure those teachers were very busy and had quite a few experiences.

But they were hardly much older than we were, is the funny part of it. Some of them did not even have an eighth-grade graduation. But that is the early history of the United States. These people that had a little education transmitted it to their students, and some of them were wonderful teachers.

And then when you got past the eighth grade, what did you do?

We either were boarded in town or the family moved to town to put us in school here in Craig, which my family did for me. I remember that I came to the Craig school at Thanksgivingtime. I had finished the eighth grade that year and came on down to go in the freshman class that year. It was tough going, but I made it. I only knew one person in Craig when I came to school.

Jennie Steele Mott

I started school in 1936. We rode horseback for the first five years. About the year I was in the sixth grade, then, we moved to Red Rock, which is just below the school about a half a mile or so, and we walked that year. The year I was in the seventh grade was during the war, and you couldn't get teachers and we couldn't leave the place. Mama had to teach us. She taught us four younger kids—well, she taught me for three years, my seventh, eighth, and ninth grades. When I was a sophomore in high school, I was sent out to Meeker to go to school. Then after that we moved to Rangely.

Estel Aicher Woolley

In 1898 Estel Aicher Woolley's mother came from South Carolina to visit her sister, who lived in Meeker. She liked the freedom she found in the West and decided to marry a homesteader. Estel was their only child.

Well, I always had a horse that I rode to school. I'd come to school every day, no matter how cold it was—even below zero—and my folks would wrap me up. If I'd fallen off, I'd have never hit the ground, be-cause I had a coat on, then I had an army coat that my dad had from Troop B, [a] heavy kind of overcoat I put on top of all of that, and they just set me up on my horse and I'd come to town to a livery stable. There was an old man down there by the name of Fred Johnson, and he had to take me off. I had so many wraps—I was such a *little* kid. He'd call my mother and—"My God! What did you send that girl out for, a day like this? Don't you know it's so-and-so cold?" But I had big German socks I put on top of my overshoes, to keep warm, and—kids don't know how it is nowadays, going places. I'd have died if mine had had to go that way!

How far was it? Were there other kids close by?

A mile and a half. There were some up above me that came down, and we met and rode together. But a lot of times I just went on. And then my uncle that had the Meeker Hotel owned Marvine Lodge, and he had his saddle horses—my dad used to winter them. He had one special, great big tall one I could hardly get up on, by pulling with every-thing, but special. I got to ride that to school when we were wintering them, you know, and I could outrun all the other kids with that horse.

Minnie Eberle James

I always liked school. 'Course, when we first came, why, I'd be so cold by the time I got to school [in Craig] I'd have to sit by this great big potbellied stove. I'd sit by that stove about two or three hours before I'd get thawed out enough to really take an interest in what I was doing. The thermometer would be way down. We'd drive—we had two horses, and we'd have some hot bricks and hot stones that we heated, but they couldn't keep you warm all the way.

How long a trip was it?

About four miles. I think [it took] about an hour. I expect the horses traveled fairly fast too, because I think they were cold. They had to keep warm.

Julia Biskup Kawcak

What about school? Where did you go to school?

South Side School. We had to go around a fence and get to it. We had to bring water to school, you know; you didn't have any water at the school. The teachers got $50 a month and they had to give $5 to some boy to do the chores—haul the coal in and clean the schoolhouse and bring a jug of water every day to school. The boys [brought] a jug of water—just a gallon of water—and we had to live on that for the day. There was an irrigation ditch right behind the school, but you couldn't drink [from] it.

And the teacher—twice we had men teachers, Floyd and Clyde Jackson, and they lived over across the river. They would come to the school on horseback. And their sister Lily rode behind either one of them, whichever one was teaching. They'd bring their lunch and everything, put their horse under an old shed—we had an old broken-down shed in back of the school. The school was about 12 by 14 feet. When Mrs. Johnson taught, they had 21 kids there.

But there was a nice hill, just south of the school, and we had our home base [for baseball] right close to the hill. We'd build a toboggan, put two sleds—just one sled here, one here [gestures]—and they had a big plank. The boys would drag that up the hill, and then we'd all get on at once and we'd all come down!

We played baseball. There would be 8 or 10 of us there. We had two teams, got a board and kind of chopped it down so you could get ahold of the thing, and played ball. We made a ball with old socks inside of another sock, and sewed. We made it real—maybe a rock in the middle, about that big, so it would go.

Ethelyn Whalin Crawford

I only went to school two months [when] we lived on the ranch. It was there on Wilson Creek, and it was a little one-room school. Wilbur and I both went; he went to the first grade and I went to the second grade. Mom taught us at home, you see; I only had two months of schooling before I came into the third grade here in Meeker. I had five years of schooling before I went into high school—five years and two months, I should say, shouldn't I?

How much time do you remember spending at home, learning to read and write?

Well, I was always very, very interested in it. I wanted to learn how to spell everything there was—everything I saw. I remember asking [Mom] how to spell *cabinet,* for instance, and she would spell it for me and she would write it out for me. She would print it for me, because I never learned to write until I was nine years old, after I came here to school—when I came here to Meeker and they expected me to do this Palmer-method penmanship. Believe me, that was hard! There were two subjects that were especially difficult for me when I came into the town school: writing was one of them, and music was the other. I loved the singing, you know, but to know where *do-re-mi-fa-so-la-ti-do*—I hadn't the remotest idea what that was all about; it was a foreign language. The ones that had done the first and second grade here, you see, they had been taught about that, and I was supposed to know it when I came into the third grade. As I say, I went five years. I skipped the fifth grade. I went to third and fourth grade. Then the seventh year, I went in at Axial [near Wilson Creek]. And then I went my eighth grade here [in Meeker], and I graduated in 1927 from the eighth grade.

How did they determine what grade you should be in?

Well, I'm not real sure but what Mom did that [chuckle]. She knew how much I knew, and she took Wilbur and I to school the first day that we went to school, and talked to the teachers. They put me in the third grade and put him in the second grade, and we'd had two months of school beforehand. I imagine that she talked to the teacher about it some—perhaps they tried us out where we were to begin with. I can't recall ever having any trouble with anything except the music and the writing.

Why did they decide to skip the fifth grade?

Well, there were about four of us, I believe, and we were in the fourth grade. Our grades were high enough, and they felt that we could handle it. There was only one trouble with this: at that time, at least, they taught fractions in the fifth grade, and fractions and me have never really had more than a nodding acquaintance. Whenever I possibly can, I change it to decimals, because in the sixth grade they taught us decimals.

Audrey Ruckman Oldland

I'd have to get up early in the morning and go and help milk and then catch my horse and hitch him up to the two-wheel cart. Then Carrie and I drove to high school that way. I never lived in town until after [I was] married.

How far was it?

About five miles. Below-zero weather. I can tell you where every downdraft was. The air froze you to death coming from here to Meeker! Down Lyon Canyon it was cold. The wind would come down that canyon—it was so cold right through there. When we were in the cart we had tanned horse-hide robes and we had the warmth around us. They provided that we did not get cold in the buggy. Carrie never liked to get out and do anything like that much. She helped in the kitchen, [but] she didn't like the horses too well, and so I was expected to do that. Carrie stayed in town quite a bit after she was a sophomore and junior and senior. She stayed in town, and I rode horseback to school.

Was that something you chose, rather than staying in town?

Well, yes, I would rather. But then, I was older and I helped with milking and I helped with the outdoor chores. So I was needed at home.

What was it like riding to school in a dress, on a horse?

Picturesque! [Laughter.] Black-satin bloomers! Homemade, black-satin bloomers that fit down over your knees, and heavy black stockings that you tucked up under the elastic of the bloomers. Your legs were sticking out except for the black-satin bloomers.

Froze both my heels, riding to school. You didn't have boots, you know—you had a pair of maybe cloth overshoes, that you wore over your shoes. When you got to the stable, which was down here [gestures] on the corner, and you got off of your horse, you were so stiff you could hardly stand up. Well, immediately you wanted to hide those black-satin bloomers, and you wanted to get rid of those black long stockings. So you rolled your stockings down—they were knee socks—and you pulled your bloomers clear up so that they didn't hang below your dress. By the time you walked from there to school, you kind of got the circulation going again.

Wouldn't that make it cold, to roll your stockings down?

Peer pressure! They all wore long stockings, but yet you still had to have them to where they were respectable. They weren't those heavy black ribbed ones! I think they were men's black stockings that I wore.

Margaret Tagert Jones

Did you enjoy going to school, and was your school far from your home in Meeker?

The school probably would have been about three blocks from my home, and I enjoyed it. It was a brick building up on where the hills started, and it was surrounded by sagebrush fields. In the spring we could go out and catch horny toads and gather buttercups. There was also an Indian burial ground in one of these sagebrush fields that we discovered, and [we] used to dig for the Indian beads—we thought that was a real neat trick, like finding Easter eggs, you know, for children. It didn't seem to bother anybody in the community, and I'm sure we didn't—well, I don't know what we did. I do remember that it was exciting to find something there when we were digging in the graveyard, I guess it was—an Indian graveyard.

When you went to school in the wintertime or in the spring when the weather wasn't good, did you go on horseback, or did you walk through lots of snow?

We walked through lots of snow. And in the spring, through lots of mud. Of course, none of the streets were paved, not even graveled: nobody had thought of doing that yet. So everything just turned to a sea of mud. I remember I wore overshoes, we called them, high rubber boots. And even though they had fasteners on them, I remember one day I was trying to get across the street—I had only one really muddy street to cross before getting to the school—and in the middle of the street, [the mud] pulled off my shoes *and* the boots. So there I was, with—just had to wade in the mud.

The onset of puberty brought many unanswered questions for these women. Menstruation and sexual relations were topics that were seldom discussed with children.

Ethelyn Whalin Crawford

When I was about 11, a little over 11, I first began to be sore in the breasts. And I thought I had banged myself against something—I didn't know I was supposed to grow there. I should have known, I should have looked at other women, but I didn't pay any attention. I just didn't think about that, and I told Mom how sore I was, you know. And so she kindly took me into a room all by myself, and she explained to me the fact that I was beginning to develop breasts and that one of these days I would suddenly start to menstruate. She also at the time told me she didn't know why. Well, she did *not* tell me about childbirth or any of these things. She simply told me that I would have these periods periodically and that I could just expect them, and that was it, because I was a girl. And for me to take better care of myself and not be so tomboyish.

How did you learn, then, about childbirth and about women carrying children and that sort of thing?

You know, I think really I learned most of it from hearing other kids talk, and, of course, most of it was misinformation.

I read everything I could get hold of; I always have. And I had a card at the library, and one day I got a book that had to do with anatomy and also with what went on—how the fetus developed and why it developed and all this kind of thing. It was written in children's language and a little bit facetiously but still quite clearly. I brought it home before I had read any of it, and I laid it on the table. And it just happened that I opened it to a place where they were talking about the process of conception, and I started to read it aloud to Wilbur. And [then] Mom grabbed that book away from me and she took it over to Dad, and I will never forget the look on her face while she underlined with her finger those lines telling about—she shut the book up and gave it back to me. She said, "You take that back to the library, and don't you open it!"

Ellen Dalrymple Dunn

Ellen Dalrymple Dunn came to Meeker with her family in 1929, when she was 13. Her parents came from New Mexico with plans to homestead. Her father, however, died of a stroke shortly after they arrived, and Ellen, the eldest of 12 children, helped her mother and brothers raise the family.

When girls changed into young women, did you know what to expect?

Yes, my mother told me. But it was hard to—well, I just didn't quite understand all of it yet, you know, when my curses came on. I didn't have any problems, but it was very dramatic, that change that goes on for any young girl.

In your generation, quite a number of the women say they just didn't have any idea—

No, and they didn't talk about it. Of course, Mother never talked about it at home and never allowed us girls to talk about anything like that—oh, we never thought of doing it. You didn't talk about it. Sex or anything like that—that wasn't known in those days.

When girls were 16 or 17 years old and got ready to be married, if they hadn't talked about it, they wouldn't even have any idea—

I don't suppose they did. I think a lot of them just went in it just like a young kid going away from home to college—don't know what it's all about until they get there! I think it was, from what different ones told me, but there they were, most of them in the family way the first month. And so—9 months, 10 months, and they had a baby.

I think about those women who had children very easily and ended up with 10 or 12. Was there any discussion of birth control?

Oh, no. Mother said they never had anything like that. I used to tease Mother once in a while, as I got older, and she was older too—Dad was dead and gone, and she lived with me. I'd say, "Mama, didn't you know what was causing all those kids?" And she said, "Well, no, I really didn't, because we didn't discuss things like that, Ellen." And that was just to shut your mouth!

Jennie Brown Spence

When you got to be a teenager, when young girls change into young women, did they wonder about that, or did that come as a big surprise?

In a way, my mother warned me, but I don't know how she—it scared me. I didn't think it was natural, and with me, my friend, well, she didn't come into womanhood until she was, I think, a senior in high school, and I came when I was in seventh grade. We were always together, and I thought it was just a curse set on me. I always had the cramps; I had to go to bed, usually, the first day; and the doctor—all he said to do was just to go to bed and keep warm. He gave me whiskey—a hot toddy. That was the cure.

I'd be about four hours or half a day that way; I'd just be in cramps, terrible cramps. I had those until after I was married. I remember—oh, I always had the cramps, even when I was teaching. I had to have a substitute on those days, if it came on the weekday. After I was married and I had the cramps, this gal from Rifle said, "Well, I've got some aspirin," and said, "It helps me; I think it'll help you." And so she gave me some aspirin, and that was the first time I ever had an aspirin or even knew about an aspirin. I was at least 21 years old, and I've never been without an aspirin since. [Laughter.] But—you just didn't talk about those things to other girls, either.

Norine Holland

Norine Holland grew up on her parents' ranch south of Meeker. Her paternal grandparents had come to establish a ranch on the White River at the turn of the century, and Norine's mother had come to the area as a teacher in 1912.

When the changes that come with young womanhood were arriving, had you been prepared for that, or—you hadn't? With the kind of mother you had?

No, not from her. But living on a ranch, and with all kinds of neighbors—well, in the first place, you'd always seen baby cows born and baby pigs born and all that, so you knew where babies came from. I think it came along with the living situation.

Tola Seldomridge and Mary Haughey at
Mary's homestead near Craig, 1915
Courtesy of Mary Haughey

Jayne Hoth's mother, Louise Farrell, and Mary Templeton. Near Maybell, about 1916
Courtesy of Jayne Hoth

And people talk, you know—the other women in the neighborhoods were always looking out. [The neighborhoods] were close-knit. When you were 13, many times they'd say, "Well, are you menstruating?" You'd stay overnight, so they'd want to know. You talked about it more freely, I think, than you do now.

Audrey Ruckman Oldland

When you became about 12 or 13 and turned from a little girl into a young woman, physically, were you prepared for that, or did it just sort of come along? And did you know anything about those kinds of things?

I was terrified. I was terrified. I cried. I cried for three days and nights. I had no idea.

You didn't know what was coming?

No. And I have—always kind of held that in the back of my mind as a censorship on my mother.

Because you wished she had told you?

Definitely. I went horseback riding with Carrie, and we went down to Mrs. Howey's. We bought some lard, and we started back. And [then] Carrie's horse bolted and ran off with her, and she was hurt. She was knocked unconscious, and she was picked up and brought home. I was terrified from that. It just frightened me to death. And I started menstruating that evening.

I thought it was something that had happened to me, not realizing—not a thing! I think it's so *terrible* that mothers can't—but anyway, I had this appendix attack at that time also, and so finally my legs paralyzed on me. The traumatic shock and everything tied in together, and so I couldn't get out of bed. See, I didn't think there was anything the matter with me—it was Carrie that I was so alarmed about, and it was her I was worried about. I was ashamed of what had happened to me. I didn't know how to explain it; I didn't know what to say; I didn't—I was just terrified, really. Like I said, I cried three days and nights!

They finally decided they'd have to get the doctor to see if I had a broken leg or broken back or something, because I couldn't move. Then was when they came about it that this was what was happening to me. Well, here I was a little old ugly, scrawny, freckle-faced, ugliest kid in the world. Mom said that I was coming into womanhood. Well, that was weeping words! That was even worse! I felt, "For God's sake! What does she mean—I have to go through life like this?"

You didn't know that it would stop for a while? You thought it was going to stay like that?

Oh, I thought I was doomed for life, maybe forever, and I thought, "I can't *take* this—just can't take this. How could the world be subject[ed] [to] something like me?"

Well, after I cried she would say, "What's the matter with you? What's the matter with you?" Oh, there wasn't *really* anything the matter with me, only I was just so distraught inside that I just couldn't even bear the thoughts of facing myself in the mirror the next day.

When I finally got it all straightened out, then that was the thing that I decided would never happen to a daughter of mine.

Did you talk to Carrie and help her with it?

Oh, yes. It came easy then after that. [I] talked to her, and to Jennie, and to Stubby, and all of them—they were all enlightened. They weren't blessed to think that they were going to be that ugly little monster for the rest of their lives.

Margaret Tagert Jones

Do you remember your mother discussing female problems—biological functions like menstruation, male-female relationships, or any of that sort of thing? Did she ever tell you stories about her experiences with that as a young girl?

No, she never did. She did tell me about menstruation—prepared me for it, in a way. However, she really didn't understand it enough to go into the explanation of why it happened. But this happened to me when I was—oh, golly, I think I was 12 or 13 years old. I should have known, but of course, no sex education [was provided] in the schools and nobody talked about this. But she did, and I was grateful to her for explaining what would happen to me at this time, and then she helped me with the pads and all of that. And there were many of my friends who knew absolutely nothing, even at that time, which would have been in . . . around 1925. Now, when *she* was a girl and this happened to her, she had no warning at all and, of course, didn't tell her mother or anybody, and worried about it, as many of them did then. She tried to keep herself clean, washed her underwear at night, but had no idea what was happening—thought maybe she'd been cut, you know. So it was certainly a dark age, as far as things like that are concerned.

Then the male-female relations, I knew *nothing* about at that point. I had a friend with whom I was very close—she had a big family, a lot of girls in the family. So we used to get together, and there were girls of all ages, of course. There was one, her older sister, who I think must have been around 17 at the time. We were talking about this, and we said, "Now how do these babies get here? What happens to us inside?" We knew they came from inside the mother's stomach, but we didn't know how that took place. She said, "You know, I think it's this thing that boys and girls do." Well, we had heard the word for that. I had a boy who sat behind me in school who drew some pictures that were pretty graphic, and I got an idea from that. Of course, we didn't talk about any of this, but I remember, a light dawned, and I thought, "Well, I'll bet that ties up."

> During the early years of childhood, most young girls had common experiences at home and in elementary school. As the teenage years approached, however, their experiences became more varied. Some quit school and began working, some continued with high school, some began thinking about a possible career or going to college, some got married. But most all of them had time for some fun.

Jennie Brown Spence

When you were in high school [in Meeker], what did you do for fun?

Well, we didn't do too much. The high school over here was just three little rooms. We didn't have dances like they have now, [but] we did play basketball, the girls did, and I was on the basketball team; I was a guard. They had public dances, and you went to the dances; your parents were always there. And, of course, you had to walk to the dances, because they didn't have cars.

When I graduated from high school, I wanted to go away to school. 'Course, girls in those days didn't work—I mean, there just was nothing for a girl to do. I wanted to go to a boarding school, [and] my folks contacted Cottey College. I thought maybe I'd get to go there, but around in late August the teacher that was teaching second grade resigned suddenly and the school was ready to start. They had no teacher, and I had taken the teachers' examination. That's what you did in those days—the state sent out the questions and you answered them, and if you passed you got a teaching certificate.

One of the members of the school board knew that I had a teaching certificate, and he knew Dad real well. He knew that Dad was a teacher, and Aunt Chat was a teacher. So he said, "Well, why don't you let her try?" Of course, that pleased the folks, because they really didn't want me to go away to school. So I taught three years, and then I was married.

CeCelia Sullivan Knott

When she was ready for high school, CeCelia moved to Hayden from the ranch and boarded with a family in town.

As you got into high school years and you were in Hayden, did you have more time then to do something kind of fun?

Oh, yes, there was a great deal more time. I enjoyed in high school all types of sports. We participated in that and all, but to, say, just go hang out, as they'd say, no.

Did kids date then about the same way as they do now?

Well, they dated, but I'm sure not as they do now, and it was at an older age. As I remember, it was more like one big party, but not a date. We would have had school dances and all kinds of activities, but you felt free to go. I mean, it wasn't a case [of] "I can't go; I don't have a date." You really weren't expected to have a date. You didn't pair off as to pairs or couples or anything like that. It was all one big—one for all and all for one. You know, the group—like a big family party.

When you were about 17 or 18 years old and looked ahead at the rest of your life, what did you have in mind?

Basically, I wanted to be a psychologist: go on to school and study psychology. I—someway I guess that got sidetracked, and I got married [at age 18].

Iris Self Lyons

When Iris was ready for high school, her parents rented a house in Craig for their daughters. The parents stayed on the homestead while the girls lived in town and went to school.

What were your favorite subjects in high school?

Oh, physiology mostly—anything about the human [body]. And then I liked Latin, which helped me a lot when I went out and took nurse's training. So many of the medical [terms] have derivatives of Latin. And chemistry, of course. In our senior year [of nursing school] we did have to study chemistry for nurses, but we didn't have to take state board on it. The girls that didn't take chemistry in high school really had it pretty rough studying.

What did you do for fun in high school?

Oh, we put on these big black bloomers and played basketball—you wouldn't believe it! Then in the wintertime we'd skate on Fortification Creek or go sledding. We kept busy.

Did young people date then?

Not particularly. Of course, they had their boyfriends and girlfriends. But I wasn't interested in boys.

It sounds like you had some designs for the rest of your life. What did you think you might do if you didn't get married right away?

Well, I knew I wasn't going to do that. But I knew what I was going to do when I was 12 years old, and that was take nurse's training. My dad was so very opposed to it, because he thought nurses just did the dirty work—sweeping and cleaning up bedpans and doing all the dirty work. But at Denver General we had maids to do the cleaning, while we learned. We really learned nursing very well, because our nursing adviser would take us out on the floor and teach us how to give shots, instead of giving an orange, like they do now.

What did the other girls in your high school class do?

Well, two of them taught school—Annie and Flora. And my sister Annie was teaching down here at Skull Creek, and my father could not stand to see me go to Denver, that terrible city, by myself. So he talked her into resigning her school and going with me.

Ina Dalrymple Eddy

Ina Dalrymple Eddy lived in Meeker during her early childhood. She was the youngest of 12 brothers and sisters. When she was 10 her father died and the family moved to Rifle, a town 39 miles south of Meeker. Her older brothers and sisters supported the family until all the children were grown.

Well, during the winter I entered all the activities at school—basketball and baseball. And, 'course, in the evenings at night when other children had the parties, I never had the clothes or the money to go to the parties. I always ran around with the best crowd in town and was accepted, but I never let anybody know that we didn't have the money or the clothes to go to things, so we stayed home. And I wasn't a child that liked to read, so that wasn't my entertainment.

I played outdoors—well, I couldn't say "play," because when you're in high school you don't play. It was more sled riding, and skiing and skating and winter sports. And in summer it was swimming—that was my life.

What did you think about high school?

Well, I think I would have liked school if I had had the clothes like other children, the money to buy paper and pencils. The one thing that I would have loved to have entered in school [was] band. But then, you had to pay for your own band instrument and, of course, my folks didn't have the money to do that.

Did that cause you some hard feelings, or was it something that you just took in stride?

I never harbored no hard feelings or resentment of any sort. I never had a childhood where I thought that I was being deprived of anything, because there was lots of love in our family.

When you were in high school, did boys and girls date, or did they just spend most of their time in groups?

Yes, they dated, and I didn't notice groups so much, because, like I said, I didn't join into the activities. I had no way of knowing whether there was a group, but they did date.

About what age did most women get married?

About 19, 20, right out of high school.

When you were about 17, 18 years old, did you have any expectations as to what you might do in life? Did you have any dreams or hopes about the next 20 years?

No, none whatsoever. Really, nothing. I never expected anything. I didn't look in the future that far, I guess was the reason; I just went and took each day as it come. When I graduated I got married, so that was a thing I hadn't planned, but it was the thing that did happen.

Did you meet your husband while you were still in high school?

Yes. We met at a dance and went together for seven months, and then we married.

Hilda Shelton Rawlinson

When you were 17 or 18 and were looking at the rest of your life, what did you think?

At that time I was working [outside the home] a lot of the time. When a neighbor or somebody in the community or maybe as far as Maybell had a baby, I came in and took care of the baby, the mother, the children—other children that happened to be in the family—[and] did cooking, the housework, the washing, the ironing, the canning, the baking: everything that the mother did. She paid me $5 a week.

They kept the mother in bed at least a week, so I would stay there probably two weeks and help.

How old were you when you started that?

I was probably 15—maybe the first one, 16—until I was, oh, 18. Then I worked at St. Mary's Hospital for one year, in Grand Junction. Then I got married in 1926, [when] I was 20.

With all this work you did, do you have any memory of having a good time during those years?

Oh, sure. We all had fun. We played cards at night, games, went to dances, and things like that. Maybe we'd ride 15 or so miles into Maybell to a dance—a bunch of us, horseback, dance all night, ride home, get home in time for breakfast, and go to work with no sleep. Dad always had something figured out after a dance; he thought we were so ambitious we could dance all night [and] could work the next day—and we always did!

Margaret Tagert Jones

Did you feel that you wanted to work to make some money when you got into your teen years?

Yes. I did work in the summers and part-time during the winter. My first job was in the local library, a very small library. That was a nice thing to do. It happened that our library was located in one of the old forts—

the log forts that were built during the time of [the] Meeker Massacre. Some of those were turned into homes, and I lived in one of those. Right next door was another one of the old log buildings, and that's where the library was. So it didn't take long to get to work or to come home. It was [a] very congenial, friendly kind of a situation, and I enjoyed my work there.

Then I worked in a dry-goods store, I guess you might say. That's what we called it in those days. If you didn't sell groceries in the store, you sold everything else. So I worked in that store for at least two summers and then after school during the winter.

Do you have memories of what you did during your teen years with some of your friends, and what kinds of activities you did that were especially fun?

Yes, the things we did on the weekends, when we weren't in school, were mostly—we'd just get together with friends. We'd talk, but we walked a lot. We had lace-up leather boots that we were quite proud of, which we walked in. So we would walk to the [Meeker Massacre] monument, three miles below Meeker, and back—six miles—and then around town for an hour or two. Just visiting and having wonderful times. I guess just nothing, but—we didn't *know* it was that, because that's what we had to do, and we enjoyed it.

What was your feeling about what you wanted to do after you graduated from high school?

My feeling was to do something to see more of the world than I had seen, being limited to the small community. The best way to do that, of course, was to go to college. I was fortunate enough to be able to do that—my parents could afford to do that at that time. It was not terribly expensive, but relatively speaking it was, I suppose. However, I had friends who were going away to school, and then getting a better education was one of the things that I felt would enhance my life. I felt that I would have a broader view of things. I'd have a better quality of life if I were able to get more education.

Virginia Shepherd

Well, our particular class in high school [in Meeker] was one that had many parties. One party was eight miles from town, at the ranch where

119

one of our members lived, and we went out by hayrack. This was, I think, probably in the early spring. Anyhow, a storm came up and the family of the host called all our parents and said, "We're not going to let them come home tonight; we'll just play games and spend the night dancing and we'll have breakfast, and when daylight comes, they can come home."

I remember "Spinning the Platter" and some of the games we played. The platter spun more and more slowly about six in the morning than it had earlier! We were always a great group to dance, and in those days, not only was it waltzing and two-step, something like that, but we used to dance the Virginia reel, which we thought was great stuff. That was almost a tradition in our class, to dance the Virginia reel.

The Masonic temple always had a Washington's Birthday dance, which was one of the big things when I was in high school, and everybody, I think, was there on those occasions.

When you were graduating from high school, what were some of the things that girls your age were thinking about doing with their future at that point?

There weren't as many opportunities then as there are today, and a girl was limited almost to nursing, teaching, possibly one or two other things. Running a boardinghouse was respectable work for a woman. Many of us did look toward teaching, and I was one of those.

How many other students in your class went off to college?

Well, that was the tragedy of the day. Some of those who could have gone to college, as far as finances were concerned, didn't want to. Some of those who wanted to didn't have the opportunity. I suppose, looking back, that I can think of 4 or 5 out of a class of 13 that went to college. So the percentage was not high.

Did most of the girls stay here and perhaps look forward to getting married and having families, or did they have any design on a career?

Well, I'm sure they had some ideas, but sometimes circumstances limited those rather severely. There were some who stayed, yes, and married and lived here always. There were some who worked in the bank or in the telephone exchange—which we did have at that time—or in the drugstore or in the budding library. But there were not as many opportunities as there are today.

Audrey Ruckman Oldland

I really wanted to be a nurse, and I talked about it at home. I had a good friend who was a nurse and was in nursing school at St. Mary's [in Grand Junction]. She was going with my brother Morris, and she wanted to take me back with her to Grand Junction when I graduated [so that] I could go into nursing school. My dad didn't want me to be a nurse. He just didn't like the idea of me waiting on sick people, and things like that. He said he just didn't want me tied down that way. And so I said, well, if I didn't do that, I would like to be a beauty operator. So he agreed that that would be all right. I went to Grand Junction with my friend Ruth, and I stayed at Jim Goff's and went to beauty school. I lacked four hours having enough hours to get my beauty certificate. I got involved with John, and we got married before I got through school.

Did you ever practice your beauty training?

Yes. I worked for Mrs. Romey here in her beauty shop—oh, say, three or four days a week, why, I'd go in, and that was when they were giving marcels.

A marcel [was given] with hot irons; you put these waves in. It was hard on the hair. You washed it and you dried it, and then you put in this hot-iron curl. I don't think anybody ever uses a marcel anymore. You had a hot-iron heater, and then it had holes in it, where you put the irons in the holes to keep the irons hot. The same principle as when you hung the iron over the lamp shade. It's an iron that has two roller handles on it. They used to be wood when Mom had one. You'd lay it up over the lamp shade—a kerosene lamp—and you'd hang the iron end on a wire or something and get the iron hot. Then you'd work with it until it cooled off. Then you'd put it back and heat it up and go on. But in the beauty shop they had these heaters, and the one I bought when I came out of beauty school had six holes in it, so I could have six irons in there at the same time.

Beryl Vancleave Richards

Beryl Vancleave Richards's parents came to Meeker in 1905 with two-year-old twin daughters. Her uncle, who lived in Meeker, encouraged her father to move to Colorado because he was in poor health and needed a dry climate. Beryl and her sister grew up in Meeker and have lived there most of their adult lives.

How about your favorite subjects in high school?

My favorite subject was history and English. I took four years of Latin, and I *never* could get enough Latin. I loved Latin.

What was your vision of what you might like to do after you graduated from high school?

I won the highest award, and so I won the scholarship to Boulder. Well, I rather wanted to go to Boulder, but Bernice [my twin sister] won a scholarship to the University of Denver, and my father would not separate us. He could not afford to send me to Boulder and [her] to Denver. I'd already had library teaching, so I decided that no matter what happened, I could do library work. Bernice went into the bank. And so we really didn't need college. If you want to educate yourself, you can.

My father was a man who encouraged reading, and he expected us to make good grades. We'd sit around the table, in the evenings when he was home, and he'd ask us questions and we'd ask him questions. If we asked him a question, he would say, "Now there are the reference books. Suppose you go look it up and you'll remember it. I can tell you, but you'll remember it if you look it up." And if we mispronounced a word, he'd say, "How about looking that word up in the dictionary?" We had one of those big old Webster dictionaries.

Ila Bowman Powell

I wish I had of been a nurse. That was my greatest desire, to become a nurse. There's something about a hospital—people say, "Ugh! I don't want to be around that smell and all that stuff." [But] it fascinates me to no end, even yet. I loved it. If I'd have only gone ahead. That's my greatest disappointment, I think, in my life for myself—I would have liked to have been a nurse.

Aunt Hattie would have sent me to school as far as I wanted to go, if I'd had just done it. She had money that was put away. She had gotten a settlement from the railroad company where her husband had been killed. She would have sent me to school, and it just like to broke her heart when I got married.

FOUR

Marriage, Pregnancy, and Childbirth

Getting married and having a family were what most of these women expected to do with their lives. Most were married between ages 16 and 22. Often their husbands were men they had known since childhood. Young women who came to the area as teachers were courted by the young men and were usually married in a year or two.

Weddings were often simple ceremonies in someone's home, with only close friends or family in attendance. Being married secretly, sometimes on the spur of the moment, was also common. After the wedding, couples were sometimes surprised by their friends with a shivaree and party.

Julia Biskup Kawcak

As the daughter of one of the Eastern European immigrants who settled in Moffat County, Julia was expected to marry within the Catholic religion, preferably choosing as spouse a young man who was also of Eastern European descent.

I got married when I was 16.

Was 16 about the usual age girls got married?

No. My sister Kate did, and so did I. She married John Hoza, and I married Paul Kawcak. That's the only guys were around, and Dad always said he wanted us to get married in our own church.

How did you meet your husband?

I'd known him from the time I was three years old. He came from the old country then, in 1903, and my sister and his brother were getting married that fall. So he came, and he was 15 then. When he came there, he played with us but he couldn't talk, you know. He couldn't talk American, from Austria, and so we talked to him in our language and we had a lot of fun. He never did have anything like that in the old country, because when they had a wedding there they went to the saloons to dance and all. Nobody had a place to dance at home. They'd go down to the saloon, and the kids had to stay home. So this was a treat to him. We had the dance right there in the home. They'd sing there, and play that accordion. My brother, he had a big accordion. He played for my wedding. We danced all day and all night in the old house.

There was even a shivaree. The VanTassels and Breezes and Tuckers—they lived further down the river, you know. They all came, and they were pounding on all kind of things. Well, nobody was outside, and it really did kind of give us a scare when it first started. They each brought some little thing. The women brought me a doily or something like that—a bowl or something. I never got much gifts; that's for sure. Nobody had the money. Judge Finley and Judge Breeze, they were both judges and they came—all of them came up there that night. They rode up to the VanTassels' on their wagons, and then they come walking up in the dark. So when they got there, we had cake and chicken and everything on the table. Mother had everything piled up around there. So they all took something to eat and had cake. I didn't have a wedding cake—just had a cake. Mother baked it.

Jennie Brown Spence

How old were you when you met your husband?

Well, I was in the seventh grade, and he came from Rifle into Meeker to live with [the] Joe Neals. And he was in the eighth grade. So I knew him from the time he came into Meeker. I used to go down there, to their ranch on Piceance.

How did it come about that you decided to get married, then?

Well, I don't know—like most girls, I just decided I wanted to get married, and my folks, of course, they didn't approve of it right away. But I got married anyway. When I got married, I didn't want a wedding, and so we just decided—Joe lived out [at] Piceance, and there was a lady cooking there and she broke her ankle. He brought her to town to get her ankle treated, and we had decided, since my folks didn't approve, [that] the next time he came to town we'd just get married, because I wasn't going to teach anymore. This was April 17th, [when] he brought this gal in to get her ankle fixed, so we decided to get married that night.

He got the county clerk out of his home and took him up to the courtroom and got a license. Joe said he signed the marriage license in the men's toilet, because he didn't want anybody to know that we were married. I told Ethel [my girlfriend], I said, "Now, we're going to get married tonight." And she said, "Well, I don't think you will. I'm going to wash my hair." And I said, "Well, you better not wash your hair"—she had great long hair—"because we *are* going to get married." And so when Joe came after me, we went down there and sure enough she had her head all wet. So her friend that was living there with her went with us to the church. And the minister, of course, he knew that we were having troubles, and so he came and married us, and we didn't tell anyone. We thought we were going to keep it a secret from April to the end of May, because it was just a few weeks till school was out. But years later we found out that there was a young couple that was in our crowd and they saw the light on at the church that night, about nine. So they went over, and there was a crack, I guess, in one of the windows, and they peeked in and they watched the whole ceremony. [Laughter.] They never did tell it, though, until years later, but they told us that they had witnessed it.

Why did you keep it a secret?

Well, they were doing that a lot in those days. My friend Ethel, she was married in October over at Glenwood, with her husband, or fiancé. We were over there on a picnic, and they just skipped away from us and I just had a feeling that they got married that day.

You didn't live together then?

Oh, no—I never saw Joe again until May, when he came in and we went on our honeymoon. I just came home [from the wedding] and went to bed, and got up and taught school the next day. And he went back to the ranch.

Was there a reason that schoolteachers shouldn't tell about it?

Well, at that time they didn't hire married teachers. I don't know why—I think they thought that they'd get pregnant and have families and they wouldn't make a good teacher: you know, they'd be interrupted with their family. I just don't know of any married [teachers,] until later. They were all single.

The feeling was that if you got married and had a family, you shouldn't work anymore?

No.

But at the same time, your mother did many things to earn money.

Well, she didn't go out of the home, though. She worked from the home, see.

Beryl Vancleave Richards

After graduating from high school, Beryl operated the Meeker Library for 12 years, until she married.

In those days, every girl wanted to get married because the spinsters, as they called them, usually had the drudgery of the house, and the hard work, and everyone felt sorry for them. So every girl wanted to get married. Well, with my obsession with books, I could not find *anybody* that I would really marry. So this clergyman, [an Episcopal] priest, came to Meeker, and he was single, and I was a good church girl, and we were married.

I was 30 years old—I never found anyone I would even have. I went to all the dances and everything, but they were not for me. So I waited for him. And after I was married we moved to Glenwood Springs. I had taken music, [and so] I became the substitute organist in the church. I taught the junior choir; I taught the Sunday school.

Ila Bowman Powell

I really didn't want to get married when I got married. I really didn't. But my brother had chummed with Les [my husband] all these years, and we had gone together some, and in the summertime he was there a lot at the ranch with my brother and we used to go to the dances together and all. But I really wasn't thinking seriously about getting married. But they had come in for Cowboys' Reunion at Fruita [near Grand Junction], [where] I was going to school. I even had my homework for the next day. Then he talked me into going and getting married. In them days you could just go and get a license—you didn't have to wait three days, didn't have to have a blood test. I think that's the best thing that ever happened to people: had to have a blood test and they'd think it over a lot of times, you know.

But I was kind of unhappy at my folks', because I needed some new clothes and I was clothes-crazy, I tell you. All the kids that I seemed to fall in with and run around with—their folks had money, and they had clothes and I didn't have them. They shared everything with me, but, you know, you get tired of that all the time. I'd never had a prom dress or anything like that. When you get to be a junior, you look forward to having those things. But my dad, he wanted me to have things, but he didn't think all those fancy things was necessary. He thought if you went to school and you were clean and neat, why, that was enough. You went there to get an education, not to dress up. And so I was down a little bit—really down—when they came in to go to Cowboys' Reunion. We went to the dance that night, and then we went home, and the next day, before the rodeo started, we decided we'd just go to Grand Junction and get married. And to this day I don't know why I was stupid enough to do it, because we were both just kids. He was just a few days past 21, and I wasn't 17 yet.

Do you think you did it because everybody else did it and it was kind of the thing to do?

Well, kind of. I do too think about that, because several of the girls I chummed with here in Rangely had already gotten married. Of course, that was big stuff then—they were going here and there, and they didn't have to get up and go to school. They had good clothes, and they had a car to drive.

But if I'd just gone on and finished the junior year, then I know I would have been leveled off, I know. I would have said, "Well, old girl, this is it for you from now on, so you better dig in there and get your teeth into it and go." But I've regretted that I didn't. However, most of my married life was a happy marriage and—I mean, you wouldn't take anything for your family.

Mary Birovchak Levkulich

Who was most important to you in your whole life?

Well, my husband, I guess.

You must have gotten to know him and like him, because you didn't know him very well when you married him.

Well, you know, you got to—our people, they don't believe in no kind of divorces. In Europe [when a] girl married [a] man she got to live with him until they die. That's it. There was no—they didn't believe in divorces those days. Sometimes you have quarrel, you know, with each other, but you make it up again—it's all right. And now they get mad at each other, they get divorced! I live with my husband 54 years. I didn't change my husband—now they change them! He got to be an old man, he knows me, and—it's all right.

> A pregnancy in the first year or two of marriage was common among these women because birth control was not generally practiced. After giving birth to several children, some women tried using common methods of birth control to avoid conception, although large families were looked on with favor.
> The births took place in the home, whether on the homestead or in town. Those women who lived on homesteads or ranches usually had to depend on husbands and neighbors for help with the birth. Even if the doctor was called, he or she often arrived after the birth, especially if the homestead was far from town or the weather was bad.
> Even when the doctor was present, however, there was little he or she could do for the woman if complications with the labor occurred. Nonetheless, these women remember few deaths in childbirth. Most women seemed to deliver their children with relatively few problems, the greatest of which was a long, painful labor.
> After the child was born, someone usually came to help the woman for several weeks with the care of the home and family. If a woman had

129

Inez Whalin and daughter, Ethelyn Crawford. Near Meeker, about 1915
Courtesy of Inez Whalin and Ethelyn Crawford

Doris Warren's mother, Goldie May Stephenson. Near Meeker, about 1918
Courtesy of Doris Warren

daughters who were old enough, they assumed the work of the household.

Julia Biskup Kawcak

That first winter, I stayed with my folks, out in Breeze Basin [near Craig], because I was expecting my son, Steve. So he was born over there. And after that they were all born up at the ranch. I never did go to a doctor, or examine, or nothing else.

Did you have anybody help you—come in to help you?

Just the neighbors. The neighbor lady would come and take care of everything. She'd come for a couple of days, to bathe the baby and wash the diapers, you know, and all that. I didn't have any Loveys [disposable diapers] or anything to put on the baby!

How many children did you finally have?

Sixteen. Nine boys and seven girls. And I love them all!

Did you have any trouble with any of the pregnancies?

Nothing, nothing. No—like that's what I say. All these women go to doctors for examinations and go to the hospital, have the doctor there, and still something will go wrong. I just thank God everything went right.

Jennie Brown Spence

When you had your own children, did you experience any difficulty with that?

No, I didn't. That's odd, too, because when my daughter was born I didn't know anything about prenatal care, at all. I lived down on Pice-ance and I rode horseback. She was born in August, and I came into

Meeker in February to a dance, rode horseback about 35 miles, didn't think a thing about it. And danced, and just as normal as could be. Never even thought about a miscarriage or anything of that sort. Or any special diet or anything. I was terribly sick—had morning sickness, and I think that's one reason why I just have two children. I just hated to think [of] going through all that.

I didn't go to a doctor until I came up to Meeker to stay with Joe's aunt. And I stayed there to deliver. I had [a doctor] from Colorado Springs. And he was to take me—he never did examine me, but he said he'd take my case. And so he went to Colorado Springs and I came into Meeker. And the morning I took sick was on a Sunday morning, and he wasn't in town. He'd go over there and get drunk and would never come back, you know.

He wasn't here, and I didn't know what in the world [to do]. Aunt Emma said, "Well, we've got to have a doctor." And so they called [another doctor]. He was a doctor here, and I'd never been to him, and he didn't have too good a reputation for success. I didn't have any faith in him. I said to Aunt Emma, I said, "Well, I'll just live or die; that's all there is to it."

So they called him, and, and, oh, I had an easy delivery, much easier than when my son was born. When he was born, I had a lady doctor, and she didn't believe in medicine, didn't believe in any help at all, you know, just the pure—just grin and bear it. And it was a long delivery and all, but I got through it. I didn't have any medication. They just didn't do much of that.

Did women die in childbirth?

Oh, yes. My mother helped with a lady here in Meeker. She had three children, and they had advised her—she was an older lady when she had these children—not to have any more, [and] they had to perform a cesarean. My mother went and assisted with her, because she was a very good friend of ours.

Mother said she held her foot all through the whole procedure. Dr. French operated on her, and took the baby, but the baby didn't live. And, of course, at that time they didn't know anything about blood transfusions. They had no way to give them, and she lived, I think, until about the third day. She was so hungry, and she just insisted on eating. Of course, she had a trained nurse there, but she kept begging for food. So they finally let her have toast and tea or something, and she started vomiting and hemorrhaging. And she just hemorrhaged to death.

Ethel La Kamp Chrisler

Ethel continued to live on ranches in the Meeker area after her marriage.

When you had a baby at the ranch, did you have a doctor for that?

I came to town. They brought me to town, and I stayed with Mrs. Jennie Spence's mother.

And she was a nurse-type person?

Yeah, uh-huh, she was. Dr. Lumm was my doctor, and then the next time, when my youngest son was born, I was at Mom's and there was no way to get to town, so Dr. Lumm came up there and stayed—well, Dad had the car and was gone. [Mother] wouldn't let me drive—I guess that was it.

Right when you were having the baby—I can understand that!

So [the doctor] came up there—she caught a ride up there—and then my dad took her back to town the next morning.

Did you have any trouble having either of your children?

I don't think so.

Margaret Tagert Jones

The only other child that was born [to my mother] that I would be able to remember was a little brother. He was six years younger than I, so I would have been six years old on the night that he was born. I had not been told anything about this, and I seemed to be very unobservant. I had no idea that there would be a new member of the family. I had not noticed any difference in my mother's . . . physique, I guess you might say. She was overweight, and maybe that had something to do with it. But I was treated to a very nice thing: I couldn't understand, even at the age of six, why this happened, but two of our most attractive teenage girls came to our house, got me, took my pajamas along, and I was to spend the day and the night with them. It was a wonderful day. They treated me to everything I wanted—played with me, had a lovely dinner—and the next morning, when I went home, I had a baby brother. I was completely amazed, and I don't know how I felt about it, because there were four of us already in the family—that would make five. Even at the age of six I realized that too many children were very hard for families of our kind to take care of, and also that my mother's health would be affected, at least temporarily, which I worried about.

So I don't remember feeling overjoyed about the birth of the baby. I do remember that I had a lovely time the last day—the day that I spent with the girls.

Did you have any idea as to whether there were any birth control methods, or whether women in your mother's age-group just had to have as many children as they had?

Not in the early years, but it must have been around 1920, maybe, that I believe she started using a diaphragm. In her case, whether she used it properly or not I don't know. But it didn't seem to work, and so she had a baby [a miscarriage], after this baby six years younger than I.

My brother, three years older than I, and I were aware of this. We were wakened up in the middle of the night. I must have been about 10 years old—I think he was about 13. We both worried about our mother's health, always, and we knew that there was something going on with her that night. But we weren't allowed to go into the room. All this happened at home, always. The doctor was there. And so then the next morning, she was in bed, she was ill, but nobody told us. But we figured out later it was a miscarriage, and she did hemorrhage. I think she may have told me this later on. She hemorrhaged, and just escaped death, I guess, by a miracle.

Audrey Ruckman Oldland

How many children did you have?

Three . . . Jack, and then five years later, why, Frank was born, and then 21 years later, lacking a month to the day, Mary was born. I swore I was going to have a girl. I always wanted a girl.

When you had those births at home, did a midwife or a doctor come to the house?

Dr. Farthing was the doctor that came. He came here and then my nurse friend from Grand Junction came up. But she was late getting here—she didn't get here until after Jack was born, and that was about an 18-hour delivery, with Jack.

With nothing for pain?

Nothing. You just worked your way along. And then with Frank, we were at the ranch and it was the last of April. It was March, or something, and—we had beautiful weather. I had all my garden in. I felt real good, and the night that I went into labor, it started to storm, and it stormed all night long. And John [my husband] went after the doctor, and the hired man went after the nurse. By the time they got back there was 18, 24 inches of snow on the ground, and they'd lost a tire, and—my!

I had a girl working for me, and she had just been with her mother all alone when her brother was delivered. Mary knew more about it than I did, and so we decided to start moving beds so that we could have me off by myself, away from the other bedrooms. We started moving beds, and we just laughed and played and moved beds all night, until Frank was born the next morning! [Laughter.] Just between pains we'd move beds, and played at it!

Well, that probably helped you feel better.

Oh yes—like a sedative! If I had to lay there and think about it, you know.

June O'Connell Sweeney

What about the time you were pregnant with your first child?

Oh, that was the tragedy—that was the tragedy in my life, because he weighed 10 pounds and 6 ounces, and I just couldn't have him; he was just too big. They went to Lay and called the doctor.

Well, I sat in a chair. My mother had come over for the delivery, of course. I sat in the chair, the big chair. I should have gone to bed or something, and all I did was pull my hair out. Oh, the pain was excruciating. I sat there for several hours, until Dr. Driscol came and put me to bed, and I had a 10-pound, 4-ounce baby.

But you finally did have him naturally?

I had the baby. But they had to pull him with forceps, and he had great big sores on the side of his head from the forceps, they had to pull so hard. In fact, the old doctor couldn't pull him out—he wasn't strong enough—and Henry [my husband] had to do it.

I'll bet that was a very upsetting time for everyone.

It was terrible, because Gilbert then screamed. He screamed and he screamed and he screamed for the first six months of his life, and I was distraught. I just said I didn't have any trouble, but that was the very worst time in my life, was when that baby screamed and screamed, and clawed at his head. We put little mitts on him, of course, but day and night that baby just cried and cried and screamed and screamed, and I was an absolute wreck. Because if I'd had sense enough, or somebody had sense enough to tell me to stop feeding him—see, I breast-fed him, and I'm certain he got all of that nerves from me, as well as me getting all the nerves from him. But I went on feeding him by the breast. I should have known better, but I didn't.

Through that pregnancy, did you have Henry's mother or other women in the community to talk with about getting ready to have this child, or about some of the changes that went on during that time?

I don't think I did—no one that was specially close to me. And, of course, me, I just thought, "Well, this is just a baby, I can just do this." You know: "Everybody has babies—I'm just going to have a baby." But I gained about 30 pounds [June was a small woman], which is too much, of course, because I thought I should feed the baby everything that he should have. [Laughter.] So . . . I was pretty silly on that first baby. But I wasn't so silly on the second one that came four years later.

Were you hesitant or concerned about having a second one, given your first experience?

Of course I was, yes. But I had learned. I had learned from the first one not to eat so much, not to think that I had to make the baby perfect by eating everything I thought that the baby needed, and he only weighed seven pounds, which was a good weight. I came to Craig a week early, and it went fine. It went very, very well. I think after my first pain, the doctor was taking the baby in a half-hour.

Lana Gregory Idol

My last two children were born when I was in my late thirties, so they were born in hospitals. My first five were born right in our little three-room house down here on Ninth Street [in Meeker] and did very well. When our second son was born, the doctor was drunk as could be and his wife was on the phone every few minutes telling my husband, "I'm trying to sober him up." But my husband and a lady by the name of Lulu Hall—[she] used to come and stay in your home for 10 days, take care of you and the baby, cook the meals, and she charged the whole sum of $50! But anyway, Lulu and Loren delivered our second son, because the doctor never did get there until after he was born. [She] was just ready to tie the cord when the doctor showed up. He was out like a light! But when our third daughter was born, I went across the street to visit my auntie. I ran back across the street, and there was a puddle of mud. My little boy was two, and I reached down and scooped him up in my arms and jumped this puddle of mud, because I didn't want him to get all wet, and my water broke. I had this baby at seven months. And there was no—well, there was a county nurse, and she came, but old Doc Brewer grabbed that child up and gave her artificial respiration with his mouth. And he broke one of her ribs—she always had a little knot on her rib. But pretty quick she let out a little squeak and [he] turned around to me—he was an old southern doctor, and he always called everybody "Miss." He said, "Miss Lana, she's going to live!" And I hadn't even thought about it at that point, you know. So she was tiny, tiny. She weighed four pounds and three ounces, and no eyebrows and no fingernails. But anyway, this county nurse said had she been born in a big hospital they'd probably just said "dead baby" and not did a thing about it, because she was blue as could be.

But see, he did that—he knew that, you know. And then Grandmother Idol said you put them in swaddling clothes; you don't handle them. So she fixed cotton, and my husband got a big wooden box and brought it in. They put cotton in there, and she put a hot-water bottle under there and laid Arlene in there. We opened the oven up; we had gas—no, we burned stove oil. We set the oven down real low, and we kept her on the oven door. She wasn't strong enough to nurse, but I had gobs of milk, so every two hours we'd pump my breasts and feed her with an eyedropper.

Hilda Shelton Rawlinson

My mother had three children after we came to the homestead. Down at the first homestead, Marjorie, my sister, was born in the dugout. Our neighbor lady lived down about two miles from us. She took care of Mother, delivered my sister, and that was the way. My mother had nine children, and she was never in the hospital until the week before she passed away, when she was 84.

She must have had children pretty easily. You hear these days about so many complications.

Don't you think it's our food and the way we live and things like that? I don't think work hurts anybody. Everybody [was] in tune.

In tune—so that you could have children, maybe more easily?

Well, the same way with cattle. If you take an old cow and keep her locked up, she's going to have trouble calving. And we found out with our cattle as we went on—these old cows that have a mountain to climb and go to roost under a cedar tree have no trouble having their calves. So why wouldn't it be the same for a woman? We baby ourselves too much.

Inez Ely Whalin

Inez Ely Whalin came to Meeker after marrying her husband in Illinois in 1912. They established a homestead on Thornburgh, near Meeker, and had eight children. Her daughter, Ethelyn Whalin Crawford, speaks for her because she has had larynx surgery.

Did your mother tell you any of the experiences about having children on those ranches?

Well, usually the children arrived before the doctor did; no matter how soon you would call the doctor, it took him too long to get there. Even when my sister who is four years younger than me was born, she got there before the doctor did. So it was just to be expected. Mom was lucky, in a way. When I was born, her mother came from Illinois to be with her several months before I was born, and she was a practical nurse. Then on a ranch adjoining Dad's, there was a visiting RN and she helped take care of Mom. But the doctor didn't get there until several hours after I was born.

Your mother must have been very fortunate, with eight children, not to have had any complications during the births. Did she tell you any stories about women who did have problems?

No.

Was there a fear of pregnancy among your mother's friends, people she knew? Was birth control practiced, or was it effective?

I think that there was no particular fear of childbirth. It seems to me as I recall hearing talk that it was considered a part of life and that a family was expected. When you married, you simply expected a family, and the person that didn't have a family was rather pitied. A woman's place in those days was in the home, and to have children, and usually she accepted that quite well. Of course, there were some rebels. Birth control was not practiced as a usual thing. I suppose that in some homes where health was a problem doctors might have helped people to secure some kind of knowledge, or perhaps in the Catholic homes they might have secured some kind of knowledge. But among my mother's friends, as far as I've ever heard anything, they absolutely had no birth control practiced. They just expected children, and they were loved, and they were taken care of. And this is one of the most marvelous things I remember as a child, is the security and the warmth and the knowing—no matter if I was really bad and I knew that I would be scolded, I knew I would be loved. This I felt from my mother, always.

FIVE

Community

At the turn of the century homesteads were often far apart, and neighbors saw little of one another. As more homesteaders arrived, they gathered together to build one-room schools for their children. The country school became the center of rural community activity, and the homesteaders looked forward to occasions when they could meet with neighbors for a picnic, a dance, or some other social gathering.

People also visited with one another as they traveled from their homestead to town for supplies. Women on the homestead were expected to have food ready for any neighbors or travelers who might stop by for a meal or a place to sleep for the night.

Virginia Shepherd

How often did your mother visit with neighbors?

Well, always, going to town. I can remember her telling once about stopping at the Wilber ranch, and she wasn't going to get out of the conveyance. My father went in to tend to some business, and the neighborly westerners came out and unhitched the horses and put them in the barn and said, "Now you'll have to come in and have a meal with us," which was very thoughtful and very kind, but also it was a surprise to her.

Was she surprised when people would come to her house and just stop and stay awhile?

Well, that was part of it too. I can remember taking a walk with my mother when I was very young, and we came home to find 14 guests for the night: the horses had given out. We lived at a crossroad, and they were very nice people. And when Mother came home, she said, "Have you had dinner?" "Well, no, but don't fix us anything—just give us what you have."

She was not accustomed to having the cupboards ready for 14 people, but somehow or other she managed it. I can remember that the men slept up in the loft of the barn, and the ladies we were able to accommodate in the house. So that was a part of western hospitality that was necessary in those days.

Norine Holland

These rural schools were the center then of most of the social activity. When I was a kid, at least through the eighth grade, they had an activity at least once a week in the school—most of the time, a dance. Of course, the school itself would have a lot of programs where kids would be in the programs, and parents would come and they'd bring all kinds of foods—I can always remember this food. They would put these tables down through the middle of the schoolhouse floors, and these tables would be *laden* with all kinds of food. And I can remember at the dances that we'd stay until morning, and they would eat at midnight. Then they'd take all this food and put it away again, and they'd dance, and then they would get up and get all this out again before you went home in the morning.

We stayed lots of times most of the night. And in the wintertime we always went by sled. We had hot rocks to keep warm. The kiddies used to have costume parties. I can remember going to costume parties. When I was in about the third or fourth grade, my brother and I won a prize. He was George Washington and I was Martha Washington.

[The old Holland ranch] was at the crossroads for people going from Meeker over by what they call the Thornburgh route into Craig, so we had lots and lots of people stopping at our house all the time. They would come from Craig to our place and stop and then go on. I can always remember there was lots of cow people, and lots and lots of people all the time.

I can remember my mother making a pie or cake every day of the world—not one pie, three or four. Three or four pies every morning, because people were always stopping, and neighbors were always there, even if people didn't stop, coming from Craig or someplace.

Julia Biskup Kawcak

In the winter we had dances. After we built a school up there, we had a dance every two weeks. But even before that we'd had dances, and different ones had a nice living room and pretty good floor. We'd go to the different houses, and sometimes mud was so deep we'd put four horses on the wagon and we'd go anyway. Took all the kids, and when the kids got sleepy, why, whoever's house you was in said, "Well, put that boy over there, the boys over there." And they were all sleeping in rows on the bed. We'd all bring cake, you know, or sandwiches. The people where you went to, some of them would make oyster soup or something, and coffee.

Then finally when we got our school, we bought a big wash boiler with a copper bottom, and we'd boil a whole boilerful of coffee—just take and fill a bag with coffee and set it in there after it was boiling, [and] make our coffee. We bought 100 tin cups and kept them in a certain place. Whoever had them brought them to wherever the dance was.

We'd dance till seven in the morning. We sure did. Then, of course, when we'd get home, the kids [had] had their sleep. And the husband, he'd go out and do the chores, eat his breakfast, go to bed. I had to stay up, because the kids were up! It was hard to get a nap. But when the kids were bigger, they'd watch the little ones and let me take a nap, until milking time, chicken-feeding time, and all that. But we went every two weeks, we had a dance. We had neighbors way up there on Elk Head, *way* up there. There used to be a high school clear up there at Pilot Knob, and that's where Hayden used to go for high school, until they built theirs. Anyway, those people lived up there on a ranch—they bought an old homestead of somebody's. The mother had an organ, the dad had a violin, the two boys had a mandolin and guitar, and they'd bring all that with them in the sled or the wagon. Every two weeks they'd bring it. Everybody was into it that way. And whether they got a penny or not, they done it anyway. Because nobody had money.

It was something, I'll tell you; we used to have the good times. All the square dances, circles, and everything. But it was all dancing together, not like they do now, one over there and one here. That's not dancing! No, it isn't! But they wouldn't know how to get out there and waltz and two-step and everything like we used to. Gosh, everybody knew how to waltz.

Hilda Shelton Rawlinson

How did the county fair get started? Why did you decide to have fairs?

Well, this goes back to the old homestead days. We used to maybe grow a great big pumpkin—or a big watermelon or a big beet or whatever, you know—and they thought it would be fun [for] everybody [to] go to Maybell; that's where it was held. [They'd] all take their big pumpkin or whatever. It was nothing—no set rules about a fair. We'd all bring our best, you know, and it was beautiful, and put them up, and take a picture of it. And that's how the fairs got started in Moffat County.

Chloe Bunker Vaughan

Esther [Campbell] lived a lot like I lived. She had come from Denver, and she was a schoolteacher, and she came out to teach school, you see. And so we enjoyed each other a lot. If she had company she'd bring them down and I would entertain them, and if I had company she would entertain them—and that would help us out entertaining our friends from out of state.

We had a telephone between us. We put a wire up between us on trees. And some places they had to put up poles, but most all the way they would cut the limbs and put it up on trees. Of course, they had to put it up high enough so the stock and things—there was no cars up there, so we didn't have to worry about that.

They had one phone at their house, and we had a phone at our house, and that was the only one in the country. If something happened to them, like during the hard winter [of 1949] they needed hay, why, they would phone to us and we would go to Maybell and phone on into Craig or, you know, we'd deliver their messages. And then Minford and I would go over and get the mail every mail day. We had two mail days a week, and I'd get her mail too, and I'd come home and tell her what letters she got. If they were letters she figured that she couldn't get answered very soon, why, I would answer for her. She would tell me what to write, and I would answer for her.

How far was her ranch from yours?

Oh, I imagine it was maybe eight miles or so.

So being many miles away from somebody really didn't interfere with getting together and doing things together?

No. Some of us made horse blankets, even. We'd take an old gunny-sack and make it big, you know. We'd lay it on the floor, and we'd pick horsetail. We'd pile it up maybe six inches deep, and then we would put another gunnysack on top of that. Then we'd tack it here and there like you would a quilt, and after it sat on the horse's back for quite a while, why, that just stayed put. Never moved.

And then we made hair ropes. We picked hair, the horse's tail, and then we had to turn—I turned and turned them until I got turned out, on this little machine. It had a hook on it, and my husband would put that [horsehair] over the hook, you see, and he'd walk out that way [gestures], and that would twist that. It would make about six rows of that. We had nails out here [gestures] that we would nail it in the dirt until we got six done; then we'd put them together, and rolled it. If they were two different colors, why, we would put three blacks together and three whites together, or three browns, just whatever it may be. And we'd wind them up. Then we would put them all together, and that made the rope. We used them—the boys made hackamores and everything else.

What's a hackamore?

Well, it sits on a horse's head when they're breaking them, leading them, or something like that. And we used hair ropes an awful lot. We sold lots of these ropes, and—he didn't really sell them. We would trade them. We'd make a bunch and we'd trade them to the Two-Bar Ranch for wool sacks and things like that.

Women who lived in the small towns of Meeker, Craig, and Rangely began to form clubs in the early 1900s. The first groups were usually called "The Woman's Club" and were formed to read and discuss books. Later, in the 1920s, such groups as the Eastern Star and the Rebekahs were formed.

The women living on homesteads or ranches didn't have time for most women's groups. In the 1930s, however, when home demonstration clubs were introduced to rural women by the agents of the state land grant colleges, these women made a special effort to attend. They were learning skills that would help them in their work at home.

The women's clubs gave women an opportunity to develop interests other than home and family. They found satisfaction in learning new things, performing community services, and providing support for one another.

Virginia Shepherd

Meeker had many early families that were English, and some had come directly from Scotland, for instance. There were some who had come by way of Canada. Some of these people were very musical, and some had been carefully educated elsewhere in our country or in Britain. I think it was rather amazing that one of the first clubs to which my mother belonged in Meeker was a reading club, and of all things, they decided to read Shakespeare. I doubt if that would happen at the present time!

My father bought my mother a set of Shakespeare, small, leather-bound copies which she treasured very greatly. And in looking through those I find that she put down the dates of some of the plays that she was in attendance when they were read. Sometimes she jotted down the part that she read, because they read them aloud. Sometimes she jotted down quotations that they discussed afterwards. And I find that they were reading Shakespeare from 1910 to 1915, because she put the dates in the back of the volume as to when they were read. Also, some of them subscribed to a magazine which was called the *Mentor,* the editor of which was Hamilton Wright Mabe. He did most of the writing when it was about literature, but when they published an issue about architecture or art, or in some other field, then he called in other people to write the articles.

They seemed to have had a very good time with their reading, and they must have liked it, if they continued it for five years. So I thought that that was unusual in a pioneer and almost a frontier community— that they should spend so much time on that. And I do know that at least one member of the club remembered the quotations, because often she would come up with a quotation from Shakespeare that fitted some current happening in the town, and that always amazed people.

Most of these women had a high school education, or less than that?

Well, of course, schools were different then, and it's hard to say. I know that this person who remembered all the quotations went to a country school down on White River [and] always was most grateful to at least one of her teachers that she spoke of very often. But some of these people who lived in Canada or Scotland—I don't know how much education they had.

Julia Biskup Kawcak

What about up there on Elk Head—did the women have any kind of club or anything?

Not in them days, nothing! Everybody worked.

Did you ever belong to a club?

I never did—except the church. After we had our car, I used to come down once a month for our church meeting, and then we'd have dinners, and all the farmers, all of our people, would give chickens. The priest would come around. Mrs. Panak always come with the priest, and everybody'd give them two or three chickens. We'd cut their heads off and put them in a sack, and then got all of that together and brought them into town. Then the town ladies got together at my brother's house, at Joe's house—they had an old shed behind their house. They'd all get together and have a boiler of water on the stove, because you had to have that. They didn't have water in town then, either.

They'd put a boiler of water on the stove and boil it. And then the men would set it down on the floor, and they'd just dip those chickens and put them in a tub. And a lot of ladies were there. They'd get the feathers off, you know. And then when they had some of them cleaned already, they'd singe them by the stove, and after they singed them some of them got busy and cut them up.

They got ice from Harry Hansen—he had ice. They'd put the chickens in the tub and put a lot of ice on them, and they had to keep them cold. It's the only way we could. And then we'd have a big dinner in town. I'll tell you, the whole town would come and eat with us. We'd make $200 or $300. We thought we made a lot of money, to help the church. And that's the way we got started with our church.

Ruby Rector Kirby

We organized a Woman's Club in Rangely. We finally joined the Federated Women's Club, and we read books; we had all kinds of crafts, if people wanted to do them. We met regularly—of course, not everybody was there every time.

What kinds of books did you read?

A lot of them had to do with history of different places and of the state, and we had discussions. Of this Woman's Club Babe Hinricks [my sister] was the first president; I was the second president; and Mom was the third president. We have records from about 1934 to 1938, and it was awfully nice in the late thirties.

Stella La Force Rector

Since you did spend most of your married life in the Rangely community, I wonder if you could give me some idea of women's clubs and activities, particularly those which you would consider clubs or activities that contributed something to the community.

Well, actually, as far as clubs, after we had over 200 people in Rangely—before that, why, Mrs. Purdy used to have a little literary club that met, oh, maybe once a week, or sometimes if the weather was good, and in the wintertime, why maybe once a month. They discussed what was going on in the world, and literature, if people were interested in [those] thing[s].

Other than that, I understand that one time they did have something they called the Woman's Club. But when you live out on a ranch and you don't have any transportation in, other than a horse, why, I never was involved with any of the women's clubs. Then after I moved to town my children were in school, so I became involved in the school activities with the children. I was 4-H leader for 10 years. After the churches became established and things, why, I did spend a lot of time with the church work, and teaching Sunday school and working to get our church started and all these kinds of things.

Mrs. Purdy had, oh, a library of about 200 books, the books that she'd collected over her lifetime. Occasionally somebody would get a new book and give it to her, and this was the library that Rangely had up until the time the college came. Of course, the schools were well supplied with library books, and I bought a great many books, hardbound books, for my children and read to them, until they got to read on their own.

About what date did she have this literary club?

Well, she was having it when I came to Rangely in late 1939, up until they had a library. She even carried on clear up until in the late forties, I think, and tried to involve some of the oil people that came in in her little literary-type thing.

Jennie Brown Spence

When I went into the Eastern Star [in 1922], I had made me a pink organdy dress, and Mrs. Iles went into the Eastern Star with me. I didn't really want to go in Craig, but she was older and she said, "I just don't want to go in alone, so you come go with me." So we joined together. I made this pink organdy dress, and it was above my knees.

You were in the Eastern Star and perhaps some other things. What were some of the activities of those organizations that did something for the community?

Well, I don't know as the Eastern Star—it was more a social deal, I think. If you belonged to the Eastern Star, or the Masons, you were special. And they paid a lot of attention to manners, you know.

Were you supposed to have the manners when you got there, or did you learn them after joining?

No, you were probably not even accepted unless you were . . . pretty well polished, you know. It was quite an honor to be voted into the Eastern Star, and a lot of people got blackballed, which was a tragedy. Oh, yes. Someone had to put your name in, and they voted on it. If you got so many blackballs, you didn't get in, and there was a lot of heartaches over that.

My mother joined a reading-circle group, where they read, and that was the beginning of the Woman's Club [in Meeker]. I've been a member of the Woman's Club for many years, but I wasn't a first member.

[The Woman's Club] was more cultural. They started the library and collected books, and things of that sort. I suppose when they joined the federation, they did what they had to do to raise money. And that was about all they had, was the Eastern Star and, of course, the Rebekahs. I didn't belong to the Rebekahs but I did belong to the Eastern Star, and I got my 50-year pin not too long ago. And then I've been a Woman's Club member for a long, long time.

Our membership has fallen off. The younger girls just—they've got their families and their activities, and they're just not too interested in it.

Lena Ely Stoddard

The way our book club started [in Craig] was one summer I had had company, and we played tennis. We went to Steamboat and went swimming, we went fishing, we went hiking, and everything. After they were gone, I was just—I collapsed. So the doctor said, "Well, you'd better go home and start a quilt—piece a quilt, kind of relax." I said, "OK, I will." So I had a quilt—I made a log cabin quilt, and it was ready to be quilted—and I was talking to some of the PEOs [a women's philanthropic organization], I think it was. I had joined the PEO when Joe was a baby.

Mrs. Cowen said, "I'll tell you what we've got." They rented books. There was no library or anything, only that little thing over on Yampa [Street].

She said, "I'll furnish the book." Alta [my sister] said, "I'll do the reading and the rest of them can quilt the quilt." So we set up a quilt here on those long things that they have [a quilt frame], you know. And that's the way the book club got started.

We had the book club and the DAR—I belonged to the DAR and PEO and Republican Women. We used to go to rallies at different schools in the country and dance with all the country people and make speeches and everything—campaign.

Community rodeo. Maybell, 4 July 1910
Courtesy of Hilda Rawlinson

Louise Farrell, Jayne Hoth's mother, and Emma and Pete Farrell. Near Maybell, about 1914
Courtesy of Jayne Hoth

What did some of those organizations do? What was their purpose?

Well, you know PEO. And the book club, we met once a month, I guess it was, and read good literature. [We] had lunch at the lady's house—there were 10 of us that did it. The Republican Women, of course, we met once a month, had programs, and helped elect the [candidates]. And what was the other one? Oh, Navy Women. For a long while, they had an auxiliary.

Then when the hospital was being built [in 1950], you know, getting active, I belonged to the auxiliary and we'd go over to the hospital and do volunteer work. Once a week we did that.

And to help get the noon lunch program going for the schools, we'd go over and help serve the meals and do the dishes, even, and clean up the kitchen afterwards, until they could afford [to hire people] and the government started in to help, you know. So we did a lot of volunteer work. I was a room mother, and we'd make cookies for the little parties that they'd have. And [I] belonged to the PTA—of course, that's a thing of the past.

Hilda Shelton Rawlinson

I think it was in 1933 or 1934 [that] the home demonstration clubs came into being in Colorado, or in this area. I belonged to one of the first clubs in Rio Blanco County, but I did live in Moffat County at that time—in 1934. Our little club was organized on Strawberry Creek [northwest of Meeker]; my neighbor invited me to come. It was the second meeting this little club had, so I was one of their charter members— the second time they had met. The name of this little club was the Harmony Club, and it went for a good many years. We had *many* good lessons on home demonstration work. They call it extension work now, but in the beginning it was called home demonstration work. We all learned a lot from this work. [The home demonstration agent] from Fort Collins [at Colorado State University] started it.*

---

*The Home Demonstration Program was initiated in 1914 by the Smith-Lever Act (38 Stat. 372, 7 USC 341) to offer rural women information concerning new methods of homemaking. This program is conducted through the state land grant colleges.

Do you know why it was started?

Well, I don't know why, only that—a little higher education for the women is what I think. Things that we needed to know, learn.

And you did learn things that you didn't know how to do before?

Oh, sure, they came from the college. We got the experts from Fort Collins would come, and each club would have their project leader, they were called. We would go and get these lessons from these teachers from Fort Collins—they would teach us to do whatever it was we wanted. Canning—everything in home work. Sewing—all kinds of sewings, and—oh, just anything you can think of. Baking. Fairs, and things like that.

Chloe Bunker Vaughan

Although the Brown's Park home demonstration club wasn't founded until the early fifties, it was the first opportunity the women had to gather in a group.

We had us a little home demonstration club, and there was 17, and I think everybody belonged—everybody that lived there [in Brown's Park]. And some of them were 100 miles apart.

I know when the Solaces came in here, they lived on the road to Rock Springs, Wyoming, and she told me that I was the first person that had ever asked her to come and visit. I had them over for—I don't know whether it was Thanksgiving or Christmas or something, and that's the way we got acquainted. We were always very dear friends.

But that's more or less the way we'd do. I know the Dickensons—they lived up on the Wyoming line—and the Buckleys, they used to have us come to dinner and spend Sunday, and then we'd have them to our house, you know.

There's a little old lady that lived down in the canyon all by herself, and she belonged to our club.

Did she take care of her place by herself?

Uh-huh, all by herself. She had a few cattle. Her son came quite a bit, I think, and would help her, and then the neighbors, you know. She was down near the school that they had down there, and everybody kind of looked after everybody.

Could you tell me about the beginning of the home demonstration club? How did that get started, and what did you do?

Well, I had to move to Craig to put Elmora [my daughter] in school, because we lived so far that it didn't pay me to drive, and so we just bought our home in Craig and put her in school. I belonged to the home demonstration club in Craig, and so I told the girls about it down there [in Brown's Park], and they all thought that would be wonderful if they had it.

We formed a little club there in my home [on Sundays], and then they just joined. I don't know just how we did, really, but we had our husbands involved too, so that when we went to our meetings, they could take [us]. Because a lot of times it was so bad—we didn't have hard roads; we didn't have *anything*, you know; the roads were terrible. And so the men would do—oh, they would maybe brand or they'd maybe hang some gates or do something [else] while we had our meeting. And then we always had a lovely big dinner. Everybody went out to bring nice things to eat.

We had [a meeting] once a month. And when it was snowy, a lot of times we'd have to go in a pickup—somebody would take a pickup. We'd walk in; we've walked to get there—every other way to get to the house. We've had quite a time.

And you just went ahead and did it through the winter?

We enjoyed that winter business! [Laughter.] We'd walk, and sometimes we went in on sleds, and—I don't know, we just managed.

We conducted our meetings just exactly like they conducted them in Craig. In fact, I think we worked harder, because we had projects. There were so many people buried just anyplace. We found who were buried in the different graves, and we'd put up little headstones for these, and they were scattered all over the country. Then we used to go clean the little cemetery down there. There was quite a few notorious people down there. Like—have you heard of Tom Horn coming in and killing this person and that person because they rustled cattle? They were cattle rustlers and so on and so forth. Everybody knew about them. They've written about them for years.

Our home was sort of centrally located—the Smelter ranch was—and we had a big old hill there. We'd take the fence down, and a lot of [the club members] started up at the head of the hill and then they just went

153

on down through the meadow—they could go for a long ways and ski. And then we had a big pond. We had that, and it was all froze over and some of them liked to skate. We'd clean that off of the snow, and skate. Then they would bring things to eat—we always ate; I never seen such a place to eat! I'd always keep a lot of coffee—or something—on for them when they came in, because they were cold.

We used to play games—Esther Campbell taught school there, and she made fun for everyone. She'd have parties over at the schoolhouse, and we were always making fun of each other, and different things—drawing pictures, you know, and things like that. Esther was just full of ideas.

Ethelyn Whalin Crawford

As an adult, Ethelyn lived in the Meeker area first on a ranch and later in town.

I belonged to the Rebekah Lodge—I went through all the chairs. I was the secretary of it for years and years until I left here, and I belonged to the White Powell Club. I was president of the Woman's Club. This was mostly after my kids were grown, though, of course—not while they were small—although I joined Rebekah Lodge and White Powell Club while they were still small.

What is the White Powell Club? When did it start?

It's a home demonstration club. [It started] in about 1936 or 1937, I imagine.

What is the purpose of that?

Well, a home demonstration club is to help women in homemaking, really. It brings canning and clothing and upholstering and interior decorating—all kinds of the crafts that might go into making a home more pleasant.

Where did you get that information about how to do those things?

We had a home demonstration agent. There's a whole lot of the clubs in this county, you know, and they would meet with this agent at a given period and be given the material [on] how to do it, and then show [the representatives from each club], and then we'd take it back to the club. Part of the time I was one of the demonstrators, and other times somebody else was. It was very interesting—I remember the upholstering particularly.

SIX

Medical Care

Homesteaders were often far from town and the local doctor. Even when a doctor was available, most people relied on home remedies for common illnesses. Remedies were made of ingredients found in the home, obtained from wild plants, or purchased at the town drugstore. Recipes for these remedies were passed from one generation to the next. Women usually nursed the sick and were expected to know which remedy to apply.

Mary Gates Haughey

Do you remember illnesses or accidents that happened and what kind of home-remedy treatments people knew about to take care of these things?

I can tell you what my dad did when we had the flu—what he gave us. Sagebrush and Oregon grape root tea, and I tell you, you got well, because you got to keep from taking the stuff! Oh, mercy! That was in 1918, when all of us had the flu.

We never had any of the childhood diseases—we hadn't had measles or smallpox or chicken pox: any of those things. However, my brothers had had whooping cough when they were younger. I didn't get it. I waited till my kids had the whooping cough, then I took it.

But you didn't get any of those other things, ever?

Not till we come to school. Then we got all of them in high school, and my brothers in grade school. We took all of it. At the time we were growing up, we were up on Black Mountain, miles away from town, and there were no vaccinations for anything. Possibly there would have been for smallpox, but measles and whooping cough and all these others—no, there were none. And we just didn't have them until I came to high school, and [then] I got everything—measles, chicken pox, smallpox, everything but mumps. I had to wait to take mumps until *my* family boys took the mumps.

Do you remember any home medical remedies from your mother?

[Mother] may have given us something—I know she was kinda heavy on quinine, which was something fierce to take. She would give us castor oil—my grandmother was strong on that—for various things. And also sulphur and molasses. What good sulphur and molasses ever did us I have no idea, but she used to poke it down us.

If we got a bad cold, we were well greased with some kind of an oil—with turpentine and kerosene or something—that had a real bad smell. They greased us with that. And mustard plasters—oh boy, they'd plaster us with that!

Norine Holland

Us kids, every time we got the croup, we always got a tablespoon—a teaspoon, must have been; a tablespoon would kill you, I think. But I can taste that stuff yet. A teaspoon of coal oil. Coal oil out of a can. Coal oil is what you put in the lamp to burn. A teaspoon of that and sometimes a little sugar on it, and I can *still* taste that and still feel it going down. But you woke up the next morning without any croup. I never went to a doctor all the time I was a little kid.

We had measles; we had chicken pox. Well, if we had pneumonia or a real bad cold, which you'd get, we always had mustard plasters.

To make the mustard plaster, you get a cloth that's big enough to put over [the chest]. You put that powdered mustard in there [on the cloth], and you put just a little bit of water with it and just make a paste. Then lay it on your chest. It'll cure a cold. It burns, [and so] you have got to be careful you don't burn.

And what were some of the other remedies? . . . Sassafras, we drank sassafras tea every spring to clear out your blood.

Ila Bowman Powell

My mother was part Indian, and so she knew all about all the old remedies and things. And most of them worked, too. Maybe it was a little psychology up here [gestures], but most of them worked. We used to have different things that we put on—she made a liniment, and now the Watkins people put out some of that white liniment. We'd take like the white of an egg, and vinegar, and ammonia, and camphor—[and] something else; I can't remember what it was right now. But anyway, she shook it all up and beat it up together and put it in a bottle. It was pretty good liniment.

What did you use that for?

Just sprains and things like that—sore places, you know. It was not really open sores, but it was really good. Then we used to have different things we poulticed with. Just old ordinary pitch off of a tree—like if you got a deep sliver or something, if you could melt that and put it on a cloth, [melt the pitch] with a match and put it there. It'll just almost draw the sliver right out to where it drew it up and you could get ahold.

What about just ordinary colds, or bronchitis?

My mom used to put camphor, turpentine, and lard. She always brewed it up together, and yet when my kids get sick or when they have a cold, I always have a big jar of Vicks. I take out a big spoonful of it, and where I took it out I put mustard oil in it. You take mustard oil and Vicks, and melt it together, and put it on their neck and chest and on their back and under the arms—it goes into the lungs easy under the arms, the fumes, and that is very good.

We used to use old mustard plasters. I knew a doctor over at Vernal—he cured my husband with mustard plasters. You mixed that up with flour and dry mustard and an egg white, and a tablespoon of baking soda, to make a thick paste and spread it on a cloth, on both sides of it, and leave it for 20 minutes' time. That's really a good remedy. But people always tried to get a supply of things in before winter came, [things] that would be good in case you got really sick.

Were there any kind of herbs or anything you got outside that you cooked, or—?

The flu, in 1918—the best thing people brewed up was this old sagebrush tea, and I mean it was nasty, and it was bitter, but it was something that they brewed up and they drank. I think several of us would probably have died if my dad hadn't fixed that sagebrush tea and kept giving it to us.

Oil of eucalyptus was another thing that [Mother] used to put on us if we were ill: mix it with some lard or something.

Mom used to get that old red bark and brew it up and make us drink it in the spring of the year. She said it thinned our blood. Sassafras bark. Pretty good if you put a little sugar in it.

Why did you want to thin your blood?

I don't know, but you should do it in the spring of the year because your blood is so thick in the wintertime. You lose a lot of your energy and everything—it needs to thin in the spring.

Chloe Bunker Vaughan

Well, I was surprised at Alan Hurd. He was an old fellow who lived by himself and, you know, he got tick fever and, oh, he was very bad in those days—it was awful. And he was alone, and he told me himself that he didn't know what to do. He couldn't come out of it. He crawled out and picked sagebrush in his yard and took it in the house and boiled it. He drank sagebrush tea, and he come out of it.

There was different women at the time that had studied more or less for nursing, but that was before I come out here, because they knew, you know, if anybody was real bad sick. I know Minford [my husband] fell putting up hay, and he hurt his back real bad, and we took him over to his sister's home. Mrs. Buffam that lived around here, she'd studied nursing, I guess, because she sure knew a lot about it. She came over, and she took hot towels and put [them] on his back, and then she rubbed him and did what she was supposed to and he come out of it.

Hilda Shelton Rawlinson

Always the turpentine bottle was the main thing. If you had a cut, run a wire through your foot—one time I did that. I jumped off the horse—I was barefooted. We always had to go barefooted in the summertime. And I ran this wire clear through my foot—I could hardly pull it out. We went and poured it full of turpentine. There was no tetanus shots. If there was anybody going to have tetanus, I should have had it. But just the turpentine was all there was—and it healed up with no trouble.

Did you have many colds?

There again was your turpentine and lard. You rubbed it on your neck if you had a sore throat, and if your throat was really sore, why, you had to have a little turpentine, or just a little bit on sugar. And also for parasites. [My Mother would] get a spoon of sugar and put about five drops of turpentine in it. How often she gave it to us, that I don't remember—I think maybe after so many days after the first dose, and then have a second dose because of eggs that had hatched.

[During] the flu epidemic in 1918, a neighbor lady, who lived in a tent on her homestead in Dry Lake, took sick and died. This is in 1918, the flu epidemic. I think this was in March. She was in the family way, had this child, and she passed away there in the tent. OK, we have no undertakers, no preachers, no nothing. The neighbor lady that had delivered my mother came and my mother helped her. They took care of this lady after she passed away. The neighbors had built the coffin and had put [her] away. Mother had to help dress her and get her ready for burial, and they had the funeral. [The neighbor lady's] husband was sort of a minister—he sort of preached.

My mother was a bit skeptical about being in where this was, because she was in the family way, and my sister was born in August of that year. So she was afraid for herself. But she went and helped.

What happened to this woman's other children after she was gone?

She had two boys in school, and they came to our house and they stayed with us and went to school.

So the father felt he couldn't take care of them, after she was gone?

They eventually went back to Nebraska, where they came from. But the boys finished that year of school with us. There again, you got no compensation—you took care of them because they needed care.

Oma Jensen Graham

The first winter we were up at Wolf Creek, the men were gone; there was just Grandma Hackett and Mother and I. And I got pneumonia. Grandmother had never been very good at skiing, but she was going over to Jack Springs [to get help]. Somewhere Mother was going through books, and she read where flaxseed poultice was good. And [before she left] Grandmother told her, she said, "Now, Mary, don't do anything desperate if we lose the baby." By the time Grandmother got over there and the Miltons got back on snowshoes, I was sitting up. Mother had put the flaxseed poultice, front and back, on me, and it loosened the pneumonia. She just took boiling water and poured it over this flaxseed until it makes kind of a syrup. She got it pretty thick and just put it on a cloth, a thin cloth, and put it front and back and then covered it.

She just happened to have flaxseed?

Yes, we always had flaxseed, because if you got anything in your eye, you'd put flaxseed in there to float [the] object out of your eye—it would come to the corner of your eye.

Do you remember other kinds of home remedies these people used?

Well, we have lost so much is the thing of it, because nobody passed it on down. We didn't have aspirins. All we had was sweet spirits of niter, and turpentine. Sweet spirits of niter was good for a fever and was also a diuretic. And, of course, we had Epsom salts and castor oil. Everybody had those. We didn't have very much to doctor with, but we didn't get sick like they do nowadays. We didn't have all these viruses, and we were off kind of alone. We didn't see other people. They didn't know what a virus was, you know.

161

Did you have colds?

Oh, I suppose so. Every kid had a cold. Every kid usually had a gathering of the ear, but you didn't go to a doctor. All you did was—oh, Mother'd mix up a hot salve with menthol crystals, and I suppose eucalyptus oil, and fixed it with Vaseline. She'd put some of that in your ear, and then you'd lay on the hot-water bottle and that was about all. If you got gathering of the head, you used a syringe with warm water and just rinsed it out.

What is gathering of the head?

Well, that's where you have this earache, and then it gathers in your eardrum. What they call a gathering of the ear—ear infection.

Rosamay Hodges Savage

Rosamay Hodges Savage was raised on a homestead near Juniper Springs, between Craig and Maybell. Her father died when she was 10, and her mother moved to Maybell and started a drugstore business to support herself and her two daughters.

I can remember the salt sides, sewed on a sack, on a thing around my neck for sore throat. It was a strip of bacon sewed onto a strip that went around your neck. That was a sore-throat remedy.

Did it work?

It worked, or something worked—it smelled, and it was greasy! [Laughter.] It smelled awful and it felt awful!

Lana Gregory Idol

They always said Grandmother Idol saved Chuck White's life. His mother was much younger than Grandmother, and she had these two little boys, and the father came one evening and said, "You've got to come help us—Chuck's very, very ill." And she got up there and she knew he had pneumonia, because Loren [my husband] had had pneumonia back in Missouri and she had seen it. She wrapped that child in blankets and greased him good with Vicks Vaporub, just soaked it into him. She had Shorty White build up the fire in the stove, and then she laid a heavy blanket in the oven and put him in there with a pan of water, and every two minutes she'd open the door. Well, you see, what she did, she broke that congestion loose.

Oh, she put the child in the oven?

Yes. She laid the child in there on a blanket, and then she put a pan of water [in] there. She had this heat just even, and she'd open the door, and then she'd close it, open the door and close it. She didn't want him to steam, but it opened up his lungs.

Audrey Ruckman Oldland

If you got the croup, you got goose grease and turpentine rubbed on you at night. If it was pneumonia, you got turpentine and the whole works—goose grease and onion poultices and mustard poultices and all of those treatments. If it was flu, it was the same thing.

[When] we had that flu epidemic there were so many people around here that died with it. We were all down with the flu at one time. I was one of the last ones to go down with the flu, and I must have been about 10, 12 years old at that time. Mama was down, and Dad. Dr. Sopenheimer was the doctor, and he'd come down and he'd say, "You got to have fresh air—fresh air. You've got to have fresh air." It was in the middle of the winter, and he wanted the windows open. We had no heat—it was just a coal stove in the dining room, and the kitchen stove. We all piled down in bed, all of us running fever and everything. I remember Daddy was a fresh-air fiend too, and he would leave the windows open. But you didn't dare get out from under the cover: you were just like a little chicken out from under its mother—you were freezing if you got out. We stoked the fire all night along. Alice Eliasen—bless her heart—she came down and stayed with us. She didn't get the flu, but she stayed there. Then Aunt Allie came down, and she stayed with us. If it hadn't been for them, I don't know. We were a hearty bunch, or we wouldn't have all made it. The doctor said, one time when he went down, "Well, they're all going to recover, because," he says, "they're all fighting and quarreling down there now." So he knew we were all going to make it by that time.

Ethel La Kamp Chrisler

Did a lot of people up in the Buford area get the flu?

Oh, yes. A lot of them passed away with it. There were some people—they lost two or three of their family. It was a big family.

If the doctor couldn't come up from Meeker, what were some of the home remedies?

They'd roll you in hot blankets—I remember that distinctly. I had the flu, and Mom said I kicked the flatiron out of bed and I turned over and went to sleep and I felt better. [Laughter.]

The flatiron was to keep you warm?

To keep the blankets warmer—they'd wring them out of hot water, and they'd get you to sweat. They'd try to get you to sweat.
One of the neighbors did the laundry one week for us, and then she helped.

Do you remember any other kinds of home remedies that your mother had?

Oh, she had turpentine [and] goose grease—rub it on your chest. I guess any kind of grease would had been all right, but they used goose grease if they could get it.

Did you have to buy it?

Well, the turpentine you would. Usually people raised geese, and then they'd save the geese when they butchered one of them, like for Christmas or something like that. Render out the grease.

Nellie Warren Parks

Do you remember the flu of 1918 and how that affected your family?

My mother didn't do anything but feed us onions, and she figured it's the onions that kept us from getting the flu—maybe the odor of the onions chased the flu away! Mother cooked them, and she'd make a broth out of them, and then we drank that. And then she'd put a little sugar on the onions, and we ate them.

There was one family we went to see, because they needed help, needed food. People would bring them in food and things like that. They were awful bad off. We went to see them, but we never ventured in the house or anything. I can remember it so well, passing this food and sacks of stuff through the window for them.

Did anyone in their family die from the flu?

No. But there was a lot of people that died around us.

Virginia Shepherd

Were you living in town in 1918, when the flu came?

Yes, I do remember that. By that time Meeker had two doctors, and we had a Ford with a Ruckstell gear which was one of the few. The worst of the flu epidemic came in a period when the roads were so muddy, and the Ruckstell gear was able to make it through the mud when some other cars couldn't.

Stores were closed for a period of time. I can remember when my father and mother and brother were all ill. We were just across from the church, and I can remember pulling the blinds down so that they couldn't see the funerals that were going on across the street at the church. That was a rather desperate time. It affected our school work too, because there were some things that I was taking—I think I was taking beginning Latin at that time, and we missed a little that we should have had as a background. It was hard to make up when we finally got back to school.

Of the people who died because of the flu, were most the elderly or the very young? Or did it seem to matter?

I think it was both. I remember one young couple, both of whom were taken, and the children then had to grow up with their grandparents. So that was one of the funerals that stands out in my memory—probably one of the ones for which I pulled the blinds.

Margaret Tagert Jones

We had a doctor [in Meeker]—there might have been two at that time, when I was very young as a child. But there was nothing such as preventative medicine—no penicillin, no antibiotics of any kind. I can't even remember aspirin. I do remember one experience, when I was probably about five years old, of losing a little companion who died from diphtheria. There were several times in my childhood when diphtheria had broken out in the town, and it was as if there was a pall over everything— terribly depressing, because people were losing their children, and they were friends: we all knew each other. So it took its toll on all of us. But I had a little friend called Chad—his father was a doctor, and I don't believe that I realized that Chad was sick. He and his little brother and my friend, another girl, and I played together so much. And then one morning they told us that Chad was gone; he'd died of diphtheria. The way the diphtheria seemed to act was that it affected the respiratory system. And, of course, there was nothing that could be done—no oxygen, nothing of that kind. So the children literally choked to death from that disease, or that was my impression of it at that time.

The other thing that happened in my family [was] a very tragic thing. My three brothers were in their adolescent years when I think it must have been an epidemic of scarlet fever that swept through the town. I wasn't really conscious of that at the time, and I'm not sure, of course, at this point whether that's what it was, but I feel sure, in many ways, that it was. Our home was very small, so we had what we called the tent house in the backyard, and the three boys lived there, coming into the house for meals and many other things. [So] they were isolated when they had this disease, because of our living arrangements. They had temperatures, I remember; they were very ill. My mother was taking care of them as best she could, and the doctor was looking in on them.

But as I remember, it was never diagnosed as scarlet fever. All three of them recovered, but in a few months their hearing seemed to be affected. They began losing the hearing so rapidly that by the time they were in their early twenties their hearing was so impaired that now they would have been labeled as handicapped.

Ina Dalrymple Eddy

When my first baby was born, I had phlebitis and the doctor didn't know what to do for me. And so Mother used her home remedies and brought me out of it.

My breasts swelled up real big, and they burst. She put pancakes—she made pancakes and put salt in [them] and she drew all the infection out.

Do you remember, with that many brothers and sisters, that they had accidents and cut themselves, or broke bones or otherwise hurt themselves?

One of my oldest brothers broke his arm, and it was set crooked. But that's all—we were a very healthy family, very healthy. We had to be. It was sort of fittest survive in our family. I had two older brothers and sisters die when I was probably—well, I wasn't even born. They had the flu. My oldest brother had the flu, and he didn't take care of himself, and of course it went into TB [tuberculosis]. His youngest sister caught it from him, and she died from it too. But there was no cure. And then I had a sister when I was in the twelfth grade die of spinal meningitis— my youngest sister that was two years younger than I. We were close, played together all the time, and when she died with such a terrible disease it was the most dramatic thing that I have ever had happen to me.

How long was it from the time she got the disease until she—

About a week—and her little back was bending then. They took her to one hospital and they wouldn't even accept her, so they had to go to another hospital—it was very contagious.

But no one else in your family got it?

No. They fumigated the house, and they told us to gargle our throat with Listerine, and to sorta note the signs. What my sister had was like the flu. She felt like she had the flu. At the time I was sleeping with her, and, of course, that worried me because—again, losing her in such a terrible, terrible way. My saddest moment in my life.

When people became seriously ill or had accidents on the homestead, the doctor was summoned from town. Because it often took several hours to reach the injured or sick person, the individual sometimes died before the doctor arrived.

Norine Holland

My father was up riding for cattle, way back up on what they call the Flattops, in February. Somebody had called him from that part of the country and said, "I saw three or four of your cattle out here." My daddy went up there, and he was stricken with appendicitis. He was very, very ill, but the horse took him down to the nearest farmhouse and they kept him there. The snow was so deep that they called down to Dr. Lumm and Dr. Brewer, the two doctors in Meeker.

[The doctors] kept telling Mrs. Murray what to do, and so then the next day they tried to get him out of there. They got him down as far as the road, because the snow was so deep. And then finally they got Dr. Brewer up there, and my father died. [The doctor] couldn't get the appendix out and couldn't get him to a hospital. Seventy-five miles was the closest hospital.

Virginia Shepherd

We moved to town when winter came—in fact, Mother and I had spent winter in town, and most of the time my father had to stay at the ranch to feed the stock. But after my little sister had died at the age of

Freddie Blevin's mother, Pearl Aiken,
about 1905
Courtesy of Freddie Blevin

Jayne Hoth's mother's family homestead. Near Lay, 1922
Courtesy of Jayne Hoth

two and had been very ill of pneumonia, Mother and I were always sent to [Meeker] for the winter. The neighbors there again were kind at what was a very tragic time for my parents. They had relays of horses all the way to town. There was a telephone—my father had put [one] in. There's only one doctor in Meeker, by the way, and that was the only one available for the whole area. And so the idea was to get the little girl to Meeker as fast as possible.

We started with our own conveyance and horses, and at intervals of 8 or 10 miles, maybe less, there were people waiting with new horses to make a quick change. But that didn't save her. This was before I was born, but I remember my parents [had] very fond memories of the little girl, and I know what a blow it must have been to them.

Oma Jensen Graham

Did you ever go to a doctor, when you were growing up?

Not until I had my leg broke, I don't think.

How old were you when that happened?

Oh, not quite four years old. Mother's horse jumped on me. I was about the only girl on Blue Mountain—that was just after we moved to the homestead—and there was always a bunch of cowboys around. So for Christmas, they didn't buy me anything for a girl: they bought me saddles, bridles, blankets, leather cuffs, a quirt, spurs, and a hat. I already had a little pony.

The first time that spring that Dad and Charlie Mantle were going to move the cattle out to Cuckleburr, I should have gone to church that morning, but I decided to ride my horse. So we helped them out about eight miles, just moving the cattle slow. After we left them, why, I said, "Well, let's do something besides walk." So we started out in a trot. The next thing I knew, we'd broke into a gallop. Well, I could handle the horse, but Mother got afraid. And if she'da stopped, instead of trying to catch me—I wasn't about to let her catch me, as long as I could outrun her—old Vic would have slowed down. But she shoved my horse off of the road, and when he jumped the wash, I fell off and her horse jumped on top of me.

What did she do with you?

Well, she had to pack me about six miles! And in those days you wore those old heavy corduroy divided riding skirts, you know. The horses stayed just a little ways ahead of us. If they'da gone on, somebody from Jensen would have come back—they knew that we'd gone; somebody would have come looking for us, see. But no, the crazy horses stayed just a little ways ahead. And so finally Uncle Seymour Snow, he looked out and saw, here come the horses. And so he had a light buggy, and here he came and picked us up, and we called Dr. Christie at Vernal. They did have a few telephones then, and he came down.

They put a weight on my leg. They didn't put a cast on it for a long time; they weighted it. And of a morning, when I'd wake up, I'd be pulled clear to the foot of the bed. This weight would pull me down [and] it would take three [people] to move me up and move the rock up to where I was supposed to be. I was 60 days in bed, but I think I was that way about, maybe two weeks, and then they did put a cast on it, but I still had to lay flat on my back. But I came out with a straight leg.

Katherine Warren Rector

Do you remember any accidents or any sort of emergencies on the ranch? If you couldn't get to town, you just had to deal with it the best you could?

Well, I remember my brother falling off the haystack, and ran an iron bar through his leg. The doctor operated on him on the kitchen table. Oh, I think he was goofing off, probably, and fell off the side of the stack. And that stacker was fastened down with these rods—there were some back here and some on this [gestures] end of it. Then when that hay went up, it would hold that till it would be sturdy. And he fell off that stack, and [those rods] run through his leg.

Ila Bowman Powell

When you lived up there on Douglas Creek, were there medical emergencies or illnesses you needed to deal with without any medical help?

I'll tell you, there was a lot of them, because there wasn't any doctors closer than Fruita or Vernal. We had no doctor, no hospital—nothing—here at the time. You just learned to take care of your kids, in whatever problems that arose, before you let it get out of hand. Like they started getting a bad cold, you got on it and doctored them right then. You didn't wait until he got pneumonia—you knew you didn't dare neglect kids and things.

One time my daughter—her brother was down under a bank, and he was making him a bridge, and he was coming down, chopping with this ax, but his finger was sore, so he couldn't hit very hard. He slid off the bank right above him, and he chopped her right in the head with that ax. The ax was sharp enough—it cut her hair off. My mother was there, and a girlfriend of mine that used to live in Meeker. She was there with me, and one of the cowboys, [who was] one of the boys that I grew up with up there. I could hear [my daughter] saying to Wallace before I saw her, "Wipe that old blood out of my eyes—wipe the blood out of my eyes!"

Well, he got to the house. He jumped this wire fence—how he did it, I don't know—with her in his arms. But I wiped it off and saw how bad it was. Jim Eidson came along about that time, and my mom says, "Oh, we'll have to cut her hair," and he said, "No, don't do that, because if you do it'll make a real bad sore."

So I took care of that myself. There was no cars, so there was no way to get to town or anything. You run into those situations sometimes. I just disinfected it, and I kept care of it myself. She's got a scar about that long [gestures] in her head, but it doesn't interfere with her hairline or anything. I said, "Well, just put some Mentholatum on it." The kids said, "Yeah, if I got a broken leg, you'd rub a little Mentholatum on it!" But it was scary sometimes, when you stop and think about it—that you didn't have any doctor or anybody around.

Lana Gregory Idol

Mrs. Idol discusses what sometimes happened to children when their mothers died in childbirth or from other causes. Her aunt was one of the women who offered to care for these children. Mrs. Idol lived with her aunt while in high school because her mother had died of cancer.

Aunt Lilly at one time had 13 children in her home, and she had only one [of her own]. Her sister, Rose White, passed away, and they had five children, and that winter [Aunt Lilly] had the five White children and us and her own boy, which was 11, and then she took—there was a druggist here in town that had two children, and she took them through the winter. She was an organizer. She really was. We each one had our chores to do: we knew what we had to do; it was our responsibility. We shared, and we shared alike. My dad had furnished her with a good milk cow, and the older boys milked the cow, of course.

Mr. Crockett paid her for his children, but Daddy didn't—he helped out on groceries and stuff, but he didn't pay her any sum. Then [when I was] in high school she boarded a lot of teachers. Of course, Lois [my sister] and I were big enough then that we were good help on that. But she was just a very wonderful woman, Aunt Lilly Purdy was.

Doctors sometimes performed surgery in people's homes because they were unable to move the patient to a distant hospital.

Estel Aicher Woolley

Dr. French was known all over everywhere with his ability as a doctor. He did marvelous operations and things that they didn't hardly perform in hospitals. He'd come in and put your dining room table out and operate on that, have everything clean. I can remember my dad having a hernia operation. Gee, we took the rugs out and scrubbed, and they used the dining room table for an operating table.

Were there many occurrences of people dying, or did most of them make it?

Most of them made it.

Do you remember how they sterilized the instruments? Did they do that in your home when they came in? Where did the family go while they were doing this?

Uh-huh, boiled them in water. The family usually stayed around. I can remember when my dad was operated on, Mother—she walked the floor in the other part of the room, or something like that, and when I came home from school he still wasn't out from the ether and all, and I can remember him talking crazy.

I can remember down here—Strehlke's had a drugstore about where the photo shop is now. They had [a] great big window, and they had a tumor, in a big washpan there, that this doctor had taken out of this Mrs. Saltmarsh. She lived, and boy, it was quite something that medical science could hardly believe—that he did it here.

SEVEN

Working Women

Women were expected to stay home after marriage. Nevertheless, more than half the women interviewed worked outside the home at one time or another during their adult life. During times of financial need, women often found it necessary to seek employment. A few of the women worked just because they wanted to, and derived great satisfaction from their jobs.

The types of jobs available to women were limited. Without special training, they could become secretaries, store clerks, and housekeepers. Those who received special training or a college education became nurses, teachers, librarians, county clerks, and beauticians.

Leona Rector Hinricks

Leona ("Babe") Rector Hinricks was born on her parents' ranch near Rangely in 1905 with the help of a midwife. With the exception of a few years away from home for high school and college, she has spent her life in the Rangely area. She taught in a one-room school for several years and then worked for 13 years as a secretary.

I lived in a little one-room shack, in the yard of a Mr. and Mrs. Carrigan. It was about a quarter of a mile from the schoolhouse. In those days you were your own janitor. The heat for the school building was coal, and we had to carry our own water from the creek. The snow on Morappos gets five feet deep on the level in the winter, and you have to walk to school.

How cold does it get?

Oh, about 25 below. I had 14 children in all eight grades, and I never had a better time in my whole life. We just had a wonderful time. I loved the kids, and they loved me. And we played games when it was so bad we couldn't get outdoors. We had jack tournaments; we had marble tournaments; we played "Pussy Wants a Corner." We did everything we could think of. And we sang. Those children walked as far as two and a half miles to school, and some of them didn't have overshoes—they wrapped their feet in gunnysacks to get there. I was really proud of them, because they walked so far and worked so hard.

Did your husband live there with you?

No. He was working on [a] ranch.

So you lived apart. Did you see each other often or live together during the summer?

Not very often, because the snow was so bad and nothing came up there except a sled in the winter. However, I broke my arm Election Day, and Mr. Hinricks came up and stayed. We borrowed a team of horses from some friends of ours in Axial Basin, and we would go down to see Lois and Wood Spence at Iles Grove on the weekends. We'd drive down in the sled and drive back. So we did get out of there once in a while.

Did you have children during that time when you were at Morappos—of your own?

I have one son, and he was born in 1928. He was with my mother and my sister, Mrs. Kirby, while I was teaching on Morappos. He was not of school-age yet, so they kept him here in Rangely while I taught. I came to Meeker one Saturday for a teacher's meeting, and Ruby brought Jimmy up to Meeker to meet me. He looked up at me and he said, "Mother, I hardly knew you—you've been gone so long." And it almost broke my heart.

Was this job you took as a teacher not just because you wanted to do it, probably, but because you really needed to do it?

It was because of the Depression. We needed the job. I could make $85 [a month] teaching school.

Janet Mortimer Eberle

My mother was a schoolteacher, so the first summer, we went to a school that she taught on Little Bear, which was about three miles from us, and my father built a little shack for us to live in. She taught that summer school until September. During that time my father worked for one of the neighbors, and then he went to road construction. He was a teamster on the road construction.

Did you live in that little house he put up through the winter?

Not that one; we lived there just during that summer. A lot of the schools in the Little Bear and Dry Fork area, and [in] a lot of areas, were summer schools, because of the difficulty in getting to school in the wintertime. Because the snow got a little deeper in the fall of 1921, in September we moved to the Sand Springs area. That was a winter school in that part of the county.

How far did you go to school, then, from where you lived?

At Sand Springs it was about a half-mile.

So you didn't get too cold before you got there?

Well—you dressed for the weather. After it froze up in the fall and my father couldn't work on the construction, he came and he was a really good house husband—he could do everything. It was a *big* school,—I think there were seven grades in that school—so it was a *lot* of work for my mother. My father did the washing and the cooking. Then he would go to the school in the morning and start the fire in the furnace—they had a floor furnace. That was a *really* nice school there, and it would be warm when we got to school.

It sounds as though it was a very fortunate thing that your mother was a teacher, so that they could kind of work together. What kind of education did she have?

She had a high school education, in Kansas, and then she went to a normal school, which is what teacher-training institutions were called in those days. In Colorado you would take a test in each county where you taught, and you would get a certificate.

177

When you did get the homestead [in 1925, north of Craig], then your mother didn't teach anymore?

Yes, she did. That was a nice cash income to get started. And it helped a great deal, because homesteading was bad enough anyway.

In some cases the woman would stay home and keep the things going, especially if she had older children, and the man would go away and work in the wintertime. But if a woman had a job, like my mother [did], then she was the one who did the [working].

My mother taught me in the ninth grade, at the Williams school, which was right on the highway west of Craig, about six miles out. If the teacher didn't have too many students, the teacher would teach maybe one year of high school, and then I would come in to Craig and take my quarter and semester exams. By then we were on the homestead, so my father was holding down the homestead and my mother and I lived in the cloakroom at the school.

There was no place to rent in the neighborhood, so we got by, the two of us, in that. It was a nice school, too. It was a large school, and it had two nice cloakrooms. So we had our bed in one, and we had a little coal oil stove that we cooked on.

Then the next year my father built us a little house in town—it was a little two-room house. My father held down the homestead, and my mother taught out at the Williams School. She rode with Elmer Trevenen on the truck. He was hauling Gilsonite from Utah. He made the trip down there, and when he came back he would pick her up from school, because it was right along the highway. So that's the way we did for the next two years.

And then when I was a senior, my aunt and uncle lived in town and I boarded with them.

Did your mother say things to you that would encourage you to do the same kind of thing, or did she talk about plans for your life after school?

Well, she certainly did stress the fact that every woman should be able to make a living for herself.

And we could see some of the neighbors. The man died, and [the wife] had to sell her place, at a sacrifice, and the only thing that she knew how to do was cook. She moved to Craig, and she cooked in a restaurant, which was fine, but she was not that young, to be doing that kind of work. But that was what she had done all her life, was be a homemaker— which was fine. Some women would look for a new husband right away, or some women would stay on their farms or their ranches and look for a husband—or try to run the ranch.

Velma Burdick Deaver

The first year I taught, I taught at [the] Thornburgh [School] [near Meeker], and I just loved that year—we had so much fun. I had seventh and eighth graders that were not too much younger than I was. I boarded with the Lough family. I enjoyed them so much.

Then I went down on lower White River and taught. I taught down at Rangely; I think it was three years I taught down there. It was a one-teacher school, and I had as many as 34 children. And that's where I met Hoyt [my husband]. He was working for different cow outfits—riding.

After you married, where did you live?

We lived on different ranches down there, wherever Hoyt could get work and I could get a school. I went right on teaching. It was never difficult for me to get a school. I always was able to get one, and, of course, the wages were not good at that time. But then, we got by.

I can remember that I did teach for one year for $75 a month, for eight months; that was the least that I ever got. Then there were times when we were down in that lower country that Hoyt was the foreman on the road construction, and a time or two he was unable to get a job because I was teaching.

Oh—there was an income already, and so they would give it to someone else?

That was during the Depression. That's the worst that we felt the Depression at all, was that he was denied work because I would be teaching.

Did you like teaching as well as you thought you would when you were a first grader?

Yes, I did. If I had my life to live over I'd do the same thing. I just loved it! And the best part of it all was after I went back to first grade.

The last 15 years I taught first grade, and I just loved it. Giving them a good foundation, and oh—they just progress *so* rapidly, and it just thrills you!

Mary Gates Haughey

I went to teaching school the fall after I graduated in 1921. [I was a] green kid—I'd be scared to death to try it now—but . . . it's wonderful to be brainless and have lots of nerve! [Laughter.]

If you could pass the state test, you could teach school.

Where did you teach?

Down on Big Gulch [west of Craig]. Altogether, during my teaching career, I had taught in that district five different terms—[although] not at the same building. And these were just small schools—3, or 4, or 5 people, sometimes as many as 15 or 20, or just the group that was there.

Where did you live when you did that?

We bached at the schoolhouse. Part of the time I was with families. Out here west of town I boarded with [families] by the name of Cathey, McFarland, and Mobley. One term I lived with all three of those, and their children went to school to me.

What was it like when you lived in the schoolhouse?

It was another little room, usually, away from the school building. Some of the teachers just had a curtain back of—in a corner with a stove and a bed back there, and that's the way they did at that time. There was no money for buildings to be provided for people.

So when the kids went home, you were there all by yourself. What did you do?

I'll tell you, when you had 15 or 20 students from the first grade all the way through, you had plenty to keep yourself busy, because you had papers to grade, plans to make. And the worst part of it is that a teacher as dumb as I was had to keep ahead of the kids, if possible! Which some-times is not so good.

Do you have any memories that stick out in your mind of particular times during that teaching period?

Down on Big Gulch, teaching that term, I was staying with a family by the name of Short. And there's about five of the family that was in school to me. And we had went to school that morning and it was bad—the weather was bad in the winter—and they had said, "Well, if it doesn't get any better, we'll meet you tonight." It was about three-quarters of a mile to school. And he said, "We will come with the team and haul you home so you don't have to walk."

But it began to storm. I sent some of the children that drove home early, because it looked like it was going to be a bad storm. And we weren't fooled: it stormed all night, and it drifted until the drift on the north side of the school building was up to the eaves of the building. Such a storm! And it blew [into] these shacks that people lived in at that time. Insulation was unheard of, and through the cracks in the floor and the keyholes there were drifts [of snow] from the way it blew. It was a terrible storm. The next day, when we went back to school—of course, they took us, with the team that day. And here was this big old drift, and those kids would get out on top of that drift and get on top of the roof, you know, and slide! Oh, that was really something! That was one thing I remember.

And at that time, that same year, friends and neighbors—[a] tragedy. A man and his daughter froze to death, which was something you don't forget. They were taking a load of hay home, and they froze. So—just things like that happened. I can't tell you what year it was, but it was bad.

Later in her life Mary worked in the county clerk's office and even-tually became the county clerk.

I was chairman of the Democrat party in that area up there [on her homestead, north of Craig], in that precinct.

You're the first person I've talked to that was really interested in politics. Why do you suppose that was?

I had never heard anything *but* politics all my life. Mother and Dad were strong politicians. Mother was more involved—that is, she felt it

181

deeper than my dad did. But they were Democrats, and I have been asked *why* I'm a Democrat. Of course, you don't dare belong [to another party], when you're raised in a family like that—you have to be!

Was political interest unusual for women? How were the women received when they got that involved in politics?

Very [unusual]. I didn't notice any difference. Not here, no. You were [just] interested. 'Course, they didn't hold any high political positions at that time. And even the superintendent of schools was a man at that time. However, my mother-in-law was the first elected county clerk in Moffat County when it had been divided from Routt County [Moffat County was formed in 1911]. She was not the first clerk, but the first *elected* clerk. And she served several years, and then there were men in between, and a woman or two.

I think it was 1920 [when women were allowed to vote], and Mother always saw that she voted, and she served on election boards and things like that. She was interested, but she never held an office.

[My husband] died on June the nineteenth, 1952; he was 51 years old.

So that all of a sudden left you without adequate income? How did you handle that?

I was very fortunate in working in the county clerk's office at that time. I was deputy county clerk, and that was my salvation. I was elected then as county clerk.

Did you campaign and all that sort of thing?

Sure! I drove over a good area of Moffat County and went to visit people, and I spoke at different places. If there was a meeting of some kind, I tried to get there. I didn't make an awful big impression, I'm pretty sure, [and] I don't know why I was elected, unless they felt sorry for me . . .

I didn't spend very much. I decided that if you couldn't be elected on your merits, you didn't have any business being elected on the amount of money that you went in debt to raise.

I was 16 years as county clerk. I was 6 years deputy and 16 clerk, making 22 consecutive years in that office. I retired in 1970.

Norine Holland

My mother [Josephine Fitzpatrick] came into the county as a teacher—from Denver. She was born in Louisiana but came to Denver to live, and finished Denver University. After she received her degree, she came to Rio Blanco County, in 1912.

She was the first teacher to teach at Miller Creek. They had by this time built a school at Miller Creek, which was close to where Grandma and Grandpa Holland lived, and my father, and that's how she met my daddy. She taught at Miller Creek the first year, and then she went to teach at the Miller Creek Ranger Station—in those years you taught people wherever they were. And then Mother went to Piceance Creek to teach, and she taught at the Rock School in Piceance Creek for a couple of years after that. Then she and Daddy were married, and she went to live on the White River [at the ranch].

After my father died, which was in 1933, my mother ran for county superintendent of schools, and she was county superintendent for the [next] 20 years.

Was she able to keep the ranch?

No. After my father died—and this was during the Depression—the bank came out and settled everything that there was. My brother was only 15 and still going to school. There was no way we could keep the ranch. That's when she ran for county superintendent of schools.

She had 25 to 30 rural schools scattered all throughout the county [to supervise]. When you stop to think, that's not all that long ago, and the only people that went to the town schools were the people that lived in Meeker. [Each of] the rural schools had a teacher—some of them even ran summer schools. There was a rural school way up outside Oak Creek that ran in the summertime. They ran from Oak Creek to the top of Douglas Pass. And she did most of [the traveling] in the early days in a Model-A Ford. I've often heard her say that Rio Blanco County, the county she covered, was [the size of] the state of Rhode Island.

She had to visit those schools every three months. Many of those rural schools had a teacherage at the back of them. The teacherage is this little room in the back, and the teacher lived there, or if she didn't live there she boarded with the nearest neighbor and maybe walked to school.

A teacher's life was certainly not easy. [She] had to keep up the school, had to clean all of it and oil the floor and keep the schoolhouse warm. My mother left office in 1951, and they still had a number of rural schools in the county at that time.

Did she ever travel in the wintertime?

Oh, she always went every three months [to each school]. She went in the wintertime [in order] to make the rounds of the schools. She was traveling all the time; she was constantly traveling.

I can remember when she went up in the summertime. I went with her [one] time, up to the rural school up there by Oak Creek. And good Lord! We went out over what they call Dunckley Pass now. We went up over that old road, and a big rainstorm came and washed the road out. I can remember that we walked back to this farmhouse, and we must have walked for five hours to get back to the farmhouse, because we were afraid of running out of gas if we started [out in the car]. So we walked and walked and walked down there [and] banged on the door about one in the morning—people always let you in, and they'd give you a cup of coffee. They got up at daylight and got us out.

In the early years, like in 1933, how in the world did she get to some of those schools, with the roads like they were, by herself?

The first years that she was in office she went mostly by herself. Then Mr. Purdy drove her for years. She went in that old Model A; I don't know how, but, well, I *do* know how—she was stuck by the side of the road half the time. When we were kids in high school, we never knew when she was going to get home. She might not get home for two days. Somebody would finally come along and dig her out, and she would go on. I can remember once she went to Douglas Creek, and she said, "Well, I *know* I won't be home tonight, but I *may* be home tomorrow night." Well, she never showed up for three days, because she was stuck down there, and she was *always* off to the side of the road all night. That was nothing to her, to be off to the side of the road, and she seldom ever took very much food, and she hardly ever wore overshoes. She had an awful lot of stamina.

In the later years of being county superintendent of schools, she had drivers drive her. She and Chuck Hossack were coming down out of Douglas Creek [near Rangely]. They had killed a buckskin. My mother was always stopping, always doing something, and Chuck saw this buckskin and Mother said, "Well, get out and shoot it so we'll have it when we get home." So Chuck gets out and shoots the buckskin and sticks it in the back of this old Model A Ford, and away they go. He was going pretty [fast]—Mother kept saying, "There's a car following us." She looked back, and before they got to Rangely she kept seeing this car and she said, "Well, Chuck, you've got to step on it, because there's a car following us, and for heaven's sake, don't let them catch up with us!"

The more they stepped on the old Model A, this car kept trying to catch up with them, and they finally saw it was a truck. And Mother said, "Well, my God, get back on the Meeker road before it catches [us]—it might be the game warden."

So poor old Chuck—he stepped on the gas, and that old Model A just wouldn't go any faster, and finally this car [caught] up with them. Lester Kenney drove up; he said, "God Almighty! Josephine, I've been chasing you all the way down the river!" He says, "Good night! I wanted to catch you before you get out here, before the sheriff picks you up, because blood's leaking out of your car!"

Well, they hadn't even paid any attention to the blood, and I guess he was coming along, and he could see the blood—

He said, "Get rid of that, or take it down to my house and we'll do something with it—you know, get it packaged up so you can take it to Meeker before you get out on the highway with the blood dripping out!" [Laughter.]

Oh, gosh! Well, I guess they all were trying to stay away from the game warden all the time, weren't they? Because they did shoot deer out of season quite often?

Oh, yeah. Oh, a lot of times. We lived on buckskin, a lot.

They had a school [in Rangely]—that was the only rural school they had when the oil boom hit in 1945 and 1946. People were living in tents and they had to get that school building built as soon as they could. They had kids all over town going to school in any room they could find until the schoolhouse could be built.

Stuart McLaughlin was an oilman, and [he] had some pumping wells. He was on the school board, and they had a school board meeting [one] evening. As I remember, it was in the summertime, and I guess he said [to my mother], "Now come out, I want you to see what's going on out in the field." And so she went out, and there was a new derrick going up. She said, "I want to go up on it." And he said, "Well, now, I don't guarantee anything," and he was very fearful she might fall, you know. But knowing my mother as he did—she was doing this [sort of thing] till the day she died; she was out in the hay field just the day before she died. She got up on this derrick, and the men were drilling, and the thing came in, as she was up there, and [it] just *completely* covered her with oil. He had to get her down off from there, and [she had] oil in her hair, and—it's a wonder it didn't put [out] her eyes; it's a wonder it didn't drown her!

That oil just shot up! It came in, and there she was. But I guess they took her back to Stuart's place, and it took two days to get her cleaned up enough to get all that oil out of her hair and her eyes and everything else! [Laughter.]

Do you remember any kind of attitude in the community toward women who continued to work after they were married?

In all those early days, and until my father died, no woman worked [outside the home] where I lived. Now, they did in town, I guess. I don't think very many worked in town. A woman's place was in the home—cooking! With that kind of setup, with men stopping [at the ranch] all the time, you didn't have any time to do anything but cook.

I often heard my mother say that she wasn't all that domestic. She *loved* to be out doing what she was doing when she was county superintendent of schools. I know that. She did it because she had to do it, but she never really liked that domesticity. She loved to talk with people, and she was very bright. She was always reviewing books, and stuff like that. But on ranches, no women worked [outside the home]. They had too much to do. They did not work, and it was not encouraged. My attitude growing up was that what you did [was] you went away to college. But you [also] got married. You either got married in college, or else you marry a local boy. Because *that's* the thing you're supposed to do, so you'll have somebody to take care of you!

My mother always kept saying, "Now, you have got to go to college, even if you have to work your own way. Look what would have happened to me if I hadn't had my college education to fall back on." But it's only to fall back on. Women did not pursue a career actively.

June O'Connell Sweeney

First you can picture me in the dormitory room in Greeley, just ending my college quarter—summer quarter. And I thought, "Well, now I have to get a job someplace." So I had the map of Colorado in front of me, and I looked around, and I said, "Maybell—isn't that a pretty name? I think I'll send an application to Maybell."

So I did, and I sent some others, too. I don't know how that letter ever got from Greeley to Maybell as fast as it did, because in a day or two I received an answer from Dr. Arborgast, who was the secretary of the school board in Maybell, with a contract: "A hundred dollars a month, [and] you can have the junior high. There are three schools. Maybell is the second largest town in Moffat County. You can stay in the hotel, [and] we'll be very pleased to have you as a teacher."

I thought, "I'll answer this and send it back." So that very day I signed the contract for the $100 to teach junior high school in Maybell, where he mentioned they had three schools, and sent it back. So there I was [ca. 1925].

When it came time for me to go to Maybell, my mom and dad brought me over to the Dotsero cutoff and I got on the Moffat Railroad. And when we got almost to Steamboat, there was a rock slide. So they unloaded us and told us we'd have to stay at the hotel for they didn't know how long.

I went to bed that night just wondering, but when I got up in the morning [I thought,] "I must call Dr. Arborgast and tell him I can't get to Maybell to start school." And when I went to the telephone, here was Walter Ketchum, who was going to Maybell, and I could go with him.

So in his little Ford coupe car we started. When I got to Craig and I saw Craig, I began to cry! Anyway, we got to Maybell, and Walter drove up in front of the hotel, and we went in, and he said, "Hello, Mrs. Miner," and all that, and I said, "I'm the teacher that's come to teach school." "Hmmmppp! You are?" "Yes, and I think that you have a room for me here." "Yes." And Walter said, "Could we have a little bit to eat, Mrs. Miner?" "No."

It was a quarter to seven then. "No!" she said. "You know that I serve meals at six in the morning and twelve at noon and six at night." "OK." "I'll show you to your room." So she took me up the stairs and showed me this room. It was a front room, and the wonderful thing was it had a window that looked out on the street. Had one of these enamel iron beds, a dresser, and that's all. I think it might have had one chair, but I'm not sure.

And she said, "The bathroom's down the hall." And she left me. So— I was a little bit dumbfounded.

Oh! Where had you grown up?

I had grown up in Leadville.

So you were kind of used to a frontier-type town?

Well, but it had paved streets! You know, it was way ahead. So much money had been made in gold in Leadville, and then, you see, I'd been to school in Greeley and all that, so I wasn't quite used to this.

After a little while, Walter came to the door and knocked, and he said, "She's going to give us a little bit to eat." So she did—she warmed some roast beef, and that was the beginning.

Well, anyway, Dr. Arborgast told me there were three schools and I could have the junior high. So—there were three schools. There were three one-room schoolhouses. And I was to have the middle one. But when it came time for school to begin, the district had gone broke. So they only kept one teacher, and that happened to be me.

I was to have the third grade through the eighth, but the rest of the high school, and the primary, were just going to be left out for that first year. I enjoyed it very much, and it was lots of fun, just getting those children to learn.

Of course, the cowboys used to stop in to Mrs. Miner's for lunch or something, and I thought, "Well, they stopped in to see the new school-teacher!" One cowboy that stopped in was Henry Sweeney, who, the following June, I married.

I had saved my money at Maybell, to go back to college. My husband, Henry, was a regular saint, I think. He let me go back to Greeley for the spring quarter, and he came after me the first of June. [So] I had that much more toward my degree.

Then I taught that next year at Lay. I rode horseback seven miles to Lay, on a beautiful big palomino stallion that Henry brought to the door every morning and put me on. And Mr. Menninger over at Lay, where they used to have a big frame two-story hotel, was always there to help me off and to take my horse and put him in the barn. He never failed to have that horse ready for me to go home at night, and help me on.

It was a winter school—it was nine months. I remember the cold. I had about 12 or 14 children to teach at Lay. One girl was [in the] first year [of] high school, and I had to teach her algebra. I had to study it every night myself. I'd had it in school, but algebra was never one of my favorite subjects. She was especially good at algebra, and she used to get the right answers, thank goodness! [Laughter.]

I know you later taught just one grade in town. What was the difference between the country school and teaching in town?

Well, of course, I had just one grade; I had the third grade. That was when we moved to Craig. That was one of the hardest decisions I ever made in my life, was when the older boy was ready for junior high school. I had taught them, even in my own house, for several years. I knew it was time they were getting out and getting somebody else to teach them besides mother. So when he was ready for the seventh grade, I said, "Shall I board these two boys in town, or shall I move into town with them?" Well, my decision was that I would move to town with them. Henry would have to come in on the weekends. That was a sad breakup.

I thought, "Oh, my goodness! I'm so tired! I'll be so happy to have a rest." And the house we got had the gas furnace, and it had the toilet and the running water, and it was a lovely little house. I thought I was in heaven, in a way, except that I'd left my husband down there to do everything and be without me. But I was only there, I think, three days when they came after me to teach school in Craig.

So I taught for six years, and Henry did come in on the weekend. And then I went to the ranch in the summers.

And, of course, going to the ranch meant cooking for the hay crew and cooking for the hired man and all that, all the time, which was fun—I didn't mind it. And we had a wonderful garden, so those meals that I got for the hay crew were all those fresh vegetables. Now, Mother Sweeney had always had help when they had the hay crew. So I said to myself, "I'm young and strong—I can do it without help." And then I said to myself, "Don't be a fool. Get help." So I did. I had help all the rest of my life.

After you taught for those six years, what did you do then?

Well, let's see. I think I was just home one year—yeah, I wasn't even home that long. I was home during the summer, and here they came: "Mrs. Sweeney, will you run for county superintendent of schools?" And I said, "No. No. My husband doesn't want me to, and I've been away from home for so long that I won't." The three ladies went out the kitchen door, and here came Henry from the barn. They jumped on Henry. And Henry said, "OK. It's all right if she runs for county superintendent." [Laughter.] Maybe he thought I wouldn't be elected! So, I was all ready to stay home and here I run for county superintendent of schools. [June was elected in 1954 and continued to serve in that office for many more years.]

I had a wonderful husband. He was so even-tempered, and he put up with all this stuff that I did and didn't mind me teaching. I think he was really kind of proud of the fact that I did teach, that I was a teacher, and he a rancher and a cattleman. He knew all about cattle from A to Z.

You know, I never remember—and this sounds ridiculous, but it's true. I never remember him being angry with me. I don't ever remember us having a fight. We just got along. I guess he put up with me and loved me. He loved me very much, and I loved him very much, and yet our lives were apart a lot of the time, because I was teaching so much, and he was the one that kept the home fires going a good deal, while I was coming and going.

Did you continue the teaching and the other things that you did just because you wanted to, or because you felt that the money would come in very handy?

I just wanted to teach. From my earliest childhood, I was going to be a teacher. And so I was.

Catharine Craig Coles

When Catharine was 20 years old, her family moved from a ranch near Steamboat Springs to one near Craig. She taught in the neighborhood one-room school for a year before she married.

[In 1921] I taught school out at Pagoda, which is at the junction of two highways east of the little place called Pagoda. There was just a store, a post office, and a cemetery there, and they had this school on farther up the road quite a distance. They didn't have a teacher for the summer school, [and so] Mr. Saunders [who was on the school board] called up. As was the custom in those days—or because he wanted to do the correct thing—he asked to talk to my father. So my father was called to the telephone, and Mr. Saunders said, "Mr. Craig, I understand you have a daughter who can teach school," and my father said, "Well, she has a certificate. She has not had any experience yet." And he said, "Well, I would like to talk to her. We need a teacher for the summer school at Pagoda very badly." And so my father said, "I'll bring her up and you can have a visit with her." And that was how I got my first teaching job. It started on the fifth day of April and was out on the 24th of November. But we managed to get through the year, and I loved my students—they were dear youngsters. I never have forgotten a one of them.

How did you travel to school?

We didn't have a car at that time, and we lived on what was called the Hughes Ranch, and there were lots of horses. I drove this buggy, and sometimes I would drive our old horse and the buggy, and at other times Mr. Saunders would put up the horse—I would use one of his. His old horse was called Flaxie, and she was very, very hyper, as we say today. And oh, she was a problem. To get Flaxie into the shafts at the end of the day, and hitched up, and get those four children loaded in—I took the four, because I took my little half-sister and half-brother, Ada and Joe, and then when I got up to Pagoda I picked up Cora and Gretchen [Saunders].

Esther Anderson Campbell

I came in 1922 to Skull Creek to teach the Skull Creek School because they were paying good wages down here. I got $90 a month.

I taught in the Skull Creek district about 10 years, but there were two or three schools in the district. In Skull Creek proper I just taught two different years.

When I first came, I boarded with a family running the Skull Creek store. They had two daughters, and I lived [in] a little bedroom built on—a little lean-to. They were very nice, until, in January, I got married.

The schoolhouse was right beside the little trail leading down from the mountain, Blue Mountain. He was a cowboy, and as he'd drive by I could see him ride past the open door—he usually came by at about the time school was out and I would be sweeping and doing my janitor work. So after a while, a few more of those trips, he began to stop in, poke his head in the door and talk, and offer to sweep and so on. In January we just came to our home and got married. Then we moved into a little dugout.

Duard was my housekeeper, while I taught school. Everybody began to kind of get a kick out of it, because he'd come down from up there—we had two horses, our saddle horses, and he'd ride one and lead the other down to water them every day at the creek by the schoolhouse, and then I'd get a chance to ride home from school in the evening. He'd always come with a dishrag in his hind pocket [chuckle], and that dishrag was a multipurpose piece of equipment. He dusted with it and washed dishes with it—used it for everything handy. It was right there so he could grab it [laughter]—everybody laughed about him carrying that dishrag around with him.

Mary Haughey, teacher in a one-room school. At Dowden Bridge near Craig, about 1923
Courtesy of Mary Haughey

Leona "Babe" Hinricks and son in a wheat field. Rangely, about 1940
Courtesy of Leona Hinricks

Did you have children?

We had one boy. And my mother kept him a big part of the time, until he got to be school-age. I had to keep teaching, that was really the way we had to make a living. We had a few cattle, later, after we got over on Douglas Mountain [near Brown's Park], but then we got—oh, about 100 head of cattle was all, not very many, but we could stay up there and keep them winter and summer. There really wasn't much profit in them, and so I'd decide every once in a while to teach school during the winter to help out. It did help some, but then we had to find someplace to keep the cattle for the winter. Duard didn't want to stay up there alone. He'd come along; wherever I taught, he was right there too.

So we'd get someone to take our cattle and feed them or graze them on their range or something like that; then we'd check on them every once in a while. And so we made it that way.

I guess the schoolhouse, particularly when all those rural schools were in business, was kind of the center of the community?

It was. That was about the only entertainment, outside of dances, that they had, especially for Christmas programs. They made a big thing of Christmas programs and invited everybody.

It was lots of work, but it was fun. But really, I considered these programs a big part of education. They needed that: to get up in front of people and speak their pieces and act. We had little skits and plays, and singsongs, of course.

If you had to describe the advantage of a rural school over that of an elementary school in Craig, what would it be? Are there disadvantages?

I really think the rural schools did a better job [chuckle]. You wouldn't think so, but in the first place you were closer to your pupils there every day. Year after year, on up through the grades, you knew them and what they needed the most. With fewer in the grades, maybe one or two in each grade, they had to know that lesson before we could go on to another one.

We got our sports and fun at recess and noons. Everybody went out to play. If there was a nice pond, we'd skate at noon. In the summer we'd play other games or have swings, or whatever. They moved a schoolhouse down in Brown's Park closer to where more of the people were located. But they set the school in quite a patch of greasewood. There was no playground, of course.

So to get a playground, we'd all go out and grub brush at recess. Their reward was that we would have a playground someday. It took all fall, really, just a little bit at a time, to get a cleared space.

How far did some of your students come to school?

We used to have more rural schools, and they'd be closer. But in later years they did away with quite a few, and they'd have to come as far as 25 miles, some of them, after we got cars and so on. It wasn't so bad, but then in the early days, when they didn't have cars, they had to be within walking distance.

I guess in Brown's Park the winters were a little milder?

It was nice. There wasn't any deep snow in Brown's Park, except one winter. In 1949 we had the highest [snowfall]. They kept plowing [the roads] out until they were just tunnels, almost tunnels up above the height of the cars. All through Brown's Park. It was pretty hard. But that year some of my pupils came to live with me in the teacherage—the ones that had to come any distance. They had also arranged that summer to move some extra cabins up closer so that the children maybe could move up to school and live there through the winter. Maybe grandma or somebody came to live with them and cook for them and so on: keep them there. Most of them went home for weekends but [came] back Monday morning and stay[ed] through the week.

But in that winter—1949—it was the big snow came just about Christmastime. The children were all home for the holidays. By the time school was supposed to start after New Year's, it was so deep no one could get there.

So the bulldozers and the snowplows and everything got as much as possible; as far as they could go, they would clear the roads out. By Wednesday or so, most of the children were back at school. And then they'd go home Friday, and it would snow again. So it was that way about five weeks [chuckle]—they couldn't come to school till Wednesday.

One family lived about 19 miles or so from school, and they would drive a truck to bring them to school. But during that hard winter, [the mother] tipped over in the road trying to come after them after school was out. She wasn't even halfway, I don't think, where she tipped over with her two little ones that weren't school-age yet. She had to leave them there with the truck, and they didn't have any extra coats. It was cold in the wintertime, so she gave her coat, I guess, to the little one, and the sleeves dragged the ground. [She] told them not to move from there, just to stay right close to the truck. She ran the distance from that truck back down to the schoolhouse, and when she came to the schoolhouse she just fell in the door. She just bumped against the door and was so all in that she couldn't hardly talk for a while, all out of breath. She said, "I tipped over and the two little ones are up there waiting, no heat or anything."

Her oldest boy was going to school, and she had come to pick him up. So we got him and took her back up to where the truck was tipped over and got the little ones and took her home. The next day, she got someone to help her tip it back on the wheels.

But things like that did happen sometimes. It made it hard, so I kept that boy the rest of the winter. And then I kept a girl [who lived] in the other direction. I kept her the big part of the winter, until it began to clear up a little. And anybody else that couldn't get home, they always stayed all night with us.

Since you did have a career and worked so hard at that, how did you manage your home responsibilities, like cooking and washing?

Well, my husband helped with the housework; he'd cook the beans, for instance, when he'd hear me turn [the children] out, or [when he heard me] call them in from recess in the morning, 10:30, why, he'd start getting lunch. Probably it was a couple of weenies. And he'd fry them until [noon] [laughter], so when I came home to eat lunch he'd put them on there, and "clickety-clickety-click," like two rocks! [Laughter.] He did his best—what he could do best was cook beans, and they were very good, but he wanted to change once in a while. He always bragged that he could cook breakfast for me in 10 minutes any day, or 5 minutes, I guess he said. He just stirred up a cup of hot chocolate, poured hot water in it, and there I had my breakfast!

Did he cook dinner too?

Yes, he started it, usually. But whatever was cooking at the time I came home, he sat down and that was the end of it. If I didn't get there right away, the potatoes would scorch or something else would happen!

He would clean—he kept the house looking very neat. He swept it out every day—that is, a trail through the middle [laughter]. Anything that was in the way, magazines or anything, he'd poke them behind the couch or somewhere where they didn't show [laughter], so it always looked in order.

Did you ever have to do a more thorough job?

Yes, on weekends I had to do that—on my Saturdays, when I was there; sometimes we had other places we had to go. And my washing. I did move my washer over there to Powder Wash the second year, and so I washed evenings. Before that it was rub-a-dee-dub on the washboard. But I had the washer there that year, and I could wash in the evenings, in the bathroom or somewhere.

And my ironing—of course, we didn't have no-iron clothes at that time, and so I would try to iron, oh, about 15 minutes before school every morning and gradually get it caught up. He would help me iron the flat things, like pillow slips and so on. Once in a while he would iron his older shirts, press them out a little bit. So he helped me—he was pretty good at helping.

I taught about 35 years. I was kind of tired by that time, but I do look back on those years as being fun. And my contact with the youngsters, and they're still so close to me. They look me up, and they write to me yet, lots of them do, and keep in touch. All these that live in this area here come to see me now and then.

Eleanor Rugler Service

Eleanor Rugler Service came from Missouri in 1928 to teach at the Pagoda School, which was south of Craig on the Williams Fork River. She found it difficult to adjust to such an isolated area but soon found that she liked the people and decided to marry and make northwestern Colorado her home.

I taught school in Missouri. We didn't get very much money for teaching, so I heard that school districts paid more out here in this country. I had a friend that had taught out here, and she gave me a school directory. So I applied for some schools. The first year I could have had three or four schools. They needed teachers in those days [1927], so I took the one up on Williams Fork, Pagoda [School].

I had two years' college. And then I got a lifetime certificate in Missouri and I had some more college courses that I'd taken, but it wasn't enough for a degree at that time.

I just taught [at Pagoda] one year, and it was a nine-month school. And, oh, I got *so* homesick, because we were snowed in all winter. And so somebody said, "Why, you ought to be here in the summertime." I [was] snowed in all winter, and, oh, it was just simply terrible. I wasn't *used* to that.

Where did you live when you got there?

I boarded with the Scotts. They were about half a mile east of the school. She was real good about taking me to see the neighbors on weekends and things like that. She tried to entertain me, as much as she could. And then we always played cribbage, and we'd have a game of cribbage every night: she and her husband, and there was an old man that lived with them. The four of us, we just had a real good time. But, of course, we couldn't do that all the time.

That was 1928, and some time after cars were available. Did they use cars in the winter?

They couldn't very well; they had to use sleds and horses—it was about the only way to get around. They didn't keep the roads open at that time.

Did they have any community get-togethers?

Oh, yes, yes, they would. We always had our Christmas program, and everybody in the community could come to that. And then they would go down to Pagoda every once in a while, and they had dances down there, even in the winter. I remember one time they went down there— it was daylight before we got home.

We were all bundled up, and we were in the sled. Usually when we went to Hayden, they would heat big rocks and put [them] in the bottom of the sled, and then we'd put our feet on them and cover up. We'd stay nice and warm.

I taught nine month school over there [at Pagoda], and they said, "You ought to teach the summer school; see if you can find a summer school." There wasn't any in that county, so they said, "Well, try Rio Blanco County." So I wrote to the superintendent at Rio Blanco County and asked if there was summer school. Boy! I got an answer right back. They said yes, they had summer school, and would I take it. So I took it. I closed school up there on a Friday and started this one on Monday. That was Lime Kiln; [it's] up here on the hill [near Meeker]. They had kilns there, you know.

This was a summer school because it was so high. It was over 8,000 feet. The snow was just too deep in the winter, so they had summer school. It was nice and cool up there, and, oh, it was so nice—I really enjoyed that nice summer. They wanted me to come back to teach the next year, so I went back and taught the next year.

197

Do you have any memories about—oh, the children that you had or some of the things that you did, special things that stand out in your mind in any of these schools?

Well, let's see. [At] Lime Kiln School, one of the neighbors had a pet deer, and the pet deer stayed at the place where I boarded. And of a morning when I'd go to school, the deer would follow me to school. There wasn't any shade around there, because there wasn't any trees, and so the deer would stay in the shade [beside the school], and then when the youngsters would come, she would get up [and] take to them. She would raise up on her hind feet and come down on their head.

Oh, the kids didn't like Old Bumps, oh, no! And there was a fence around [the school], and when they would come to the gate they would call me and they'd say, "Mrs. Service, we're here." And if I'd go out and meet them, they could walk with me; it would be all right. But they wouldn't go out by themselves.

[Old Bumps] used to come to town. Jim's dad used to bring grain down, and she would jump up on there—they'd bring it down on the sled. She would jump on the sled [and] they'd bring it downtown, you know, [and] she'd wind around downtown. And, of course, he'd have to stay all night and then go back. One time he couldn't find her. So somebody probably put her in the pot.

Was it a lot of hard work preparing for all those different grades?

Yes. And then they didn't have all the things that they have now. You know, you can get *so* many things already printed or hectographed (duplicated) or stuff like that. I had to make myself a little old hectograph to make the stuff off on.

How did you do that?

There was a certain kind of material you could get, a little pan, I guess about the size of . . . [gesture]. And then you had to have a certain kind of ink to wipe on. Then you just put it on that and just took one sheet off at once.

But that was a big help when I got that, because otherwise I had to do it all, you know, and, like, if I had three youngsters in third grade that had to have some arithmetic, I'd have to make three copies. I usually would use carbon paper. But then two copies was about all you could do.

How did you meet your husband?

Oh, he lived up there on Lime Kiln. He would come riding by there, you know, see the schoolteacher.

Did you want to continue teaching after you got married?

Well, I did. I taught—oh, I don't know how many years after that.

They asked me after my youngest baby was born—they wanted to know if I would finish the term. And I said, "Oh, my goodness." I said, "The baby is just two weeks old." And I said, "I nurse him, and I'd have to take him to school." They said, "That's all right." And a woman said, "Why, my kids have got a nice big doll bed, and we'll bring that up there to school and you can put the baby in it." 'Course, as young as he was, he just slept most all the time. I don't remember how many weeks I taught—I think about five or six weeks like that. Took that baby up there to school. 'Course, I put him in there, and, of course, the youngsters knew that they had work, and they didn't play much with him.

They worked. They were busy; I saw to it that they were busy. And as long as you keep them busy, then you don't have any trouble. And [if] you get the youngsters to like you, you don't have any discipline problems. They knew they were coming to school, and they knew they were there to work, and that's what they did.

I taught at Axial for about 17 years, and then when they closed that school I went to Hamilton and I taught there for 2 years. Then my certificate ran out, and they said I'd have to go to school to finish my degree before I could teach, because I had to have a degree. But then at that time I thought I couldn't teach but just a few more years, and it just wasn't worth it. Besides that, I had two foster children at home, and so it would have been hard for me to go away for a whole year. I had taken all the correspondence and extension work that I could, and the rest of the time I'd have to be in school. So I didn't think it was worth it.

You were at Axial for a long time, then. What did your husband do while you were there?

Oh, he had a business [in Meeker].

And so you drove [the 20 miles] from here to Axial? Was it a summer or winter school?

Winter. Oh, yes, every day. I never thought anything about it. I'd just get up of a morning, [thinking,] "Oh, it's just kind of snowing this morning"—never thought a thing in the world about it.

One time I had to go up to Strawberry [to teach school]. [Strawberry is about 25 miles west of Meeker.] Well, they came down and wanted me to finish a school term, and I wasn't teaching that year, and there was a half-year left. They had an old lady out there that was teaching, and she couldn't make it to the school anymore, so they needed somebody. They just came down here and just *begged* me to take it. They said, "We'll fix a place." They had a house—it was a three-roomed house, and they used the biggest room for the school, and they put two schools together. At that time they paid $75 a month for the teacher, you see. But each district put in $75, so I got $150. I could not turn down that $150, and the superintendent down here found out about it, and she said, "Eleanor, don't you tell anybody what you're getting up there." She said, "You're making more money than the people up here in high school are." Just had about half a dozen kids.

One time [when] I drove over there, it had snowed during the weekend, and I got more than halfway over there and I could not go any further, just simply couldn't make it any farther. So I just thought, "Well, I'll take the key out of the car and let it sit there, and if anybody wants by, they'll have to go around, or do something."

I couldn't walk home; it was too far. And I *could* walk over [to the school]. And so I just started out afoot. I had a bag that I had put some food in, and took what I really, absolutely had to have.

I knew the kids, by the time I'd get there, they'd probably be gone. They stayed till noon, they said, and then they went home. But then some of the kids saw me coming, and they came [back].

But my feet were so swollen from walking so far that I couldn't wear my shoes. So one of the women that had youngsters in school sent me some bedroom slippers. So I used them, but then by the time the weekend came I could wear my shoes [again]. One of the men went down and got my car for me.

You stayed up there for the week?

Through the week. I always did stay up there through the week.

How did your husband feel about that, and your kids?

Well, he wasn't working, and he was glad that I was. Times were hard, you see, at that time [sometime in the 1940s]; he was doing carpenter work, and there just wasn't any.

What do you think are the advantages or disadvantages of the rural school?

Well, I think the youngsters really learn more in the rural school that must help them in later life: you know, be self-reliant and do things on their own. Here [in Meeker] they just depend on somebody else to do everything for them. And then a lot of times, those bigger ones, they'd have to help the little ones, and that was good for them too.

I had a girl one time—she couldn't read. She simply couldn't read. Well, here [in Meeker] she'd be in the reading class, and that would be it. There [in the rural school] she would read four or five or six times a day.

So they really did learn then—really got it?

You really got it. If you didn't, why, it was your own fault! Say that somebody had trouble with math. If they couldn't learn their times tables—boy! I made them learn their times tables! And if somebody didn't have anything to do, why, you'd go over there and spend some time with Johnny on his times tables.

Beryl Vancleave Richards

A number of public-spirited women joined the national Woman's Club. They were civic-minded women, so decided to start a public library in Meeker [ca. 1925]. One-half of the old log building formerly used as the officer's quarters during the Meeker Massacre was rented. There was very little money for this project. Books were donated, especially by families who were moving away. The books were placed on the shelves in a helter-skelter manner, and it became a "seek and ye shall find" situation. It was decided that all the books should be cataloged according to the Dewey decimal system.

As the books were cataloged, the cards were placed in a large cabinet so that each book could be easily found. It was really a work for two people: one could check out the books to the public, and the other could repair the books.

A grass rug was laid over the old floor in the living room, and several chairs were donated. The women of the Woman's Club raised the money for the rent and our salary. The room was heated in winter with a large coal-burning stove, which we had to keep going, banking the fire at night. The coal had to be carried inside from an outside coal house.

As the library grew, the town placed a small mill levy to the taxes, and new books could be purchased.

I kept the library for 12 or more years, until I was married, in 1935, and we moved to Glenwood Springs, where I was asked to catalog the books there.

Iris Self Lyons

What year did you go to nurse's training?

We went out in 1927, December, and classes started in 1928. It was a baccalaureate, and we had 1928, 1929, and 1930.

That's all they required for a baccalaureate. They knew that we were going to come home, so they let Annie and I take state boards before we finished up our required duty on the floors. So really, I was a registered nurse before I was a graduate. There isn't any such thing as a graduate nurse anymore: you're either registered or you're not.

At that time, the first year, the city and county of Denver paid us $10 a month to take our training, and the next year they paid us $15, and then the senior year we were paid $20. I wish they'd revert back to that. They graduated nurses that knew bedside care. Not administrators.

I remember very distinctly over here [in Craig], it was at night and the aide was up on OB somewhere. Some bell rang, and I went up there, and [the patient] wanted a bedpan. I gave it to her, and [she said,] "You—a registered nurse—give me a bedpan?" I said, "Why, sure. I know how." She said, "Well, in Denver they'd walk a block before they'd give you a bedpan."

Where did you meet your husband?

His dad and mother had a homestead out here in Breeze Basin, and we lived about 19 miles on south. [My husband] went to school in Hayden. But my brothers used to work for the Lyonses in Breeze Basin, and he'd come over once in a while. His dad was anxious for him to get married, and he said, "Why don't you go over there and look at some of those good-looking Self girls?" And [when I heard about that] I said, "Well, as far as I was concerned, it wouldn't have done you any good, because I knew what I was going to do." [Laughter.]

What did he do—wait around for you to get through?

Well, he went out and took a course in aviation in Missouri, and he is a qualified pilot. But when we got married, that took care of that.

We lived in town in the winter, and then my brother-in-law's folks moved off the ranch [and so] we moved out in Breeze Basin.

You were 25 when you got married. [Iris's husband was 30.] Did you want to practice the nursing you'd spent so much time on?

Whenever they called me, I went up [to the hospital in Hayden]. But it was usually people that were terminal, and they didn't get well anyway.

Did you think that if you married a farmer, you'd somehow have a chance to practice your nursing?

I didn't think anything 'bout it particularly. But when Jean [my daughter] was about three months old, there was an ad put in the paper—[it] said [they were] going to close [the] hospital [in Hayden] if [they] don't get help. And there were five people called me up and wanted to know if they could come to the ranch and have their babies. No water in the house, this and that, and I didn't work like that. I said, "Wayne, I can't do that." Because I had had one person out there [in Breeze Basin, I] knew it was a tragedy. 'Course it would have been anywhere, but I said, "I'm going up and get a job."

Well, that was one time he was angry. He wouldn't go with me. He sat down and he turned white and he was afraid to bawl me out, I guess. So I took Jean up there and got the job. Arleen and Sylvia [my older daughters] took care of her [at home]. 'Course, Wayne was always within calling distance, so I just left the children and went on to work.

One time when Mt. Harris [a coal-mining town eight miles east of Hayden] was going full, so many of them up there had thyroid conditions. They had some doctors come in from Denver, and they'd do the thyroidectomies. Of course, they needed special nurses, so I went up there and stayed day and night. My sister came over, and I told her that they wanted me to come; if she would come and take care of the kids, I'd give her half of what I made. So she came along, and she said, "You sure are nuts. I'd have come over just to play with the children and you wouldn't have had to pay me nothing."

[One summer] they couldn't get a doctor in Hayden [at the hospital], but they paid me to go up there and stay, without any patients, all summer long. So I'd take my knitting and my sewing and go merrily on my way. Then we had one doctor come in, but he didn't pan out too well, so they finally had to close it up. Then about that time [the hospital in Craig] had opened up, so I came down here [in 1950].

Wilma Crawford Smith

Wilma Crawford Smith was raised on a homestead near Meeker. She finished high school in 1918 and spent two years in college at the University of Colorado. She then returned home and married. Her husband was killed in an accident early in their marriage, and Wilma then worked until retirement to support herself.

How many children did you have?

One. And she was just two years old when her daddy died. He was hurt in an accident in the lumberyard—an accident with the machinery.

So after that happened, did you have to make a living? What did you do?

Oh, yes, I've made a living all my life. Anything that comes up. I did all kinds of work—housecleaning, baby-sitting; I went on to one thing and another. I did everything but tend bar and work in a café. I worked for the Side's Rexall Drug Store for 12 years, and I worked at [the] Meeker Laundry. I helped in the garage.

Did you have any problems with child care?

No. I could always leave her with my mother. No, I never had to have a baby-sitter. I lived with my mother, and Mother lived with me . . . one way or the other.

CeCelia Sullivan Knott

After graduating from high school in Hayden, CeCelia married and soon moved to Craig. She began working to supply extra money for her family. Eventually her marriage ended, and she became the sole source of family income.

Did you work because you liked doing it, as many women do now, or did you do it because you—

I did it for necessity: because we needed the money. Oh, I think we'd have had a roof over our head, and we'd have clothing and food and so forth, but there's always you want that little bit more. I know that [when] I started, it was just kind of I wanted the money for this and that. But when [my daughter] was three and, of course, World War II was on, it was to have that extra bit of money, so Alice could have dancing lessons and she could have piano lessons. There was no money for those things.

I'd like you to tell me a little bit about some of the things you did over these years and for how long you did them.

Well, my first working [was] as a clerk, or, as they called it then, a pharmacist assistant, with Cowen's drugstore. I was there for nearly 10 years. Actually you can't put up prescriptions, but you can sell any medication. Now if you are truly a clerk, at that time you were not to sell any medications at all; you could sell cosmetics and work fountain and so on. As a pharmacist's assistant I was able to do any of that, except for putting up the prescriptions. The pharmacist—mainly it was men then, but there were a few women pharmacists. They would actually put up the prescriptions, but then I could sell it to the person when they came in. So it was really just a clerk job, but you had to go through the state so you would be legal.

I worked for a period for the telephone company when they went to dial in Craig—at the time when we used to call the operator, [who would] say, "Number please?"

Then I [went] to work at the Palace Drug, and I was there almost 10 years. Same sort of thing. From the Palace Drug I went to work for a dentist; I worked as a chairside assistant there. Since that time, I've worked at East School as a teacher's assistant, and I've just finished my thirteenth year there.

Now you told me something that you did in addition to all those jobs, after you did those jobs—

All these years I've moonlighted, as the saying goes.

In the evening, or the early morning?

Whichever is handiest for you. Basically, evening.

I don't think if I worked all day long that I could do that.

You get in a rut when you don't do anything else. It's just like [when] the farmer has to milk the cows every evening—you go do your cleaning then. I have done other places, besides the library, but basically the public library, [for] 25 years.

Since you did have a career and you did work outside, how did you manage all those home responsibilities too?

Well, you just sort of took it out of yourself, really. You worked it in as you could, and you went just a little later in the evening or a little earlier in the morning, or both, than you would otherwise. The weekend—I always said after the weekend I was glad to go back to work to get rested.

EIGHT

Looking Back

The unspoiled beauty and sparse population of northwestern Colorado are very important to many of these women. They feel at home in the sagebrush- and pinion-covered hills, which are uninhabited except for an occasional ranch or small town. The nature of the area is reflected in the independent, self-reliant character of these women.

Lena Ely Stoddard

I loved it out here—when I first saw it, going up into the mountains and, I guess, homesteading like we did: seeing all the beauty of it. It just gets to you. You just love it.

Every summer, when my parents were living, we'd go back [to Illinois] and we could hardly wait until we could get back here—the cool nights and the beauty of the foliage and everything.

Ellen Dalrymple Dunn

What do you think is a unique advantage or disadvantage to living in northwestern Colorado?

Well, I liked it because I've always liked the mountains. I liked to hike, and I liked to fish, and I really enjoyed it. I've never cared for cities, and I don't even like Grand Junction, as far as the city is concerned, because I miss the outdoor life. Now here in Grand Junction I have to go quite a distance to fish and hunt. When we were in Meeker we could just walk down to the river and go fishing, or when we were in Rangely we could just walk down just out there a little ways and kill a deer in deer season and an antelope in antelope season. Just walk out the door there and get a sage chicken [in season]. We really loved it—my husband and I both did. Especially [for] people with children, it was very nice, because it was outdoors. [They had] small schools, and it was really good for them— they had lots of running-around [room]. You had more freedom because there wasn't any such thing as a fence or a yard. The clean, fresh air was good for all of us. We had a lot of good food, homegrown food—it isn't like shipped-in food that we're getting nowadays—and I think that's the reason we were all so healthy. I never was sick—never had a doctor for 18 years. They had a lot of advantages. Like there in Meeker, that lovely library and everything. We had everything that they had in the city.

Esther Anderson Campbell

And you say the advantages and disadvantages of living that far away out of town—I don't feel it was a disadvantage. I don't like to live near town. I think we were better off when we didn't go to town more than once a month or once in a winter. We bought our supplies in big amounts, and we were satisfied with what we had. We used the venison, killed our meat, and had chickens and eggs and milk and so on; we didn't have to go to town, only for staples. We bought enough in the fall to do us through the winter, for most things, and if we ran out of corn-starch, we used flour, I guess, and if we ran out of sugar, we used honey or syrup. So, we didn't have to have certain things. We could get along— we substituted quite often. And I like that kind of life much better than here, where you go to town every day, get one or two items.

So I think in that way it's an advantage. 'Course, there were disadvantages. If you had to go to town and the weather was bad or the roads were bad, it was kind of hard to get there sometimes.

Norine Holland

The first time I traveled from northwestern Colorado, I was 14 years of age and I saw my first train [in Rifle].

After I saw my first train, I knew I wanted to travel, and I've traveled quite a bit, you know, into all the other towns and everyplace in Colorado. I've been to Hawaii and to Alaska and through most of the United States. But I still think that northwestern Colorado is the most unique place. I think it is to this day the most uncommercialized area in the whole United States. When they felt they were going to have an oil boom, I did *not* want it to come. That was very selfish. I wanted it to come to give people jobs, but I did *not* want it to come and spoil our beautiful northwestern Colorado.

Mary Wear Villa

In the late 1800s Mary Wear Villa's grandparents homesteaded in Axial Basin, between Craig and Meeker. Mary grew up in Meeker in a musical family, and she and her brothers and sister played for many of the community dances. She eventually became a music teacher and has taught in Meeker for 30 years.

When you saw other places, and particularly larger towns and a different style of living, did you view this area differently at all?

Oh, I think [a person is] bound to. We went to Grand Junction in the spring for a school [band] trip. When I went to Utah, it was a school trip. And when we would go down [to Grand Junction] and see the roses blooming and then come back to all this snow and mess we had here, it sort of made one want to get out of here. There were bigger and better things someplace else.

As your life went on, I know you did get out, all over the world, but your home for the most part has been here. Are there some things about it that you think are unique?

Oh, I think home is always home. It smells right; it feels right. And we don't have the extremes in weather. We sort of think we have long winters and all this, but we don't have horrendous storms here, windstorms and things of that nature. It's a comfortable place to be: I like to know people. It's nice being away from people at times—even though it's fun to go to cities, it's nice to come back where it's quiet.

Regret or disappointment about their lives is not something these women think about often. When asked about satisfactions, accomplishments, and disappointments, they reveal a pride in taming the land, managing a family, and contributing to the community.

Those women who were married and had children most often mention the family as the biggest source of satisfaction and consider that their devotion to the family was time well spent. Contributions to community projects were also an important source of satisfaction.

Those women who worked in the schools, in city government, or in private business for many years felt a great sense of accomplishment. In most cases the income was important for the family; however, some women worked at jobs they enjoyed simply because they wanted to. Although social attitudes during this time implied that women should stop working outside the home after marriage, that notion didn't seem to affect these working women in any significant way. Their independent spirit may be responsible for that.

Lack of further education was often mentioned as a disappointment, whether for the sake of interest or that of career. A high school or college education is something some of them felt they had missed, usually for lack of opportunity. In general, however, most were satisfied with the direction of their lives.

Jayne White Hoth

What are the things in your life from which you've derived the most satisfaction?

Well, just having three good children. I think that's one of the main things that you're always happy with, if your children turn out well, and mine have.

I have a very close relationship with all my brothers and sisters. As a matter of fact, we have a family get-together almost *every* summer. We had one in Rifle last year, at my oldest brother's place, and 81 of us were there. I have 5 brothers and 5 sisters, and all of us are still living. All of us have been married, and only 2 did not have children of their own. A couple of us are great-grandparents now.

I've enjoyed living in this community. I think Maybell is very unique; it's a place where people really care about other people yet.

Margaret Tagert Jones

Can you think of one or two things that you are most proud of about your life, things you have done or accomplished?

I guess I have a little trouble with that word *proud*. For me it infers society's opinion, you see, and I'm not sure that if my life were looked upon by society there might be things of that kind—certainly nothing that outstanding. But I would rather use the [phrase] *satisfaction and a sense of well-being*. I've gotten that from reading, from having new worlds opened up through travel; my husband and I have been very fortunate in being able to travel to many places in the world. And then [there's] the satisfaction I have had from my family, particularly my two daughters, whom I wanted more than anything, and more than boys! I'd had four brothers—I wanted girls. I was fortunate to get those, and it's been a joy to me to watch their progress, and to continue to watch it as they mature into middle age at this point.

You were a homemaker all your life and did not have a career. Do you have any thoughts on what you were able to do in that role that you wouldn't have been able to do had you always had a job?

Yes, I do, because in that role I was able to do lots of volunteer work in the community, which I think benefited the community. And it certainly did me—it's helped me to learn about human nature. I was able always to be the homeroom mother for my children in school. I made *dozens* of cookies. I was leader of the Camp Fire group we had. I sponsored groups of young people to our church summer camp for a week.

I served on our school board and dealt with rural people who had the problem of getting their children to school.

Audrey Ruckman Oldland

Were there things that you wished you had the opportunity to do in your life but, for whatever reason, didn't do?

I wished I could have gone on and gotten more education at some time in my life: along a special line, or something like that.

Do you think you would have had time to practice whatever it is you might have learned?

Oh, probably. I have a little poem that I cut out one time that I thought fit, and that goes something like what I wanted to do at one time was to learn—"I wanted to write a book. / But what I did was learn to cook. / But when I see boys' hungry eyes, / I'm glad I make good apple pies." That's kind of the way it's been, you know, because I always thought it would be fun to be able to put into words and onto paper all of these things that go through my mind. Like when I was young and out, I felt I could fly. I felt if I just—if I could *just* get a little more speed, I could raise up off the ground and fly. And I thought, "If I could write a book, I might be able to lift somebody to that elevation where they could feel like they could fly." And I was so happy when I just felt like I was just leaving the ground almost. I did fly, you know—I did take flying lessons. Well, after we were married, when Frank was little, they were giving flying lessons. I took flying lessons until I soloed. I had about four hours' solo time flying, which I very, very much enjoyed. Oh, I felt free as a bird, and I thought it might be just about as close to heaven as I was ever going to get!

Ethelyn Whalin Crawford

Have there been any major disappointments in your life?

Major disappointments? That's . . . you know, when you're going through something that's difficult, it's a major tragedy, of course. And then, after you have looked back on it, perhaps it isn't. I would have liked to [have] gone on to school like Mom would have, but I finished in the midst of the Depression and there wasn't any money. Then I got married, and I started raising my family and working. When you work on a ranch, you usually *work,* and by the time I had gotten my family to where I might have gone back to school, I wasn't in any position to go to school at all. I mean, I wasn't where I could have gone on. [Since then] I have taken special courses in colleges and universities, [courses] that I was particularly interested in, and have enjoyed them immensely.

Were there any very sad times in your life you would be willing to discuss?

Oh, there's been some sad ones, of course. You don't go through life and get to be almost 71 years old and not have some sad moments in your life. But, you know, I don't ever dwell on it at all. I think every moment in itself is precious, and if I live it the very best I can at that moment I will be the richer. If something has happened that I haven't taken advantage of, or if I have gone astray in some way—which I have, of course, and made mistakes and all that, well, sure I have. But it's added up to what I am now, and to tell you the honest truth about myself as now, I'm not unhappy with what I am. Part of it came out of this country, you know, this very country that I grew up in. It contributed to that because I worked hard as a young person—I worked very hard. But I can't ever recall being bored. I am rich, Julie. I am richer than words can tell, and it has nothing to do with possessions.

CeCelia Sullivan Knott

As you look back on your life, what are the things from which you derived the most satisfaction, that you're most pleased about?

I guess financial security. Now that sounds silly. I think that's been the driving force, having financial security. I will ask no one for anything. If I can't do it, it won't be done.

Are there any things that you wish you had had the opportunity to do but just didn't, for one reason or another?

I didn't further my education. Pursue my dream.

Was there ever a time through those years—I don't think there was, because you were too busy working—where you could have taken—

No, there really hasn't been. It's only been in the last few years that we have had these extension courses. And I guess there's been a long time I could have got up and made the change—moved away to where educational opportunities [were]. [But I didn't think of that] up until the time I had worked as a teacher's aide, and felt that it's awful when you spend a lifetime working and yet you've got this near the end of the road before you find something you totally love—absolutely love.

Ruby Rector Kirby

I think my big satisfaction comes from hard work, putting together, I'd say, a pretty good-size cattle-ranching production outfit. We worked awfully hard, and if it hadn't been for this dear friend of ours, this president of the Bank of Vernal, we'd never have made it. See, at one time, we sold the whole outfit on West Douglas Creek. Then one of the brothers that had it died very suddenly and the other brother didn't want it, so we bought it back. We went to this president of the bank and told him we needed $105,000 down payment. And that fellow looked at us and said, "The bank can't loan you that kind of money," but, he said, "I can." And he wrote us a check for that and took no note or anything. Now that's having confidence in people.

What is it about this country that you like?

Well, I think that song "The Hills of Home" hits it: "the broken skyline."

Now at one time Albert owned some acreage over south of Bennett, which is about, oh, 100 miles east of Denver out in that flatland country. He was having health problems, and he thought maybe we'd have to sell out and go someplace where he didn't have to ride horseback so much. But I told him no way could he make a prairie chicken out of a hillbilly. That's the way I expressed it. It's beautiful, but I said, "You can see three weeks ahead out in that country, and it just doesn't appeal to me."

I had one lady one time—a young girl came to the ranch, and she looked around, and she said, "You couldn't hire me to live up here." I looked at her kind of surprised, and I said, "What's the matter with it?" She said, "I can't see another house." See, we had no neighbors up there except this one boy that's over in the next canyon. There's about 800 acres in there, and we surround him—we've got 10,000 acres up in that summer country on West Douglas and West Creek. And that's what I like about it—not being able to see another house.

214

Leona "Babe" Hinricks. Rangely, about 1920
Courtesy of Leona Hinricks

Ila Bowman Powell

I feel sorry for the kids nowadays because they don't have any conception of how to go ahead and do for themselves, to make do with other things, you know.

I get cross with them a little bit sometimes and tell them, "You have to save—you have to do these things. I'm not telling you kids this to be hateful or bossy, but I want you to learn to do things while I'm still here to teach you." Those kids—the first day they'd built a fence was yesterday. [My grandson] turned 16 on the nineteenth, and he never built a fence. They lived in a trailer downtown [in Rangely], and he's been all over the country—to Phoenix and to Denver and to Nebraska, you name it; he's been everywhere like that. But he's never helped build fence or do anything. So I was giving him and Aaron [another grandson] a deal about building a fence yesterday. They thought it was pretty neat, that Grandma would sit down there and show them how to twist the wires together, fix loops—I put in new gateposts and everything—and they couldn't believe that it would be as interesting to do something like that.

How do you dig the holes for this?

We did that with a shovel. They said, "You got a posthole digger?" I says, "That's a buncha hooey." You know, they got some kind of things that go down like this [gestures], and they got kind of blades, and you twist them around with a stick at the top, and then you lift them up, which is harder than everything. [Then you] dig the dirt out. But I just take a shovel and dig it out. We had to do that a couple of times yesterday: set two posts, and the rest of them were—the wires were just mashed down.

And my daughter down below here wants to put some cattle on my field, so we had to go build a fence—there was nobody else to do it.

Since you have spent some time in Tacoma, Washington, did your impressions and your feelings about this particular country change?

No, I just wanted to get back. You know, I was just like an old horse: where something is raised like that, you want to get back. There was too many people out there for me, to begin with. You'd go up to people next door—I had a next-door neighbor once, and I went [to her] and said, "Hi, it sure is nice this morning." She went in the house, and you could hear the door lock. Really hurt my feelings. But people [are] like that, a

216

lot of them—they don't want to be involved with you. I had in-laws, and I met a few nice people that were my friends and all, but some of them—the general feeling of people like that [is] they just minded their own business and they wanted you to stay away and mind yours. They weren't friendly and nice.

How did you manage with all those [10] children?

Well, I'll tell you. The people say, "Oh, I've got one kid. I couldn't have two—I couldn't watch them; I can't take care of the one." Well, if you've got two or you've got three, they amuse themselves more and everything. You just go along with them, and you're with them all the time. I don't believe in mothers being away from their kids. I never worked a day away from my kids. If I was in the garden, or wherever I was at, my kids were with me.

Your kids are the only thing you'll ever have that's your own. Maybe some woman can come along and take your husband, or somebody can steal your car and your money out of the bank or something. But I say nobody can take your kids away from you. In fact, they're so ornery nobody would want them, so there you are! [Laughter.] That's all you ever have that's really your own.

Leona Kaloris Papoulas

Those were the happy years, my dear. When I was living out there in the flats, up there in Sage Creek, we used to play horseshoes. We had time to play cards. We didn't have the responsibilities of today. You were happy; you had the time with each other then. We would all pile in, and we would go to the [sheep] camps. John had a Studebaker—it was a vanlike deal. And we would go with the animals—not all over, because we didn't have the roads then. We had the mules that they would pack and go. Then we'd go to Hayden. The highlights of my children were—we'd come down there, and on the corner of the main street of Hayden, John Pleasant had a service station. [Mr. Pleasant would give] my Angie, my oldest one, and Jimmy a nickel, and they would go across the street to the drugstore and have an ice-cream cone. That was the highlight of the week; they loved that. Now a 5¢ ice-cream cone to a child—but they loved it, and he was such a wonderful man.

217

There was so much togetherness in our early years. Not [just] for me but for everyone, I think.

Oma Jensen Graham

I've worked hard, but I learned a long time ago that you might just as well enjoy your work because you're going to work all your life and you'll get more out of it if you enjoy it.

I think if these young kids today, instead of waiting for sundown and payday, [would] put a little more into it, they'd get a little more out of it.

If you had to compare what life was like in the twenties and thirties with how ranch people live today, what would you say is the big difference?

Well, the thing of it was, in the old days their word was as good as their note. And they were honest. You didn't have to lock your house. Everybody was free to come. If they were hungry, they came in, cooked, washed up the dishes, filled the wood box, and that was it.

You never locked a house. Now their word isn't any good; you have to lock up everything. Neighbors depended on each other in those days. You helped each other—you traded work is what you did. When they went to brand, why, everybody went and helped out. The women took food and the men, they all got together and you traded work, even on the ranch.

What are the things in your life from which you've derived the most satisfaction?

Everything! I've enjoyed living. I've enjoyed working. And my friends—I enjoy people. And I love to tell jokes, I'm telling you. I think that laughter is the best therapeutic medicine that you can use.

Do you have anything you would call a disappointment?

I think everybody has disappointments, but I've found one thing out: as you go through life, leave the bad stuff behind and take the good with you, because if you pull all of it, you get to where you can't take one step forward. Forget all the bad times—everybody's had bad times—and pull the fun times along with you, and you can always take a step into tomorrow.

Doris Stephenson Warren

I think my grandmother had a big influence on my life, really. She was very colorful. She had such a difficult [time]—moving that far from [her] own people, you know, from Indiana to Colorado, and never being able to communicate [with them]. I think she went back maybe twice in her lifetime. These pioneer women had an awful lot of endurance and courage.

Near Glenwood Springs
Photography by Cinda Roth

Afterword

A New Historical Territory

Elizabeth Jameson

The popular image of the American West was once so overwhelmingly masculine that one historian called the region "Hisland"—a demographic anomaly populated entirely by cowboys, soldiers, miners, trappers and other white men.[1] Addressing the distortions of history and myth meant seeing people who had been excluded from the story— American Indians, Hispanos, persons of many European, Asian, and African heritages, women as well as men. As women entered the historical picture, the focus shifted from "rugged individuals" to families, from tents and campfires to communities and regional networks, from the romance of masculine adventure to the daily tasks of home building and homemaking, childcare and crops—the thousand daily activities that create and transform human society.

Histories of western women have altered our understandings of both women and the West. Common stereotypes, rooted in the role prescriptions of relatively privileged eastern women, reduced female pioneers to passive genteel civilizers, oppressed helpmates, and "bad women." We are gradually replacing these one-dimensional images with more accurate depictions of richly faceted and complex women who helped establish farms, families, and communities, sometimes with understandable qualms, sometimes with zest and optimism, sometimes with matter-of-fact competence, often in isolated and difficult circumstances.[2] The women's voices in this volume help us hear more accurately how the West was built.

Elizabeth Jameson is Associate Professor of History at the University of New Mexico.

An inclusive history is less a simple narrative of adventure and conquest and more a complex story of contested access to land and resources, of transplanting and transforming social relationships. It questions something as seemingly simple as what we call the region, since what was West for Euro-American pioneers was East for Asians, El Norte or northwestern Mexico for Spaniards and Mexicans, and a progressively threatened homeland for American Indians.[3] Adding women to the historical narrative meant more than adding stories of women's achievements in "masculine" arenas. It took us into new historical territory, to explore how gender roles were structured, how they varied from group to group and region to region, how they changed in a variety of new physical and social environments. Through women we began to see men in the contexts of homes and families, just as we began to see women as workers, community-builders, and social activists.

As historians started to search for western women, we inevitably faced the question of sources. What records would document the experiences of women of many ethnic backgrounds and economic circumstances? Some letters and diaries were saved in archives or in family attics. Some government documents, state and federal censuses, property records, and court proceedings helped describe the lives of so-called "ordinary" women. And oral histories allowed us to record the memories of persons who lived the history they helped to make.[4]

As personal accounts of "ordinary" lives, oral histories can be enormously compelling. As entries into our common pasts they demand care and caution. Interviews are interactions. Both participants affect the record; neither goes away unchanged. Interviewers bring their own cultural baggage, values, and experiences to the encounter. They ask questions. Their personalities and their preoccupations affect the exchange. The stories people tell are filtered through years and memory, filtered differently by different people and on different days. Some emphasize happy and triumphant stories, some focus on loss and hardship. What they share is affected by the audience they perceive. And most people have some accounts that are so personally significant that they have particular resonance from frequent repetition.

Besides issues of selectivity, memory, and audience, there is the additional question of sampling, of assessing what is individual in the histories, what speaks to a collective past, and what memories document changes in women's roles and relationships. We are limited by who we can locate, by who will speak with us, by who has survived to speak for others. Because oral histories narrate the experience of living people, they raise with particular immediacy questions that apply to all historical records. All documents are produced by particular people at particular moments for particular audiences. All records are partial. And for all the careful interpretation they demand, oral histories also allow us to preserve experiences that might otherwise be lost. They represent an enormous historical debt, and an obligation to interpret with care.

The women whose stories appear in this volume speak sometimes in individual voices and sometimes in chorus. Their narratives are direct, immediate, and familiar, and therefore carry particular authority. Listening carefully, we can appreciate their richness and their variety, and begin to discern common themes and changing concerns.

Historical interpretation, like the interviews themselves, is an interactive process. It locates the narratives in historical frameworks, while allowing new evidence, new voices, to alter inherited interpretations. The stories in this volume are dialogues that operate on many levels. They were, most directly and immediately, conversations with Julie Jones-Eddy, a descendant of the region who shared with the narrators a personal knowledge of the arid Colorado high country. The histories she recorded enable dialogues with a wider audience, and with the way we see the past.

The women of northwest Colorado helped make their history as well as record it. Their lives reveal a variety of experiences, preferences, and choices, all of which were partially shaped by time, place, gender, and life-cycle. They allow us to see through women's eyes a particular chapter of western settlement, settlement that was encouraged at least partly by the promise of cheap land. After 1871, when Congress established the reservation system, what had previously been Native American territory was progressively offered as "public domain" to Euro-American settlers through a variety of federal programs. The restriction of the Ute Indians to a Utah reservation in the 1880s was part of this larger movement. As they returned to the area to hunt through the early 1900s, they engaged in often peaceful exchanges with the new settlers. Chronicled in this volume, for instance, by Nellie Warren Parks, Ruby Rector Kirby, and Oma Jensen Graham, are accounts which suggest that daily encounters were often less threatening for the newcomers than they expected. Certainly they were not as threatening as the less chronicled but more wrenching consequences of white settlement for native peoples.[5] Peaceful exchanges of food and assistance partially masked the larger power relations that insured settlers' access to their new homes.

The federal government offered land through a number of laws that varied in their exact provisions, but which generally allowed heads of families to claim 160 acres (more in some arid areas), and to achieve ownership by paying a small fee per acre, building a home, clearing part of the land, and occupying it for a specified period (usually five years). Although earlier acts made no provisions for women to own land, the new Homestead Act of 1862 allowed women as well as men to file homesteads, provided they were unmarried or heads of households, at least twenty-one years of age, and citizens or immigrants who had filed for citizenship. Between 1868 and 1955, almost 250 million acres were distributed to private individuals under this act. Many Euro-American women moved onto the land and, in impressive numbers, succeeded in proving up their claims. One study based on land office records in Lamar, Colorado, and Douglas, Wyoming, for the years 1887, 1891, 1907, and 1908 found that 11.9 percent of new homestead claims were filed by women. Proportionately more women than men "proved up" and received title to their land—42.4 percent of women who filed homestead claims compared with 37 percent of the men. The Homestead Act thus gave Euro-American women an important independent stake in the land. Still, as the "homesteading women" in these pages attest, there were other avenues to land ownership, including preemption and purchase, and more women settled as wives and daughters in family enterprises than as independent landowners. The majority of all homesteaders, in fact, failed. Either they never intended to stay, and filed claims for temporary residences or for investments, or they could not wrest a living from the land and left.[6]

The "homesteading women" in these pages represent the persisters, and we see them only as their lives connected with the region. Their experiences before they arrived in northwest Colorado are sketched only briefly, and we do not hear from those who left. These narratives represent the women who stayed or who returned, and, at least demographically, they may be a fairly good sample. The chroniclers of *Homesteading Women* are fairly typical of their neighbors with regard to ethnic origins. The local population was, from 1880 on, overwhelmingly white and native born. Although one person in four was an immigrant in 1880, that proportion declined over time, to about 15 percent in 1890, 10 percent in 1900, 5 percent in 1920, and 2–3 percent by 1950. Thus, by race and birthplace, Jones-Eddy's respondents are fairly typical of the population as a whole. They are representative, too, in their family ties. Like most women in areas where men predominated, all but two were married (over 95 percent). Like increasing numbers of Americans, four divorced (9 percent); all but one remarried. They tell their lives in relationships, and their relationships to the land appear mediated by family roles, by their perceptions of the options available to daughters, sisters, wives, and widows in a relatively small, dispersed, and masculine population. In 1880, only four years after statehood, the few citizens of Routt County, from which Moffat County was later created, included only about one woman for every nine men. Women increased in numbers and in proportion to the population as settlement proceeded. In 1890 the populations of Routt and Rio Blanco counties were approximately 36 percent female, and for the next twenty years there were some three men for every two women. By 1920, Moffat and Rio Blanco counties were about 55 percent male, and men continued to outnumber women through 1950. They predominated in slightly greater proportions among adults, so that there were fewer women of marriageable age than suggested by overall population figures that included children. That reality helps explain why single men so quickly turned their attention to schoolteachers, nurses, and other newly arrived women, and why so many of the women married.[7]

The numbers of women relative to men were even more skewed in the rural areas, and in the smaller towns of the isolated farm and ranch country. Moffat County was 44 percent female in 1930, Rio Blanco County 43.5 percent. In the larger towns, such as Craig, Meeker, and Rifle, the residents were almost equally divided by sex, while in the smaller towns of Maybell, Price Creek, and Rangely the female population was 40 percent or slightly less. Similarly, as late as 1950, Craig, Rifle, and Meeker had proportionately more women than the rural areas, although the overall proportion of women to men had almost equalized. These differences were reflected in the relatively greater proportions of women than men who were married—75.5 percent of all women age fourteen and over in Moffat County in 1950, and 77 percent in Rio Blanco, compared with 67 percent and 69 percent, respectively, of the men. While one man in four was single, only about one woman in ten was unmarried, and proportionately more women were also widowed or divorced. The different representation of women in the towns and the rural areas also indicates how tightly rural women's options were tied to various family agricultural enterprises. Women who needed to earn money had to work in the small towns where the few "women's" jobs existed. While most male wage earners worked in agriculture, mining, or construction, most employed women worked in service occupations— in restaurants and bars, hotels and lodging houses, other retail establishments or private homes; in telecommunications, public administration, education, or other government work.[8] In their paid employment, as in their family roles, the women in this volume appear typical of their time and place.

But statistics are only rough approximations, scaffolding that requires further elaboration to reveal human experience and historical meaning. They represent only what we can *count* about a local population. They can assure us that people whose lives are recorded in these interviews are not wildly atypical of all settlers, and help us find larger patterns for the varieties of womanhood that are recorded in these pages. But the census figures mask patterns that occurred over women's lifetimes, and that are more clearly revealed in their oral testimony.

Two factors that emerge as important boundaries for women are their places in the regional economy and their places in their individual life-cycles. The decennial censuses, like the 1950 figures, can tell us that only one woman in four was employed that year in Moffat County, and one in five in Rio Blanco, while 85 percent of all men were in the paid work force; and they reveal the jobs available for both.[9] But they mask the in-and-out patterns of work and movement that the women themselves reveal—the need to move to town to educate children, or to earn a living (almost half the women interviewed worked for wages at some time in their adult lives). The organizing themes that Jones-Eddy chooses underscore the differences in rural and small-town options, and the unfolding experiences of childhood, adolescence, young womanhood, marriage, and old age. Rather than spinning a saga of women homesteaders, she reveals the varieties of womanhood in a region where life options were structured by the economies of farming, ranching, mining, and oil.

The patterns of human maturation and generational change occurred in tandem with regional development, and began with the contrasting reactions of mothers and daughters as they encountered the new land. Women's childhood memories of the journey focus on play and adventure. With adult hindsight, they recognize that child's play was often women's work, that coming into the new country meant cleaning, cooking, and washing in often primitive circumstances. Women seem to remember their own childhood journeys with amusement and warmth, but, perhaps with adult identification, they recount that their mothers were more apprehensive, their adjustments more difficult. It is certainly understandable that children appreciated the virtues of playing in mud considerably more than their mothers, who had to get the grime out; that tent life held greater romance for youngsters than for adults; that high-altitude baking was a challenge and isolation not always welcome. But these distinctions may also suggest ways that people sort out the meanings of memory, assigning hardship to others and claiming the joys. Whether literally true or selectively filtered, these memories document changing responses to settling, adjusting, and establishing roots in a new environment.

One pattern that emerges involves the process of settlement itself, how it was that people happened to choose to establish themselves in what might seem for some an unlikely destination. Although we may envision pioneer families journeying west, rather than isolated men, these narratives suggest even wider ties. It is striking how many families came to northwest Colorado because family or friends were already there; that women first came to the area to visit their sisters; that many brought farming, ranching, or coal-mining skills with them to an area where they might be practiced. "Home ties," whether literal, ethnic, or adoptive, suggest networks of serial migration and mutual aid that helped knit local and regional communities.

For the first women homesteaders, community seems to have waited until after the first intense years of clearing the land, building a home, and establishing livestock and gardens, frequently while bearing and caring for young children. While we cannot fully imagine their lives, we may empathize with hinted meanings in stories shared of childbearing, like June O'Connell Sweeney's story of her mother-in-law's being revived with whiskey and "thawed out" in the last stages of her pregnancy, or of the isolation of Jennie Brown Spence, who did not speak to another woman during hers. The implications of being, as June Sweeney put it, "a woman alone among all men" become more concrete as we begin to imagine motherhood in the new ranch country.

Childbearing aside, aspects of gender roles often blurred in the first years on the land. Women and children "helped" with arduous outdoor work, like clearing sagebrush and digging wells, while they continued to perform more traditional tasks. Whether the first home was a tent, a dugout, or a log house, the practical details of housekeeping were physically and emotionally demanding, as women dealt with cold, altitude, and isolation, hauled fuel and water, and "freeze-dried" laundry. "Housework" on farms and ranches involved not just caretaking, but processing and manufacturing. Women tended livestock, canned and preserved, made soap, lard, and clothing, and generated needed cash with their "butter-and-egg money."

Both rural isolation and the seasonal cycles of haying, branding, and roundup placed special demands on women to care for family, strangers, and work crews. Their descriptions of the enormous meals required to feed temporary help during haying and roundup remind us that the seasonal work cycle was domestic, too. Nurses, nurturers, and social planners, women had caretaking duties that reached beyond their immediate families to extended kin, and to the far-flung neighbors and strangers who became partially their responsibility. Hospitality, holiday planning, medical aid, and kin obligations—like Ila Bowman Powell's taking over her ailing mother-in-law's garden and housework—were all part of "women's work." Ranch hands, neighbors, and strangers all needed to be fed, cared for, and doctored by women who were more isolated and outnumbered than their sisters in the small supply towns. Presiding over birth, death, and all the major life events in between, women of the isolated slopes were the midwives of local life cycles.

Their burdens lightened as the land was cleared, flocks and herds were established, houses were built, and children became old enough to help. Then women could turn their attention to the details of "community building," teaching local schools, organizing dances and neighborhood socials, and holding religious services in their homes. Out of the networks that brought them there, the shared work of haying and roundup, the first social ties and shared family concerns, women banded together more formally to build schools, churches, libraries, and hospitals, to do volunteer work in 4-H and Camp Fire Girls, to staff the Sunday schools and other institutions they had created. Finally, after families and community institutions were established, they could focus on fun and self-fulfillment, lodges and literary societies, Home Extension, and politics.

This rough sketch of women's personal and social maturation fails nonetheless to reveal the fascinating variety of men's and women's roles that is a submerged theme in these pages. The desire to understand how gender roles are constructed, learned, and changed animates much of the new field of women's history. These are complicated topics that pose problems of sources and interpretation. There can be a considerable distance between what a culture prescribes as appropriate behavior for each sex and what people actually do, and the prescriptions of public media may reflect the values and aspirations of more privileged groups. Particularly as we expand our vision to include persons of different ethnic and religious backgrounds, races, classes, and regions, the varieties of activities appropriated by each sex require careful framing to suggest the changing boundaries of gender. We are coming to realize that behaviors and values considered appropriate for men and women are not rigid constructs, but relatively plastic ideologies that allow for considerable variety in daily practice. Thus, although most women in the late nineteenth century were expected to be "domestic," the precise meanings of "domesticity" could vary from woman to woman, class to class, culture to culture. Much that has been written about changing family roles has omitted rural areas and the West. This is true even for pre-industrial periods, and for predominantly rural areas. Some histories of western women have grappled with the significance of nineteenth-century role prescriptions for western farm and mining families, but it is a particular gift of *Homesteading Women* that we can glimpse varieties in the family roles and strategies of twentieth-century western ranchers.[10]

Even given the economic structures that emphasized marriage and that limited women's employment possibilities, there is considerable variety in the adult strategies the narrators describe. We can see in their childhoods some of the differences of circumstance and personality that grounded their varying routes through adulthood and maturity. Just as demographic particularities affected women's adult options, so for little girls the size of their family, their place in the birth order, whether they had brothers, and whether they lived in town or the country all helped shape the contours of childhood play and chores. Their memories suggest that women prepared during girlhood for their multiple tasks as farmers, ranchers, housewives, nurturers, and community leaders. Many of the oldest daughters and other girls who did outdoor chores clearly relished caring for animals, outdoor play, and outdoor work. They remember with obvious energy and fondness their childhood tasks of raising orphaned lambs and calves, planting potatoes and mowing hay. That enthusiasm is sometimes lacking in their lists of domestic work—washing and ironing, doing dishes, cooking and baking, and caring for younger siblings. Perhaps there was more recognition for outside work than for the household chores that were "naturally" theirs. Perhaps girls who preferred indoor work were more likely as adults to move to town or to leave the region than those who enjoyed outdoor labor. Certainly the domestic burden was most difficult and poignant for girls who, like Katherine Warren Rector, were required when very young to assume primary household roles—to be, as she put it, "a housewife forever and ever."

We cannot know from these accounts how children's work was divided in households with no daughters, whether sons in such families assumed domestic responsibilities just as ranch daughters worked both indoors and out. But the women's accounts of childhood responsibilities and play foreshadow their adult tasks with striking accuracy. Girls' play, like their work, combined domesticity with more athletic outdoor activities. As they played with dolls, built houses, cut out paper dolls, whittled, rode, climbed, skied, and fished, they were at home with the range of adult possibilities their region offered. Most of them did work considered appropriate for both women and men. Yet the domestic labor was considered natural, while there was a greater sense of "helping" and accomplishment when they crossed domestic boundaries. They performed in both arenas, but they did not own them equally. For some women, stretching the boundaries of girlhood extended their visions of personal possibility. For others, the blurred roles were at times confusing. Audrey Ruckman Oldland voiced both sides of the gender equation when she said, "It always seemed to me like I wasn't considered a boy and I wasn't considered a girl," but that she was "thankful that I had that rounded-out life that I had."

We cannot know from these accounts all that shaped childhood constructions of gender. Parents' role flexibility and satisfaction, and the divisions of tasks and recognition in individual households are among many factors to consider. The differing perceptions expressed even among this small group in a single area are intriguing, and suggest at least one avenue for further exploration.

The variety of tasks assigned to girls was clearly extended in adulthood, as many continued to work both outdoors and in. They describe a variety of specific strategies for dividing and sharing tasks in their marriages, and show considerable flexibility in adapting roles to circumstances. Some men clearly formulated separate spheres of work, like Jennie Brown Spence's husband, Joe, who said, "I run the outside, and you run the inside," or Catharine Craig Coles's father, who "had very decided ideas about what was women's work, and working out in the field was not one of them." Other couples divided work differently. Julia Kawcak worked in the fields, discing and plowing, and persuaded her husband, Paul, to learn to milk, sharing what had previously been her job. By contrast, Jennie Brown Spence's mother did not let her milk, and despite Joe Spence's apparently traditional division of farm labor, he continued the milking ban so that his wife would not be tied to cows, but could accompany him on roundup. June and Oma Jensen Graham shared work and companionship through frequent moves and an enormous variety of wage work, including her waiting tables and running cows, doing both female service work and labor more often considered male.[11]

Sometimes less traditional divisions of labor represented the negotiation of new primary roles, and at other times partners "helped" with work considered the other's responsibility. Seldom did primary responsibility imply an utterly rigid separation of tasks. Joe Spence was a good cook who taught his wife household skills. He helped with the washing. Lois Wells Bair's father made jack-rabbit chili and Christmas taffy, and Mary Gates Haughey's father prepared sagebrush and Oregon grape-root tea for flu sufferers. Masculine assistance with domestic chores was more common during times of illness and childbirth, and when wives worked for wages outside the home. Janet Mortimer Eberle recalls that when her mother taught school, her father was "a really good house-husband," who cooked, washed, and started the schoolroom furnace each morning. This pattern is echoed by Esther Anderson Campbell, who reports, "Duard was my housekeeper, while I taught school," and remembers with obvious fondness how people laughed about his omnipresent, multipurpose dishrag. Yet her descriptions of both their roles reveal assumptions about what was primary for each. At one point, she says, she taught school to "help out," and reports similarly that her husband "helped with the housework," despite the fact that she taught for 25 years, and he clearly shared household duties much of the time.

Such language may legitimize role-sharing and role reversals that pushed the boundaries of what couples considered acceptable, or it may provide rhetorical strategies that mediate between zones of private comfort and the anticipated judgments of others. As women entered the paid work force, they explained their decisions in a variety of ways. Many, like Eleanor Rugler Service, who took her nursing infant to school while she taught, explained their decisions in terms of family economic need and the needs of the larger community. Others, like Iris Self Lyons, risked resistance and anger at home to respond to personal and social imperatives. Some, like Ila Bowman Powell, didn't "believe in mothers being away from their kids." And still others, like Norine Holland's mother, accepted that "women's place was in the home," until necessity forced them out of it. The need for cash to establish homesteads, the hard times of the Depression, and widowhood all took women into the paid work force. That some of them relished the increased independence and accomplishment of their paid work is apparent. It is equally clear that, as in urban areas, gender roles were continually renegotiated and reinterpreted in the rural Colorado ranch country.

The various presentations of work, family, and community that Julie Jones-Eddy recorded bring to the personal and social terrains of gender the same rich diversity and complicated textures with which the women describe their lives in the expansive high country. If that rugged terrain could be cold, isolated, and sometimes dangerous, its "broken skyline" also brought peace, welcome solitude, and connection to family and community. If the land they settled, the homes and communities they built, were each woman's personal legacy, their generosity in sharing their histories leaves a rich legacy for readers and for historians. We may return to these and other oral testimonies to seek patterns in the variety, to sift further the relationships of age, family, circumstance, place, and gender. If Audrey Ruckman Oldland was thankful for her "rounded-out life," the generous memories shared in these pages have also helped to round out ours, and to round out our history as well.

Notes

1. Susan Armitage, "Through Women's Eyes: A New View of the West," in *The Women's West*, eds. Susan Armitage and Elizabeth Jameson (Norman: University of Oklahoma Press, 1987), 9–18.

2. Common stereotypes of western women are delineated in Beverly Stoeltje, "A Helpmate for Man Indeed: The Image of the Frontier Woman," *Image of American Folklore* 88, no. 347 (January–March 1975), 27–31. New works that challenge these images and examine women's active roles include Armitage and Jameson, eds. (n. 1 above); *Western Women: Their Land, Their Lives*, eds. Lillian Schlissel, Vicki Ruiz, and Janice Monk (Albuquerque: University of New Mexico Press, 1988); Sheryll Patterson-Black, "Women Homesteaders on the Great Plains Frontier," *Frontiers* 1, no. 2 (Spring 1976), 67–88; Glenda Riley, *Frontierswomen: The Iowa Experience* (Ames: Iowa State University Press, 1981); Julie Roy Jeffrey, *Frontier Women: The Trans-Mississippi West, 1840–1880* (New York: Hill & Wang, 1979); Sandra L. Myres, *Westering Women and the Frontier Experience, 1800–1915* (Albuquerque: University of New Mexico Press, 1982).

For work related to this volume, see Joan M. Jensen, *With These Hands: Women Working on the Land* (Old Westbury, N.Y.: The Feminist Press, 1981) and Teresa Jordan, *Cowgirls: Women of the American West* (Garden City, N.Y.: Anchor Books, Doubleday & Company, 1984); Edith Eudora Kohl, *Land of the Burnt Thigh* (St. Paul: Minnesota Historical Society Press, 1986); Elinore Pruitt Stewart, *Letters of a Woman Homesteader* (Lincoln: University of Nebraska Press, 1961).

3. In this chapter I use "West" not to denote the direction of migrants' journeys, but rather the area west of the 98th meridian in what is now the western United States, recognizing the contested meanings of the term and the histories of struggle it encodes. For works on women of color in the West, see Joan M. Jensen and Darlis A. Miller, "The Gentle Tamers Revisited: New Approaches to the History of Women in the American West," *Pacific Historical Review* 49, no. 2 (May 1980), 173–213; Rayna Green, "Native American Women," *Signs: Journal of Women in Culture and Society* 6, no. 2 (Winter 1980), 248–267; Lyle Koehler, "Native Women of the Americas: A Bibliography," *Frontiers* 6, no. 3 (Fall 1981), 73–101; Catherine Loeb, "La Chicana: A Bibliographic Survey," *Frontiers* 5, no. 2 (Summer 1980), 59–74; Lenwood G. Davis, *The Black Woman in American Society: A Selected Annotated Bibliography* (Boston: Hall, 1975); Lawrence B. DeGraef, "Race, Sex, and Region: Black Women in the American West, 1850–1920," *Pacific Historical Review* 49, no. 2 (May 1980), 285–314; Elizabeth Jameson, "Toward a Multicultural History of Women in the Western United States," *Signs* 13, no. 4 (Summer 1988), 761–791.

4. *Frontiers* has published two special issues on women's oral history, *Frontiers* 2, no. 2 (Summer 1977) and *Frontiers* 7, no. 1 (1983), which contain oral histories of western women, accounts of oral history projects in western states, and lists of oral history collections in western states.

5. See Susan Armitage, "Everyday Encounters: Indians and White Women in the Palouse," *Pacific Northwest Forum* 7, no. 3–4 (Summer/Fall 1982), 27–30, and "Women's Literature and the American Frontier: A New Perspective on the Frontier Myth," in *Women, Women Writers, and the West*, eds. L. L. Lee and Merrill Lewis (Troy, N.Y.: Whitson, 1979), 5–11; and Glenda Riley, *Women and Indians on the Frontier, 1825–1915* (Albuquerque: University of New Mexico Press, 1984).

6. Homestead figures calculated from *Historical Statistics of the U.S.: Colonial Times to 1970. Bicentennial Edition* (Washington, D.C.: United States Government Printing Office, 1975), 429; Patterson-Black (n. 2 above).

7. Calculated from *Twelfth Census of the United States, Taken in the Year 1900*, Vol. 1, Part 1 (Washington, D.C.: United States Census Office, 1901), 496, 576; *Thirteenth Census of the United States Taken in the Year 1910*, Vol. II (Washington, D.C.: Government Printing Office, 1913), 225, 227; *Fourteenth Census of the United States Taken in the Year 1920*, Vol. 3 (Washington, D.C.: Government Printing Office, 1922), 139, 144–145; *Fifteenth Census of the United States: 1930*, Vol. 3, Part 1 (Washington, D.C.: United States Government Printing Office, 1931), 303–304, 308–309; *Sixteenth Census of the United States: 1940*, Vol. 2, Part 1 (Washington, D.C.: United States Government Printing Office, 1942), 769, 770, 774; *A Report of the Seventeenth Decennial Census of the United States; Census of Population:*

1950, Vol. II, Part 6 (Washington, D.C.: United States Government Printing Office, 1952), 6–70, 6–71.

8. See n. 7 above: 1930 Census, 233, 236, 239; 1950 Census, 6–52, 6–56, 6–70, 6–71, 6–79–80, 6–82, 6–84.

9. Ibid.

10. For the role prescriptions of the 19th-century Euro-American elite, see Barbara Welter, "The Cult of True Womanhood: 1820–1860," *American Quarterly* 18, no. 2 (Summer 1966), 151–174. For analyses of domesticity in the West, see Elizabeth Jameson, "Women as Workers, Women as Civilizers: True Womanhood in the American West," in Armitage and Jameson, eds. (n. 1 above), 145–164; and especially Robert L. Griswold, "Anglo Women and Domestic Ideology in the American West in the Nineteenth and Early Twentieth Centuries," in Schlissel, Ruiz, and Monk, eds. (n. 2 above), 15–33.

11. For analyses of gendered divisions of farm labor and impacts of technology on women's work, see Corlann Gee Bush, "The Barn Is His, the House Is Mine: Agricultural Technology and Sex Roles," in *Energy and Transport,* eds. George Daniels and Mark Rose (Berkeley: Sage, 1981), 253–259; Joan M. Jensen, "Canning Comes to New Mexico," and "'I've Worked, I'm Not Afraid of Work': Farm Women in New Mexico, 1920–1940," in *New Mexico Women: Intercultural Perspectives,* eds. Joan M. Jensen and Darlis A. Miller (Albuquerque: University of New Mexico Press, 1986), 201–226, 227–256; and Deborah Fink, "'Mom, It's a Losing Proposition': The Decline of Women's Subsistence Production on Iowa Farms," *North Dakota Quarterly* 52, no. 1 (Winter 1984), 26–33.

Interviewee Biographies

Lois Wells Bair (1912–1988)

The Wells family moved to Skull Creek from Oklahoma in 1923 and bought a relinquished homestead; there they had 10 children. Lois attended the one-room school in Skull Creek when Esther Campbell was its teacher, and she completed eight grades. At 17 she married Bud Biles and continued to live in the Skull Creek area. In 1937 Bud got a job with the Colorado Department of Highways, and they traveled with the highway crew all over northwestern Colorado. They had two children. Bud died after 49 years of marriage, and Lois later remarried.

Freddie White Blevins (b. 1913)

In 1902 Freddie's maternal grandparents filed on a homestead near Craig. Her parents lived in Craig. Freddie attended the University of Colorado at Boulder for a year and then went on to the Chicago Conservatory of Music. Then she returned to Craig and married Tom Blevins, her high school sweetheart. They lived briefly in Montana, where their two children were born, and then settled on a ranch in Brown's Park, about 70 miles west of Craig, where she spent 20 years teaching in the rural schools. In 1967, after attending college in Greeley for many summers, Freddie finally earned her B.A. in music and elementary education.

Esther Anderson Campbell (Chandler) (b. 1899)

In 1922, when she was 22, Esther came from Denver to Skull Creek, near Rangely, to teach in the one-room school there. Her preparation for teaching consisted of normal school training in Minnesota and several summer school sessions in Colorado colleges later in her career. She soon married Duard Campbell, a local cowboy, and they lived in a dugout near the school. In 1936 they built a log cabin on Douglas Mountain, near Brown's Park, and lived there primarily in the summertime, because during the winter they were living near the school where Esther taught. They had one child. Esther lost Duard late in life and has recently remarried. She is referred to as Esther Campbell in this book because that is the name by which she is known in northwestern Colorado.

Ethel La Kamp Chrisler (b. 1904)

In 1905 Ethel's parents homesteaded near Meeker. Ethel attended a rural school through the eighth grade and later went to business college. She married Tim Chrisler when she was 20, and they lived on various ranches with their two children.

Catharine Craig Coles (b. 1901)

Catharine was born in Canon City, Colorado. When she was in high school her family moved to northwestern Colorado and lived on leased ranches; they had eight children. Following high school, Catharine taught for a year in the one-room school at Pagoda. She married Russell Coles, and they made their home with five children in Craig.

Ethelyn Whalin Crawford (b. 1913)

Ethelyn's father settled near Meeker in 1904, and her mother arrived in 1912. Following their marriage, the couple homesteaded at Thornburg, northeast of Meeker, and had eight children. They eventually moved to Meeker so that the children could attend school. After high school, Ethelyn worked on various ranches until she married Arthur Howey in 1934. They lived on a ranch in Powell Park, west of Meeker, and had two children. When Ethelyn's first marriage ended in divorce, she moved with her children to Grand Junction and worked for two years as a bookkeeper and secretary. She then remarried and lived in Meeker. In 1961 she and her husband moved to Oregon, where he died. She later remarried.

Velma Burdick Deaver (b. 1901)

Velma's parents came from Vernal, Utah, to Meeker in 1898. When Velma was six they leased a ranch along the White River and eventually had 11 children. After high school, Velma attended Western State College in Gunnison, Colorado, for two and a half years and then began teaching in the rural schools around Meeker. She married Hoyt Deaver at age 25 and for several years continued to teach in the Meeker area. After they moved to Craig, she taught for 25 years and eventually completed her B.A. in summer school at Western State. The Deavers had one child.

Ellen Dalrymple Dunn (1907–1989)

Ellen was 13 years old when she moved from New Mexico to Meeker, about 1919. After the death of Ellen's father, her mother and the 12 children moved to Rifle, where the older children worked to support the family. Ellen worked in drugstores during and after high school until she was 23, when she married Phil Dunn. Her husband worked on the state highway survey crew, and she traveled with him all over western Colorado.

Janet Mortimer Eberle (b. 1911)

Janet, an only child, came to Moffat County with her parents in 1918. In 1925 they filed on a homestead on Fortification Creek, 14 miles north of Craig. Janet attended the rural schools where her mother taught. She moved to Craig for high school and then attended college in Greeley for three years. When she returned home she taught in a school near their homestead. In 1933, at age 22, Janet married Ernest Eberle and lived on a ranch near Axial. She taught in the one-room school for several more years, until she had the first of two children. In 1962 she was elected county superintendent of schools and served two terms.

Ina Dalrymple Eddy (1916–1988)

Ina was born in Hurley, New Mexico, the second to last of 12 children. Her parents moved to Meeker, Colorado, about 1919, with plans to homestead. Shortly after they arrived, her father died, and the family moved to Rifle, where the older brothers and sisters worked to support the family. After high school, Ina married John H. Eddy. They lived in various towns in northwestern Colorado and had three children.

Oma Jensen Graham (1909–1988)

In 1902 Oma's parents came to Blue Mountain, north of Rangely, from Saratoga, Wyoming, and later homesteaded at Connie Springs, near the Utah border. In 1927 they moved to Buford on the White River where her father was a ranch foreman. After high school, Oma worked at a dude ranch on the White River until her marriage to June Graham, a ranch hand 17 years her senior. They lived on ranches all up and down the White River and in later years operated several small businesses in Meeker.

Mary Gates Haughey (b. 1903)

In 1911 Mary was eight years old when her family, who lived in Missouri, decided to join a wagon train for Oregon. On reaching Craig, they decided to homestead on Black Mountain, north of Craig. After graduating from high school, Mary taught for five years in the Big Gulch area, west of Craig. At 22 she married Clarence Haughey. They filed on a homestead and raised four children there. When her first son was ready for high school, the family moved to Craig. Mary worked in the county clerk's office in Craig and soon became deputy clerk. When her husband died of a sudden heart attack at age 51, she was able to support herself and her youngest son. Eventually she was elected county clerk and served in that office for 16 years.

Leona Rector Hinricks (b. 1905)

"Babe" was born on the family ranch west of Rangely. Her father arrived in the area in 1885, and he brought her mother from Missouri in 1899. Babe attended Western State College in Gunnison, Colorado, for three years and then married Clarence Hinricks. During the Depression she taught in the one-room school at Morappos. Later the family lived in various parts of northwestern Colorado. They returned to Rangely in 1947, and Babe worked as a secretary for an oil-well service company for 13 years. She had one child.

Norine Holland (b. 1917)

Norine's paternal grandparents came to Meeker in 1885 to preempt land and eventually, in the early 1900s, to live there. Her mother came to the Meeker area to teach in 1912. Norine's parents raised their four children on a ranch near Meeker. When Norine was in high school her father died, and her mother was elected county school superintendent. After high school, Norine attended Mesa College in Grand Junction and then came home to Meeker to teach. She later earned her A.B. in education. When her fiancé was killed during World War II, she moved to Denver to begin a Ph.D. program in social work and completed her M.A. in social work. After working for many years in Denver and California, she returned to northwestern Colorado.

Jayne White Hoth (1918–1988)

Jayne's maternal grandmother came alone from Ohio to homestead near Maybell in 1887. She married a local cowboy and raised four children. Jayne's mother grew up working on the ranch. Jayne's family moved to the Denver area when she was six, and she didn't return to Maybell until after a divorce, whereupon she moved there with her young son and subsequently married Carl "Mike" Hoth. She and her husband worked on several ranches and had two children. After her husband died, she worked as the postmistress for several years.

Lana Gregory Idol (b. 1915)

Lana lived on her parents' ranch near Elk, Wyoming, until she was three. Then her mother died of cancer, and the five children were brought to Meeker to live with her mother's sister. When the children were a little older they returned to their father's ranch in Wyoming. Lana attended the rural school there until high school, when she returned to live in Meeker. After high school she completed two years of college. Lana then married Loren Idol and had seven children. She relates several of her mother-in-law's homesteading experiences in her interview.

Minnie Eberle James (1896–1989)

In 1910 Minnie, the oldest of 10 children, came to Craig with her family to homestead. After graduating from high school in Craig, she attended one year of college at Colorado State University and then returned to Craig to teach in a rural school for a short time before moving to California. She returned to Craig in 1941 to marry Lewis James, and they lived on his ranch for a year and a half, when he died of pneumonia. She then worked as a bookkeeper in Craig.

Margaret Tagert Jones (b. 1915)

Margaret's mother, Fanny Wear, came to northwestern Colorado about 1889. Fanny's parents settled on the Yampa River west of Craig, at Juniper Springs, and later moved to Powell Park, west of Meeker. Fanny married Link Tagert, and they raised five children in Meeker. Margaret (the editor's mother) attended school in Meeker and went to Colorado State University for her bachelor's degree in home economics. She taught at Craig High School for one year before marrying Hugh Jones in 1938. They had two daughters.

Julia Biskup Kawcak (1899–1987)

In 1908 Julia came to Moffat County to homestead with her parents and four brothers and sisters. Her parents had emigrated in 1894 from Austria to Rockvale, Colorado, where her father worked in the coal mines. Julia married Paul Kawcak when she was 16. They filed a homestead on Elk Head, east of Craig, and raised 16 children.

Ruby Rector Kirby (b. 1902)

Ruby's father came to northwestern Colorado from Texas during the 1880s. He brought Ruby's mother to Rangely from Missouri in 1899, after they were married. They had three children. Ruby's sister is Leona "Babe" Hinricks. Ruby graduated from Western State College in Gunnison, Colorado, where she studied accounting and music, and then worked in San Francisco for three years. A severe attack of arthritis compelled her in 1930 to return home, where she worked until her first marriage. After a year of marriage, while she was pregnant with their child, her husband was shot in front of the Nichols' Store over a land dispute. In 1938 she married her second husband, Albert Kirby, a homesteader, and together they established a large cattle ranch. Ruby had one child.

CeCelia Sullivan Knott (b. 1918)

CeCelia's parents homesteaded on the Williams Fork River southeast of Craig about 1910. Her mother had 13 children, including three sets of twins. After high school, CeCelia married John Knott and moved to Craig; when her daughter was three the couple was divorced. CeCelia then worked until retirement as a pharmacist's assistant, chair-side dental assistant, and teacher's aide.

Mary Birovchak Levkulich (1896–1990)

Mary came to the United States in 1914 from Hudlova, Austria-Hungary, when she was 18. She worked in New York City for three years before marrying George Levkulich, a young man from a neighboring village in Austria-Hungary. Mary and her husband moved from one coal-mining area in the East to another until 1926, when Mary's husband decided to homestead in northwestern Colorado. They were unable to find suitable homestead land, and so they bought 160 acres in Breeze Basin.

Iris Self Lyons (b. 1905)

In 1914 the Self family took up a homestead on Spring Gulch, near the Williams Fork River, and raised nine children there. When Iris completed high school in Craig she went to Denver for nurse's training. Following graduation, she returned to Craig and married Wayne Lyons. They lived on his parents' homestead in Breeze Basin and raised their four children. She continued her nursing at the Hayden hospital and later at the Craig hospital.

Alta Fox Martin (1892–1984)

In 1929, with seven children, Alta and John L. Martin moved to northwestern Colorado from Brighton, Colorado, to homestead on the Great Divide, north of Craig. Shortly after their arrival, Mr. Martin and one son died of strep throat. Alta gave up the homestead and moved her family to a house near the Great Divide School and the Community Center. She and her children worked at odd jobs to provide a living. She lived there for 32 years, until 1962, when she moved to Craig.

Jennie Steele Mott (b. 1930)

Jennie's parents came to Rangely in 1931 with 9 children to homestead on Little Foundation. They eventually had 11 children, all of whom attended the Douglas Mountain School. After completing high school, Jennie married Jack Jones and raised three children in Rangely. When her husband died she remarried but was later divorced. She currently works at the post office.

Audrey Ruckman Oldland (b. 1910)

In the early 1900s Audrey's mother came to Meeker from Missouri to visit her brother. For several years she worked for Mrs. Schermerhorn, who operated the stopping place halfway between Rifle and Meeker on the stage route, and then she married. She and her husband homesteaded in Powell Park, south of Meeker. Audrey was the fourth of 10 children. After high school, she attended beauty school in Grand Junction for a short time before marrying John Oldland. She worked in a beauty salon in Meeker before the first of her three children was born. The family lived on a ranch west of Meeker.

Leona Kaloris Papoulas (b. 1905)

Leona came to Helper, Utah, in 1913, when she was eight, the child of Greek immigrants. In Utah she went to school through the eighth grade. She married John Papoulas in 1924, and in 1928 they moved to Vernal, Utah. She and her husband established a sheep-ranching business in northwestern Colorado, just across the Utah border, and spent most of their lives following the sheep from the winter range near Utah to the summer range in Hayden and Oak Creek. She had four children.

Nellie Warren Parks (1893–1985)

Nellie's parents arrived in the Meeker area in the 1880s and preempted land on Miller Creek. Her parents had five children. (Katherine Rector is Nellie's sister.) Nellie attended the one-room summer school near her home and then worked at home and on neighboring ranches until she married George Parks, a rancher. They had six children and were married for 64 years.

Ila Bowman Powell (b. 1911)

Traveling to northwestern Colorado in a covered wagon, Ila's parents arrived in Rangely on 29 June 1908. They settled on a homestead on Douglas Creek, south of Rangely. Ila attended school in Utah, Rangely, and Fruita, near Grand Junction. After the eleventh grade, Ila married Les Powell. They moved to Tacoma, Washington, for three years and then returned to Douglas Creek to homestead and raise 10 children.

Hilda Shelton Rawlinson (b. 1905)

In 1916, when Hilda was 11, her parents, Harley and Sophie Shelton, homesteaded near Dry Lake, 15 miles south of Maybell. They came from Nebraska with six children and had three more children at the homestead. After the eighth grade, Hilda cared for women who had new babies and also worked in Grand Junction until 1926, when she married John Fickle. They lived in California for six years and then returned to the Meeker area to buy a ranch. They had one daughter. Hilda's husband died, and she eventually married Sam Rawlinson. She operated a post office at her ranch on Price Creek for several years.

Katherine Warren Rector (b. 1909)

In 1882 Katherine's father, a gold miner in Georgetown, Colorado, came to the Meeker area. He married her mother in 1890 and preempted land for a home on Miller Creek, where they raised four children. Katherine's sister is Nellie Parks. When Katherine was 12 her mother left the family. Katherine completed nine grades in school and then helped her father on the ranch until she married Ralph Rector. The couple operated her father's ranch and raised two children there.

Stella La Force Rector (b. 1920)

Stella was born in Oak Creek, Colorado. Her father died when she was six, and her mother was left with six children to raise alone. The family moved to Glenwood Springs, where her mother could find work. Stella completed high school and one year of college. Then, while working on a ranch near Kremmling, Colorado, she met her husband, Jay Rector. After Jay worked in several construction jobs, the couple settled in Rangely and lived on the Rector ranch, raising four children.

Beryl Van Cleave Richards (b. 1903)

Beryl's parents moved to Meeker from Oregon with their twin daughters in 1905. When Beryl was six her mother died while in surgery, which was performed in the home. After high school, Beryl served as the librarian in the small public library until she was 30, when she married W. O. Richards, the Episcopal priest in Meeker. They later moved to Glenwood Springs.

Rosamay Hodges Savage (b. 1898)

Rosamay was born on a homestead near Juniper Springs. Her family lived there until 1908, when her father died. Her mother then moved to Maybell and operated the town's drugstore. After high school, Rosamay attended business college and worked for several years in Denver before marrying Detmer Savage. After retirement, they moved back to northwestern Colorado and lived on a ranch in Rangely. When her husband died, she moved to Meeker.

Eleanor Rugler Service (1904–1986)

Eleanor was teaching school in Missouri in 1927 when she decided to come west because the wages were better. She taught in various rural schools in Moffat and Rio Blanco counties. When she arrived, she had two years of college, although she continued to take courses for many years. Eleanor married James Service. They had three children and raised two foster children. She continued to teach in the rural schools until retirement.

Virginia Shepherd (b. 1905)

As a young bride, Virginia's mother came to Meeker from Virginia in 1901 to live in a small house at Buford. Later, Virginia's father held county offices and they lived in town. After high school, Virginia attended Colorado College and graduated from the teachers' college in Greeley, Colorado. She returned to Meeker and taught for several years, before moving to teach in Colorado Springs, Colorado, where she remained until retirement. While in Colorado Springs she earned her M.A. in education at Colorado College.

Wilma Crawford Smith (b. 1900)

Wilma's father homesteaded in Meeker in 1885. Her mother came with her family in a covered wagon in the 1890s. The Crawfords had five children. After high school, Wilma attended the University of Colorado for two years before marrying Allen Smith and returning to Meeker. Her husband died in an accident when their daughter was two years old; subsequently Wilma worked at various jobs in Meeker.

Jennie Brown Spence (b. 1897)

In 1898 Jennie's parents came to Meeker from Carthage, Missouri. Her father taught in the rural schools and worked in Meeker. They later filed on a homestead. After high school, Jennie taught in the elementary school until she married Joe Spence. They lived on various ranches where he worked and finally settled on a ranch above Meeker, where they lived for 25 years. They had two children. Jennie began teaching again in the Meeker schools during World War II and continued this work until retirement. Jennie ultimately completed her B.A. in education at the teachers college in Greeley.

Lena Ely Stoddard (1894–1991)

Lena, a graduate of Knox College, came to Hayden from Illinois in 1921 with her husband, Chuck Stoddard, who was to be the new school superintendent. Although they lived in town, they filed on a homestead and lived there in the summers. In 1927 they purchased the newspaper in Craig and moved to the home in Craig where they raised five children.

June O'Connell Sweeney (1904–1987)

June was born at Buford, Colorado, and lived most of her early years in Leadville. After attending the teachers college in Greeley, June was offered a job teaching in Maybell. She taught for a year and then married a local rancher, Henry Sweeney. June loved teaching, and she continued to teach, while raising two sons, until retirement. In the 1950s she was elected county superintendent of schools, a position she held for many years. June earned her B.A. in education at the teachers college in Greeley during summer terms.

Chloe Bunker Vaughan (1902–1990)

In 1926 Chloe came from Illinois to visit her sister, who lived near Maybell. She soon married Minford Vaughan, and they homesteaded on Zenobia Peak, in the Brown's Park area. Eventually they bought a ranch in the park. They had one daughter. Chloe formed a home demonstration club in Brown's Park, the first club for women in that area.

Mary Wear Villa (1925–1989)

Mary's maternal grandparents homesteaded near Axial, between Craig and Meeker, in the late 1800s, and her paternal grandfather was one of the very early settlers in Meeker. Her parents lived in Meeker with their four children. Mary's family was very musical, and their band played for many community dances. Mary majored in music at the University of Colorado and taught music in Sterling, Colorado. Soon she returned to Meeker and continued teaching for 30 years. She married Martin Villa, and they had two children.

Doris Stephenson Warren (b. 1923)

In 1889 Doris's mother came to Meeker by way of covered wagon and the family homesteaded on Flag Creek. She later attended college against her father's wishes and became a teacher. After high school, Doris worked as deputy county clerk until she married Harold Warren. She later worked in the bank and was elected county treasurer, a position from which she is now retired.

Inez Ely Whalin (1889–1990)

In 1912 Walter V. Whalin brought his new bride to Meeker from Illinois. They homesteaded on Thornburg, near Meeker, and had eight children. Ethelyn Crawford is Inez's eldest child.

Estel Aicher Woolley (b. 1905)

Estel's mother came to visit a sister in Meeker and met a cowboy she later married. They homesteaded on Flag Creek and had one child. During Estel's school years, the family lived for a time in Denver and Grand Junction. After completing high school, Estel attended business school in Grand Junction. She then returned to Meeker and served as deputy county clerk. When she married Raymond Woolley she moved to Craig and worked as a bookkeeper until the first of her two daughters was born. After several years, the family moved back to Meeker.

Index

The Editor

Julie Jones-Eddy is the U.S. Government Documents Librarian at Colorado College's Tutt Library.